Texts & Documents

A SERIES OF THE GETTY CENTER PUBLICATION PROGRAMS

The TEXTS & DOCUMENTS series offers to the student of art, architecture, and aesthetics neglected, forgotten, or unavailable writings in English translation.

Edited according to modern standards of scholarship and framed by critical introductions and commentaries, these volumes gradually mine the past centuries for studies that retain their significance in our understanding of art and of the issues surrounding its production, reception, and interpretation.

Eminent scholars guide the Getty Center for the History of Art and the Humanities in the selection and publication of TEXTS & DOCUMENTS. Each volume acquaints readers with the broader cultural conditions at the genesis of the text and equips them with the needed apparatus for its study. Over time the series will greatly expand our horizon and deepen our understanding of critical thinking on art.

Julia Bloomfield, Thomas F. Reese, Salvatore Settis, *Editors*
THE GETTY CENTER PUBLICATION PROGRAMS

Friedrich GILLY

PUBLISHED BY THE GETTY CENTER FOR THE HISTORY OF ART AND THE HUMANITIES

DISTRIBUTED BY THE UNIVERSITY OF CHICAGO PRESS

TEXTS & DOCUMENTS

Friedrich
GILLY

Essays on Architecture

1796–1799

INTRODUCTION BY FRITZ NEUMEYER
TRANSLATION BY DAVID BRITT

THE GETTY CENTER PUBLICATION PROGRAMS
Julia Bloomfield, Thomas F. Reese, Salvatore Settis, *Editors*
Kurt W. Forster, *Consultative Editor*

TEXTS & DOCUMENTS

Harry F. Mallgrave, Architecture Editor

Friedrich Gilly: Essays on Architecture, 1796–1799
Lynne Kostman, Managing Editor
Benedicte Gilman, Manuscript Editor

Published by The Getty Center for the History of Art and the Humanities,
Santa Monica, CA 90401-1455
© 1994 by The Getty Center for the History of Art and the Humanities
All rights reserved. Published 1994
Printed in the United States of America

00 99 98 97 96 95 94   7 6 5 4 3 2 1

Publication data for the original German texts may be found in the source notes
following each translation.

Permission to reproduce figures 2, 4, 7, 12, 17, 18, 19, and 34 and permission to translate the text for Version 2 of the "Note on the Friedrichsdenkmal" has been granted by Frau Wanda von Hugo, Berlin. Permission to reproduce figure 35 and to translate the quotation in note 109 of the Introduction as well as the "Notes on a Sheet of Sketches for the Friedrichsdenkmal" has been granted by Gebr. Mann Verlag, Berlin. Permission to translate the quotations in notes 14, 21, 23, 24, and 297 of the Introduction, as well as Version 1 of the "Note on the Friedrichsdenkmal," and Appendix 1 and to reproduce Appendix 2 has been granted by the Geheimes Staatsarchiv Preußischer Kulturbesitz, Abteilung Merseburg. Permission to translate the quotation in note 293 of the Introduction has been granted by the Staatsbibliothek Preußischer Kulturbesitz, Berlin.

Cover: Friedrich Gilly, cubes in the sand (detail). Estate of Martin Friedrich von Alten. Staatliche Museen zu Berlin, Preußischer Kulturbesitz, Kunstbibliothek, Hdz 7719. Photo: Petersen.

Library of Congress Cataloging-in-Publication Data is to be found
on the last printed page of this book.

CONTENTS

Acknowledgments

Like all scholarly publications, this edition of Gilly's essays has enjoyed the support of a number of institutions and individuals. I owe thanks especially to the staffs of the Kunstbibliothek of the Staatliche Museen zu Berlin, Preußischer Kulturbesitz; the Staatsbibliothek zu Berlin, Preußischer Kulturbesitz; the library of the Getty Center for the History of Art and the Humanities in Santa Monica; the Schinkel Archiv in Berlin; and the Geheimes Staatsarchiv Preußischer Kulturbesitz, Abteilung Merseburg, for their assistance.

Kurt Forster's high enthusiasm, Julia Bloomfield's strong patience, and Harry Mallgrave's valuable suggestions contributed much to the structural shape of this book. The careful and intelligent editorial fine-tuning by Benedicte Gilman and Lynne Kostman improved it in detail and as a whole. I owe special thanks to David Britt for his fine translation of the Gilly essays and my introduction. Thanks are also due to Victoria Beach for proofreading the galleys and to William Gabriel and Monika Wiessmeyer for their participation in the early stages of this project.

—F. N.

Introduction

Fritz Neumeyer

Entrusted for Completion: Retrospect of a Brief Career

When Friedrich Gilly died of a pulmonary disorder at Karlsbad (Karlovy Vary) on 3 August 1800, at the age of twenty-eight, it was the end of an architectural career that had barely begun. His fame rests on a creative period of less than a single decade in which this youthful architect was able to erect only a few, extremely modest buildings. Seldom has so great a name been founded on so slender an oeuvre.

The state of Gilly's reputation in his own lifetime is known to us from comments made by the members of artistic and academic circles in Berlin. A leading contributor to the periodical press in Berlin, Friedrich Gentz (1764–1832), who was Gilly's brother-in-law, painted the following glowing portrait of the young architect in a letter to another, no less eminent figure, the philologist and archaeologist Carl August Boettiger (1760–1835):

> *That he is a man of great intellectual curiosity and equally great learning in his own discipline and furthermore an amiable man in the very best sense of that word: all this I might well pass over in silence since I imagine that you would very soon have known it without being told, even if he had come to you with no recommendation from anybody. But what I must tell you because it lies beyond the scope of a brief acquaintanceship—setting aside my own love for the man—is that this young man possesses one of the foremost artistic geniuses of our country and our age. I am far from indicating the true extent of his abilities—though this in itself says much for him—when I tell you that in his twenty-fourth year he was hailed by all those best qualified to judge as the first architect in the Prussian state. Nor does it do him justice to view him as an architect alone, for he is destined to achieve the highest rank in every one of the fine arts.[1]*

Other artists of Gilly's generation were no less enthusiastic, as one can conclude from a letter the poet Wilhelm Wackenroder (1773–1798) wrote to his friend and literary colleague Ludwig Tieck (1773–1853) in February 1793—at a time when Gilly had not one single major design to his name—to describe his first meeting with Gilly.

1. Friedrich Wilhelm Freiherr von Erdmannsdorff, the mansion of Wörlitz near Dessau, 1769–1773. Photo by author.

"I have made an acquaintance that could not possibly be more pleasing to me: that of a young architect Gilly, whom Bernhardi knows. But any description must fall far short! This is an artist! Such consuming enthusiasm for ancient Grecian simplicity! I have spent a number of very happy hours in aesthetic conversation with him. A godlike man!"[2]

It was presumably through his friend August Ferdinand Bernhardi (1770–1820), a young writer and artist who taught at the Friedrich-Werdersches Gymnasium in Berlin, that Gilly acquired his close contacts with the Berlin literary world.[3] His own literary interests dated from his early youth, and he could be expected to hail a man like Wackenroder as a kindred spirit, for both men had a religious veneration of art. In 1797, anonymously and jointly with Tieck, Wackenroder published *Herzensergießungen eines kunstliebenden Klosterbruders* (Heartfelt outpourings of an art-loving monk);[4] the book met with an enthusiastic reception in early Romantic circles in Berlin, and there was, of course, a copy of it in Gilly's personal library.[5]

For its day this artistic manifesto, which critics initially ascribed to Johann Wolfgang Goethe (1749–1832), demonstrated an uncommon breadth of artistic sympathy. It paid tribute not only to the great Italian Raphael but also to the still comparatively obscure native artist Albrecht Dürer. Wackenroder was one of the first to set "Old German" and Italian art side by side as equals and thus establish a historic link between Rome and Nuremberg.

At almost exactly the same time Gilly engaged in a comparable bridging operation between the same two antagonistic worlds for art history. In his description of the castle of Marienburg (Malbork), near Danzig (Gdańsk), Gilly set this late thirteenth-century citadel of the Teutonic Order in a new light, thus opening the eyes of his contemporaries to the beauty of a neglected, native, medieval architectural tradition. It may well be that Wackenroder's "outpourings" added a new dimension to Gilly's enthusiasm for ancient Grecian simplicity; or, conceivably, the reverse may be the case: that Gilly's picturesque glimpse of the Middle Ages fired the writer's imagination and led him to embark on comparable expeditions into the history of art.[6]

The nature of the relationship between these two artists remains, like much else in Gilly's life, an open question. The biographical record is sparse. Friedrich Gilly was born on 16 February 1772 at Altdamm (Dąbie), near Stettin (Szczecin), the son of the provincial architect (*Landbaumeister*) of Pomerania, David Gilly (1748–1808).[7] Friedrich grew up there until his father was transferred to the Oberhofbauamt (Royal building administration) in Berlin in 1788 as superintending architect (*Geheimer Oberbaurath*). Friedrich Gilly received a thorough training in architecture from his father with particular emphasis on technical and craft matters, in keeping with the responsibilities of a provincial architect, who was mostly concerned with canal engineering and functional construction for agricultural purposes. After spells as an apprentice mason and carpenter and special tuition in mathematics, Friedrich went on to study at the Architektonische Lehranstalt (the architecture school of the Akademie der bildenden Künste, the academy of fine arts) in Berlin, where he joined the class of Friedrich Becherer, a pupil of Karl von Gontard. His own first teaching experience (1792–1793) was as a teaching assistant (*Repetitor*) to Becherer.

Among Gilly's drawing teachers at the newly reorganized Akademie der bildenden Künste were such well-known artists as Daniel Chodowiecki (1726–1801) and Johann Gottfried Schadow (1764–1850). He gained his first practical and artistic experience around 1790 under Carl Gotthard Langhans (1732–1808) and Friedrich Wilhelm Freiherr von Erdmannsdorff (1736–1800), the two leading practitioners of early Neoclassicism in Germany. On the death of Frederick II of Prussia (Frederick the Great) in 1786 both had been summoned to Berlin by Frederick's successor, Frederick William II. David Gilly's transfer to the Oberhofbauamt in Berlin had been another consequence of this change of regime, which marked a decisive break with Frederick the Great's artistic taste.

Erdmannsdorff, an aristocratic amateur, had been inspired to become an architect by the Palladian buildings he had seen on a visit to England in 1763; regarded as one of the leading experts on the "Antique style," he had been powerfully influenced by a number of visits to Rome and by personal contacts with Johann Joachim Winckel-

2. Friedrich Gilly, pavilions in Wörlitz Park, 1797, pen and ink, 8.3 × 13.2 cm. Lost. From Alfred Rietdorf, *Gilly: Wiedergeburt der Architektur* (Berlin: Hans von Hugo, 1940), 66, fig. 51. Santa Monica, The Getty Center for the History of Art and the Humanities.

3. Carl Gotthard Langhans, *Brandenburg Gate around 1798. City side (Das Brandenburger Tor um das Jahr 1798. Stadtseite)*, aquatint by D. Berger after Lütke. From Hermann Schmitz, *Berliner Baumeister vom Ausgang des achtzehnten Jahrhunderts* (Berlin: Ernst Wasmuth, 1914), 160. Santa Monica, The Getty Center for the History of Art and the Humanities.

mann (1717–1768), Giambattista Piranesi (1720–1778), and Charles-Louis Clérisseau (1721–1820).

Prince Francis of Dessau, with whom Erdsmannsdorff had visited England and Rome, commissioned him to build two mansions on parkland, at Dessau and Wörlitz; these signaled the final abandonment of late Baroque architectural forms. Wörlitz (1769–1773), designed on English and Palladian models (fig. 1), was the first attempt on German soil to create an architecture based on the ideas of Winckelmann. In setting out to combine beauty and utility, the design was as scrupulous in its attention to the antique as it was in providing the practical comforts of modern domesticity. With its park, laid out as an English landscape garden, and with its elaborate theoretical and educational program, Wörlitz became a total work of art, a *Gesamtkunstwerk*; and its fame as a model of sophisticated art and living reached far beyond the frontiers of the state of Dessau. It became the most celebrated ensemble of German Enlightenment architecture and garden design and attracted hordes of visitors from many countries.

In May 1797, traveling to Paris by way of Weimar, where he visited Boettiger and probably also Goethe, Gilly passed through Wörlitz and Dessau, where he found the work of his teacher not without fault. Under one of his sketches (fig. 2) he wrote, "The roofs are really a bit too high."[8] Characteristically, Gilly corrected the fault then and there, reducing the heights of the roofs in his sketches. The small buildings, which looked half like pyramids and half like porticoes, were thus released from their formal indecisiveness. With his marked predilection for solid forms, Gilly made these modest structures cubically concise and optically massive; reducing their roofs made them more effective, to his eye, as isolated features amid expanses of parkland.

Langhans, Gilly's other principal teacher, was as active a pioneer as the amateur Erdmannsdorff. The Brandenburg Gate (fig. 3), built to Langhans's designs in 1788–1791, was the outstanding example of early Neoclassicism in Berlin; it gave new impetus to the vision of a Doric revival on Prussian soil and set before people's eyes once more "the noble simplicity of the ancients," whose ruined buildings now took on new life and youth "beneath northern skies."[9]

In 1790, after working under Langhans on the construction of the tower of the Marienkirche in Berlin, Gilly was appointed a "supernumerary" supervisor (*Kondukteur*); in 1792 his training as a government architect was completed, and he was appointed a full supervisor. His first independent works date from the years that followed. In 1792 he designed the facade for a residential building built between 1792 and 1794 at Jägerstraße 14; in 1795 he provided the interior design and decor for five rooms in the castle at Schwedt an der Oder for Prince Louis Ferdinand. From 1793 onward Gilly taught architectural drawing at the private school of architecture founded and run by his father under the name of Lehranstalt zum Unterricht junger Leute in der Baukunst

(Institute for the education of young people in the art of building).

Gilly's work first reached the public with his design for "a Lutheran church to hold six hundred persons, for a court city," which was exhibited at the Akademie in 1791.[10] There, too, in 1795, he attracted great public attention with an exhibition of his sanguine drawings of Marienburg. The king himself acquired a drawing,[11] and at the end of November 1795 a cabinet order awarded Gilly five hundred *Thalers* for a four-year study tour abroad.[12] Another immediate benefit that Gilly reaped from his successful excursion into the Middle Ages was that the publisher of a journal gave him the opportunity of writing an essay on the history and architectural features of Marienburg and thus of making a first public trial of his literary talents.[13]

In 1796 came the design that made the youthful architect an instant celebrity in Berlin and beyond: the design for the Friedrichsdenkmal, the memorial to Frederick II, with which Gilly's name has remained indissolubly linked to this day. Willfully disregarding the terms of the competition, he proposed a site far away from that specified and a monument that went far beyond the equestrian statue then still compulsory for the monuments of princes; instead his design proposed a temple that would form a considerable urban landmark.

When the Friedrichsdenkmal competition designs went on display at the Akademie der bildenden Künste in September 1797, Gilly was on his way to Paris. In April of that year, he had at last set out on the long-overdue study tour, which was supposed to take him to Rome, the Mecca of the arts; however, political events in Europe forced him onto a different course. With the Lombardy campaign in 1796, Napoleon had embarked on his conquest of Italy; a year later, Rome was occupied by a French army. Gilly accordingly traveled via Dessau, Weimar, and Strasbourg to Paris, where he spent six months. From there he continued to London and then returned to Paris, where he added substantially to his library. His homeward journey was by way of Hamburg, Vienna, Prague, Dresden, and Weimar to Berlin, where he arrived back in December 1798 without ever having set foot on Italian soil.[14]

His return to Berlin was impatiently awaited by the seventeen-year-old Karl Friedrich Schinkel (1781–1841), who—so legend has it—had seen the Friedrichsdenkmal plans at the Akademie der bildenden Künste and had resolved then and there to leave school and study architecture under Gilly. Schinkel had spent the interim until Gilly's return at the private architecture school run by David Gilly, under whom, according to Schinkel's biographer Gustav Friedrich Waagen, "he felt himself not very far advanced." In return for "the usual fee," Gilly senior had offered Schinkel a course of architectural instruction that consisted of "little more than handing him this or that architectural drawing to copy."[15]

Back in Berlin, Gilly embarked on a new period in his private as well as his professional life. In April 1799 he married Marie Ulrique Hainchelin, to whom he had become secretly engaged before setting out on his tour. In May 1799 he accepted a position of professor at the newly founded Bauakademie (Academy of architecture). Initial commissions, including the construction of the Villa Mölter in the Tiergarten and the assignment to build the "dairy" of Schloß Bellevue, promised him a successful career as an architect in Berlin.

It was part of Gilly's newfound freedom that earlier in the same year, in January 1799, together with his friend Johann Heinrich Gentz (1766–1811), he founded the Privatgesellschaft junger Architekten (Private society of young architects). In this he was probably inspired by the architects' clubs that he had encountered in Paris. His Parisian experiences probably also inspired the idea of making his own library available to a small and select group of like-minded colleagues. Additionally, Gilly's membership in the Masonic Lodge "Zu den drei goldenen Schlüsseln" (The three golden keys) may well have favored the creation of social groups of this kind.

The Privatgesellschaft fostered self-education through mutual criticism, and Gilly presumably regarded it as a complement, or even as a counterweight, to the official architectural training whose one-sidedness he criticized in an essay written in the same year as the founding of the society. What was offered at the established institutions clearly did not satisfy the idealistic demands of an enthusiastic younger generation of architects. The fact that Gilly proclaimed the true purpose of the Privatgesellschaft to be the "more earnest study of art,"[16] entitles us to assume that he found the conventional education of an architect wanting in this respect. It is a hypothesis that is strengthened by the suggestion, in a recent work on Gilly, that the collaboration between father and son does little credit to the father, who seems to have exploited his son's artistic abilities while he himself remained tied to the craft and technical aspects of his subject.[17]

The Privatgesellschaft had seven members. Along with Gilly and his slightly older friend Johann Heinrich Gentz were Gilly's school friend Joachim Ludewig Zitelmann (1768– ?), now a graduate student of architecture (*Bauassessor*), and four younger architects, Martin Friedrich Rabe (1775–1856), Schinkel, the Stuttgart-born Carl Haller von Hallerstein (1774–1817), and probably Carl Ferdinand Langhans (1782–1869), son of the designer of the Brandenburg Gate.[18]

According to the commemorative essay on Gilly published by his friend Konrad Levezow in 1801, the objective of the Privatgesellschaft was "the encouragement of genius through mutual emulation, and refreshment after the labors of ordinary business through opportunities to engage in works of genius."[19] Members gathered weekly to devise impromptu solutions to small architectural problems or to select by lot an individual who would make a presentation of his work or of an architectural assignment, followed by discussion and friendly criticism. "In addition," says Levezow, "they read

4. Friedrich Gilly, sketch for the Berlin National Theater, 1799?, pen and wash, 27×42 cm (top view), 10.5×19 cm (bottom view). Lost. From Alfred Rietdorf, *Gilly: Wiedergeburt der Architektur* (Berlin: Hans von Hugo, 1940), 117, fig. 107. Santa Monica, The Getty Center for the History of Art and the Humanities.

aloud historical notes on the progress of architecture as well as biographical information that they had collected on celebrated and deceased architects. From time to time, one member of the society would read a paper on an important topic connected with the art of architecture."[20]

Dated drawings by a number of the members suggest that the meetings of the Privatgesellschaft continued as late as 1800, which means that they did not end when the Bauakademie, the first state architecture school in Germany, opened its doors on the upper floor of the newly completed Alte Münze (the Mint building) on the Werderscher Markt in Berlin. This important specimen of Berlin Neoclassicism was designed by Johann Heinrich Gentz, and Gilly was also involved in the project. He designed the figurative frieze that adorned the cubical building; whether he also influenced the design of the structure itself remains an open question.

Gentz and Gilly, the two prime movers of the Privatgesellschaft, were both appointed professors at the newly founded Bauakademie. Gentz was given the specialty of "urban architecture," and Gilly, in a letter of 20 April 1799, was assigned that of "instruction in optics and perspective . . . also architectural and mechanical draftsman-

Lusthaus über der Eisgrube zu Paretz.

5. Friedrich Gilly, *Pavilion above the Ice Pit in the Park of Paretz (Lusthaus über der Eisgrube zu Paretz)*, 1797–1800, engraving by Ant.[on] Wachsmann, 9.8 × 14.3 cm. From *Sammlung nützlicher Aufsätze und Nachrichten, die Baukunst betreffend* 4, no. 2 (1800), title vignette. Santa Monica, The Getty Center for the History of Art and the Humanities.

ship."[21] In a letter of 17 May 1799, Gilly accepted the offer "with the most respectful thanks" and undertook to "exert my utmost efforts to fulfill these obligations, which I so gladly assume, to the best of my ability."[22]

The archival file of correspondence with the Bauakademie from which the previous letter comes also contains the last extant document in Gilly's hand. It is the application for sick leave that he addressed to the director of the Bauakademie, Heinrich Karl Riedel, on 9 July 1800.

> *The long illness from which I have unfortunately suffered for some years is such that several physicians now prescribe, as a necessary therapy, that I use the spa waters of Karlsbad; and this is a prescription that I cannot oppose without laying myself open to reproach, however disagreeable I may find it in many ways—compelling me, as it does, to suspend the whole of my professional activity. However, I am left with no alternative but to make the journey, and I therefore enclose a copy of the certificate received from the physician to this effect.*
>
> *I now find myself obliged to apply respectfully to the Honorable Director of the Royal Bauakademie for a leave of absence of approximately six to eight weeks, and I beg to hope that His Honor will have the great kindness to support my application. As I keenly look forward to recovering the happy gift of perfect health, I am filled with the desire to attend with still greater application to the business entrusted to me, in which I shall spare no effort.[23]*

In a letter dated 14 July 1800, Riedel approved the application and forwarded it to the board of trustees, which approved the leave of absence on 19 July.[24] Gilly left

Berlin shortly after, and in the early hours of 3 August 1800 he died at Karlsbad.

Gilly had been unable to realize any of the major designs of his final years. Neither the Friedrichsdenkmal nor the Schauspielhaus (National theater, fig. 4) in Berlin, on which Gilly had worked unceasingly since his return from France, was ever built. For the Schauspielhaus, the king opted for the design submitted by Carl Gotthard Langhans, and, in his capacity as a public employee of the Oberhofbauamt, Gilly was chosen to supervise the construction. Work began in early spring 1800, a few months before his death.[25] The project for a new theater in Königsberg (Kaliningrad), for which Gilly had submitted plans, was equally ill-fated. In the course of construction, the client departed so radically from Gilly's designs that the architect was left with no alternative but to decline all responsibility for the building.[26]

A few minor buildings, such as the pavilion above the ice pit in the park of Schloß Paretz (fig. 5);[27] the Meierei, or dairy, in the park of Schloß Bellevue; and the Villa Mölter in the Tiergarten were begun in 1799 and 1800; all were still in progress when Gilly died. Schinkel, in his autobiography of 1825, claims that "all the uncompleted private architectural works of the late Gilly were entrusted to him for completion."[28]

Friedrich Gilly as the Founder of the Berlin Architectural Tradition

The high expectations that attached to Gilly in his lifetime were justified by the rich and eventful history of his later influence. This posthumous career is all the more surprising if we reflect that since the early years of the twentieth century, his reputation has rested on nothing but drawings and a few written documents. With the exception of a mausoleum at Dyhernfurth (Brzeg Dolny), near Breslau (Wrocław), now in a ruinous condition, none of Gilly's few completed buildings outlasted the nineteenth century.

For many years, Gilly's posthumous status in the history of German art and architecture lay in Schinkel's hands. In the literature, Schinkel was presented as Gilly's reincarnation, with the implication that in his work a tragically curtailed artistic career found its natural continuation. The smoothness of this transition was due, not least, to the hero worship on Schinkel's part that led him to assimilate, as it were, the identity of his revered teacher and friend. Even to an expert eye, the drawings made by Schinkel in Gilly's lifetime are sometimes indistinguishable from those of Gilly himself; and this fact has been responsible for the survival of a number of Gilly's drawings. Ascribed to Schinkel and added to his archive, they survived when most of Gilly's other papers disappeared.

Gilly's reputation was thus absorbed into that of Schinkel, and it accordingly passed through some strange vicissitudes during the nineteenth and twentieth centuries.[29] The very first Schinkel monograph, *Karl Friedrich Schinkel: Eine Charakteristik seiner künstlerischen Wirksamkeit* (Karl Friedrich Schinkel: A characterization of his artistic activities), 1842, written by Franz Kugler (1808–1858), presented Schinkel as a student who was in no way inferior to his master in talent, and who fulfilled his teacher's unrealized visions.[30] In 1849 the sculptor Schadow, who had immortalized Gilly in a bust immediately after his death, coined the phrase that Schinkel was "nature's repetition of his master."[31] As Schinkel rose to unchallenged historical eminence, Gilly was typecast as his teacher and gradually declined into a mere footnote to his biography.[32] As Alfred Woltmann significantly put it in his architectural history of Berlin of 1872, Gilly's "chief claim to fame" was that "Schinkel was his pupil."[33]

By the end of the nineteenth century, Gilly had entirely faded into Schinkel's shadow. George Galland, whose brief article in 1878 was the first to take Gilly as its subject since Levezow's memorial essay of 1801, defined the situation perfectly in his very first sentence. "No great or notable reputation attaches to the artist whose memory we seek to revive in the following lines, and for whom we seek to arouse our readers' sympathy."[34]

Naturally enough, amid the centennial celebrations of Schinkel's birth, Gilly enjoyed his moment of reflected glory. He did not feature in the text of Richard Schöne's official oration, delivered on 13 March 1881;[35] however, in a paper delivered to the Berliner Architekten-Verein (Berlin architectural association) on 28 March 1881, the architect Friedrich Adler took the opportunity to direct attention to "Friedrich Gilly—Schinkel's Teacher,"[36] who, as he said, had been undeservedly overlooked in the celebrations in honor of "Berlin's greatest architect."[37]

Here, once again, Gilly appeared in his traditional role as "the master of our master," who "pointed the way" or "blazed the trail" for Schinkel.[38] But elsewhere in his text Adler struck a note that suggests a new interest in Gilly while it also casts a revealing light on the state of architecture in Berlin in the early 1880s. Clearly, the latter-day representatives of the Schinkel school felt that the Neoclassical position needed defending against the rise of pluralistic historicism. Hitherto, architectural historians had presented Gilly as an artist whose output was so slender that he could be judged—as Theodor Fontane put it—only by "what he *intended*";[39] but Adler was at pains to set the record straight by pointing out just how much he had achieved "in the brief span of ten years." To this he added the question: "Of what other German architect can we say as much?"[40]

Adler was seriously trying to afford a more accurate view of Gilly's career than that supplied by Levezow. He was also anxious to safeguard Gilly's "considerable legacy

6. Friedrich Gilly, *Sketch for a Country House* (*Idee eines Landhauses*), 179?/1802, etching
by [Anton] Wachsmann, 6.8 × 11.5 cm (oval), 10.3 × 14.5 cm (overall). From Carl Zetzsche,
Zopf und Empire (Berlin: Kanter & Mohr, 1906), 1: reverse of title page. Santa Monica, The
Getty Center for the History of Art and the Humanities.

of artistic achievement" and stressed his own high opinion of Gilly's work by letting it
be known that he was a collector of Gilly drawings.[41]

Adler's attempt to assess Gilly's achievement in its own right is also interesting
because it reflects a change of emphasis in the historical evaluation of his work. Previously, the Friedrichsdenkmal design had been regarded as Gilly's most important work;
and, indeed, without ever being built, it had given a decisive impulse to the evolution
of Prussian Neoclassicism. Now, however, the rediscovery of Marienburg came to be
regarded as Gilly's central achievement. Adler presented Gilly as the pioneer of the reassessment of medieval brick architecture and declared him to be the spiritual progenitor
and scholarly founder of the modern brick architecture that had emerged with Schinkel's new Bauakademie of 1831, to which the members of the Schinkel school in Berlin
saw themselves as the heirs. In Adler's words: "Gilly's most significant architectural
achievement is and will remain the rediscovery of Marienburg and its introduction into
the scholarly literature of art. For this gave rise to the powerful wellsprings that—
through the genius of Schinkel—have so bountifully nourished the architecture of the
present day."[42]

As early as 1869, in a speech in praise of Schinkel, Adler had spoken of the "student years with his master, Gilly" and had described the "grandly austere magnificence" of the Marienburg drawings as the "slumbering seed" that bore fruit in Schinkel's Bauakademie.[43] The man who rediscovered Gilly thus saw him both as an architectural pioneer and as a contributor to the history of architecture; and this had a relevance of its own. As one of Schinkel's *Enkelschüler*—the disciples of his disciples—Adler had played his part in establishing the historicist professional ideal of the scholar-architect. Adler's own architectural ambitions lay in the insertion of medieval styles into the classical forms of building in order to create a practical synthesis of structural forms, very much in the spirit of Schinkel's Bauakademie.[44] The architectural synthesis at which he aimed had a precise parallel in his choice of topics for scholarly research. Adler was, as it were, following in Gilly's footsteps with his work on Greek antiquity and on Gothic architecture in brick in the Mark Brandenburg.

Other individual architects who subsequently set out to record and interpret Gilly's work were similarly seeking to legitimize their own work. It was not until comparatively late in the day that art historians as such began to pay attention to Gilly. In 1910 the two approaches came together and led to something of a Gilly renaissance, which raised his name to an unheard-of popularity.

The ground for this had been prepared from 1905 onward by a rediscovery of the art of the period "around 1800";[45] the motivation was a desire to purify the forms of Wilhelminian architecture through the bourgeois virtues of plainness, economy, and simplicity. Even before Paul Mebes published his highly successful book *Um 1800* (Around 1800), Carl Zetzsche brought out a triple album under the title *Zopf und Empire* (Periwig and empire).[46] Engravings of designs by Gilly, taken from the periodical *Sammlung nützlicher Aufsätze und Nachrichten, die Baukunst betreffend* (Collection of useful essays and news concerning the art of building), appeared as title-page vignettes in all three parts (fig. 6).[47] Around 1910 a rapid succession of further publications on the "early Hellenism" of the Berlin school of architecture and on Prussian Neoclassicism in general fostered a profuse growth of Neoclassical tendencies in pre–World War I Berlin architecture.[48] The expressive range extended from Spartan austerity through subtle reductionism and Biedermeier elegance to archaic bombast.[49]

By 1914, polemics were surfacing in the architectural press against the new "primitivism" and the dogmatic "simplification" that had degenerated into "a slogan for snobs." Gilly's name was one of those that appeared in this context, and he was whimsically scapegoated by one editorial, which remarked, "Gilly is in fashion, and he is, alas, 'copperplated' just as indiscriminately as the formal repertoire of Hirt was—shall we say—evoked, twenty years ago." We have to read on to find that here, as elsewhere, Gilly was suffering from the consequences of enforced Siamese twinning with his great pupil. The attack was really directed against the modish appropriation of Schinkel's ideas.[50]

How far the situation was from a consensus can be seen if we turn from this to an essay by Paul Zucker published in the journal of the Bund deutscher Architekten (German architects' federation) a few months earlier, in September 1913. Under the title "Ein vergessener Berliner Künstler" (A forgotten Berlin artist), Zucker presented Gilly not at all as "in fashion" but as "wholly unknown to the great mass of Berliners alive today, revered only by a tiny band of interested art historians and architects."[51]

Among art historians, two in particular were intimately bound up with the early twentieth-century vicissitudes of Gilly's reputation: Hermann Schmitz, librarian of the Kunstbibliothek in Berlin, and Wilhelm Niemeyer, a pupil of August Schmarsow. In 1909 Schmitz brought out no less than three articles on different aspects of Gilly's work,[52] in which he took up the subject where Adler had left off.[53] Schmitz followed these in 1914 with a book on late eighteenth-century Berlin architects, which he based on a course of lectures, "Der Klassizismus in Norddeutschland vor Schinkel" (Neoclassicism in northern Germany before Schinkel),[54] delivered at the Kunstgewerbemuseum (Museum of arts and crafts) in the winter of 1908; these lectures seem to have met with an eager response from architects in Berlin.[55] In Schmitz's book, which was widely read and went into a second edition in 1925, the bust of Gilly made by Schadow in 1801 confronted the reader on the half-title page.

From a scholarly point of view, Schmitz made no original contribution to the study of Gilly, and his interest in the subject did not last. In 1909 he enthused over Gilly as "perhaps the most magnificent phenomenon" among the German architects of the last third of the eighteenth century, a man whose "timeless," picturesque vision of the Gothic was far superior to that of the nineteenth-century Gothic revival; he went on to add that "only a painter such as Monet" could come close to this vision. For the first time even Schinkel was relativized by comparison with Gilly's architectural genius.[56]

By 1914, however, it would seem that Gilly's artistic originality had been markedly impaired. In 1909 Schmitz had announced a forthcoming book on David and Friedrich Gilly;[57] but by 1914 he had abandoned this in favor of a broadly based publication on Berlin architects in general, in which he wrote with considerably more reserve. "Valuable and filled with fine architectural ideas though Gilly's artistic remains may be, we must acknowledge that they represent an admittedly tasteful reworking of contemporary classic forms—and particularly of those cultivated in Paris—and that in all of them there is not one single, organic architectural creation of genius."[58]

This verdict was accompanied by a shift of Schmitz's historical interest away from the influence of antiquity and the Neoclassical tradition; he now turned his attention to the Gothic, whose influence he traced as far as the nineteenth century in a study published in 1921 called *Die Gotik im deutschen Kunst- und Geistesleben* (The Gothic in German artistic and intellectual life). In this, too, Gilly found his niche as the author of "the first publication on a Gothic architectural monument in our fatherland"[59]—an achievement for which he had already been given due credit by Adler in 1881.

In 1922, in a book based on prewar research, *Kunst und Kultur des 18. Jahrhunderts in Deutschland* (Art and culture of the eighteenth century in Germany), Schmitz once more expressed his reservations about those same "architects of the end of the eighteenth century" to whom, in 1914, he had devoted his undivided attention. Now, it seems, the creations of German Neoclassicism demanded "unprejudiced reassessment," and the massive forms deployed by Gentz, Gilly, Friedrich Weinbrenner, the young Leo von Klenze, and Schinkel struck Schmitz as evidence of a "loss of the sure architectural instinct" that ultimately "opened the door to arbitrariness of proportion."[60]

Niemeyer, who had discovered Gilly in Zetzsche's *Zopf und Empire*, claimed credit for having prompted Schmitz to work on Gilly and indeed for having drawn Schmitz's attention to him in the first place.[61] In 1912, in an essay on Gilly's and Schinkel's approaches to form, Niemeyer undertook a profound and strongly felt analysis of Gilly as an "architectural thinker." Zetzsche, as editor of the periodical *Der Baumeister* (The architect), rewarded this with an appreciative review in which he commented that it established a direct link with "Schinkel's sources," from which the path might lead onward "to something newer and higher."[62]

Niemeyer had given proof of his understanding of architecture with a dissertation in 1904 on problems of form in late Gothic buildings.[63] He then joined the library staff of the Kunstgewerbemuseum in Berlin before being called to Düsseldorf by Peter Behrens in 1905 to teach at the Kunstgewerbeschule (School of arts and crafts). His view of Gilly was not so much that of an art historian as of a committed participant in the evolution of contemporary architecture. Articles on Behrens and Alfred Messel, published in 1907 and 1908,[64] reflect his commitment to the evolutionary triumph of a Modernism that he regarded as a new Renaissance. As the "most idiosyncratic representative" of the "Northern Renaissance," Gilly fitted neatly into this view of contemporary architecture: he became the protagonist of classic Modernism.

It therefore comes as no surprise to find that in Fritz Hoeber's monograph on Behrens of 1913 (intended as the first volume in a series on "modern architects"), a publisher's announcement mentions Niemeyer as the author of a forthcoming monograph on David and Friedrich Gilly. Under the blanket heading of "Moderne Architekten," the last page of the Behrens monograph carried the names of those precursors and pioneers of modern architecture who were to figure alongside Behrens in the series: Theodor Fischer, Messel, David and Friedrich Gilly, Schinkel, Otto Wagner, and the sculptor Adolf Hildebrand. The accompanying copy announced that further volumes on Henry

van der Velde, H. P. Berlage, and Josef Maria Olbrich were in preparation.[65] The out-
break of World War I put an early end to the ambitious plans for the series, and not one
of the promised volumes ever appeared.

Niemeyer regarded Gilly's designs not at all as "dream architecture" but as "the
most deeply considered products of a reflection on first principles," which possessed
lasting value as "architectural methodology, as the laws of thought." In Gilly's architectural conception, "two quite distinct intellectual currents," namely "rationalism and
Neoclassicism," combined and took visible form.[66] In Gilly's designs, there was a simultaneous sense of structural and dramatic vision, a keen feeling for both the truth and the
expressive force of a form, all manifested "in crystalline purity, with an almost propae-
deutic sense of system." In Niemeyer's view, Gilly was living proof that "harmony of historic form and pure function" was possible. It was a possibility that lay within the reach
of contemporary architecture. His readers had only to think of Behrens and his work
for the electrical concern AEG. Gilly's quest for the "rationality of form" and the "harmony of elementary values" made him a model for others to follow, cutting across all
barriers of chronology and style and justifying his inclusion among "modern architects."

A further step in establishing Gilly's modernity was taken by the architect Paul
Zucker, fresh from his doctoral thesis on "Raumdarstellung und Bildarchitektur im Florentiner Quattrocento" (Spatial representation and pictorial architecture in the Floren-
tine quattrocento), and thus well versed in the examination of drawn and painted
architecture, which he described as "a kind of intermediate terrain of art."[67] In his article—which appeared in 1913, only a few months after Niemeyer's—Zucker credited
Gilly with an "astonishing degree of contemporary relevance"; in this he was thinking
not only of the competition of 1912 for the Berlin Opera House but also, with reference
to the Friedrichsdenkmal, of the Greater Berlin competition of 1911. He credited Gilly
with a hitherto unremarked "modern approach to urban planning."[68]

In Zucker's view, the formal conception that he associated with Gilly offered
an opportunity to continue the tradition of the "great Berlin architects" into the present
day with the aim of creating "perfect expressive forms of our time." Among the architects
who had trodden this path with success and had "continued in the direction indicated
by Gilly," Zucker counted "Schinkel, [August] Stüler, and—after an interval of more
than half a century—Messel."[69]

The key role in the reassessment of architecture "around 1800," and presumably also in the rediscovery of Gilly, seems to have fallen to one member of the "tiny
band of interested art historians and architects" to whom Zucker referred. This was an
architect famous far beyond the confines of Berlin, the designer of the Wertheim Department Store, Messel. Unfortunately, since posterity has continued to deny Messel
the monograph that was promised in 1913,[70] this aspect of his work, along with many
others, remains obscure to the present day.

As a young government architect, winner of the Schinkel Prize in the centennial year of 1881, Messel paid his own tribute to architecture "around 1800" when, in 1886, just before erecting his own first office building on the site of Johann Heinrich Gentz's Alte Münze building (with its frieze by Gilly), he conducted a careful survey before demolition began in order to save the building for posterity, on paper if in no other way.[71] Messel had a similar encounter with a Gilly building in 1906, when the Palais Solms Baruth on Behrensstraße, with its facade by Gilly, was demolished to make way for his new Nationalbank building.[72] The motif of inset Doric columns that Messel used on the doorway might be seen as a melancholy reminiscence of the architecture of Gentz and Gilly.[73]

Around 1910 the critics were hailing Messel as "the true grandson of Langhans and Schinkel (after a generation of degenerate sons)."[74] It was his "influential achievement," according to Karl Scheffler, to have carried architecture back beyond Schinkel, to the creative period between 1780 and 1800, and to "the art of Schinkel's immediate predecessors," in which the "living germ of the tradition" resided.[75] In Scheffler's view, Messel's "best and most profound buildings" harked back not to Schinkel but "to Langhans's Brandenburg Gate, to Gentz's Alte Münze, to the buildings of Gilly, and to the old town houses of the years around 1800."[76]

Scheffler said that Messel had "opened the eye of the age."[77] This suggests that with Gilly in mind we can pursue the Neoclassical current in modern architecture from its roots until far on into the twentieth century: to Behrens, who spoke of Messel with deep respect and who was the most convincing interpreter of Gilly's massive forms,[78] and to Behrens's pupil Ludwig Mies van der Rohe, who according to his own words valued Messel more highly than Palladio.[79]

The ambivalence at the heart of this whole notion of a "Northern Renaissance" was made explicit in a widely read book by Arthur Moeller van den Bruck, *Der preußische Stil* (The Prussian style), which was written in 1916, at a moment of nationalistic euphoria and German military success. In a detailed and well-illustrated chapter, Moeller van den Bruck introduced Gilly to a large readership and presented him as "the first modern architect," the Proteus of the Prussian style. From the outset, Moeller van den Bruck made it abundantly clear that he regarded this Prussian style not as a merely national phenomenon but as something universal, "a principle in the world."[80]

The synthesis of rationalism and Neoclassicism, which for Niemeyer had been a compelling union between logic and beauty, was now twisted into a marriage between Prussianism and Grecism, celebrated at the altar of history. Its ruling idea was no longer the yearning for grandeur as an idealistic motivation but the driving force of aggrandizement as the vindication of imperial ambitions. Moeller van den Bruck followed his chapter on Gilly with another on "Monumentality," in which, with brutal candor, he proclaimed the extension of art into power politics: spiritual dominion finds expression in a monumental style, and this displays a mastery of forms "that begins as self-mastery and can become world mastery."[81]

Conducted on an industrial scale and by industrial methods, World War I shattered the prewar dream of a humanistic synthesis of art and technology that would constitute an "industrial civilization." The period after 1918 was marked by a total rejection of the Neoclassical tradition, which even Behrens branded in 1920 as "monumental art, aesthetic imperialism."[82] With the rise of Expressionism, which found its closest affinities in the Gothic and the Middle Ages, the avant-garde temporarily closed the file on Neoclassicism. In 1921, instead of bringing out his projected monograph on Gilly, Niemeyer became editor of the Expressionist art periodical *Kündung* (Proclamation).[83] The way in which Schmitz shifted his ground, criticizing Gilly's dependence on the antique while praising him as the discoverer of Marienburg, is part of exactly the same pattern.

To the modernist architects of the 1920s, Neoclassicism was synonymous with academicism, representing an outworn inheritance that they forcefully disowned in public, even though in their own work they continued to feel an allegiance to the abstract rationality of classical forms. In 1923, with his spectacular juxtaposition of the Parthenon with a sports car, Le Corbusier showed just how abstract this continuing tie could become.[84] The art historians of the 1920s had only a few fresh insights to offer on Neoclassical architecture, and they took little interest in it. They contented themselves with reaffirming Gilly's role as a precursor whose influence persisted far on into the nineteenth century, and this became enshrined in the canon.[85]

Not until the 1930s was there a new Gilly revival, in which his legacy was both academically studied and ideologically updated. In 1931 Horst Riemer wrote a doctoral dissertation on Gilly and theater construction.[86] In 1932 Wolfgang Herrmann, in the first part of his history of German architecture in the nineteenth and twentieth centuries, studied Gilly in detail as an important innovator.[87] Then, in 1935, came the still-unsurpassed Gilly monograph by Alste Oncken.[88] In this, her doctoral dissertation, Oncken cataloged Gilly's artistic and literary works and widened his context from late eighteenth-century Berlin to European Neoclassicism as a whole. Her book remains the most important source of information on Gilly, not least because it refers to extensive archival holdings, most of which were lost in World War II. Since Oncken, Gilly scholarship has found very few new sources.

The ambivalence of the process of rehabilitating Gilly's reputation and the transition to a very different attitude toward him are most tellingly documented by the case of the Berlin architect Wassili Luckhardt. In 1933 Luckhardt wrote an article entitled "Vom preußischen Stil zur neuen Baukunst" (From Prussian style to modern architecture), an account of the continuity between Prussian Neoclassicism and Modernism (*Neues Bauen*), in which he reexamined Moeller van den Bruck's presentation of Gilly. In 1934 he republished "Vom preußischen Stil" twice, with revisions.[89] The modernists, wrote Luckhardt, were very much opposed to the idea of "associating the name of Moeller van den Bruck with the new movement"; but in his view there was much to be said for doing just that. Moeller had after all regarded Gilly as the "first modern architect," and in his "line of thought" he had anticipated many of the ideas in contemporary architecture—and this at a time "when the new movement in architecture was barely detectable even in its very first stirrings." Luckhardt therefore considered it both justified and worthwhile to engage more closely with this conservative thinker.

As presented by Moeller, Gilly's "cuboid world" revealed a "new architectural impulse" that had much in common with Modernism. In both, wrote Luckhardt, architecture turned its back on ornament and evolved instead a style of "the primitive in its noblest embodiment," marked by a new feeling for planar form and for a sculptural conception of the architectural whole. Gilly had freed architecture from the formal repertoire of historical styles and had made it rigorous, practical, and sober; and this, Luckhardt continued, was in total agreement with the principles of the new architectural movement of the 1920s.

Luckhardt called on "present-day architects" to see Moeller van den Bruck's statements "in the light of the situation in which we find ourselves at present"; logically, this would have meant crediting Moeller with the foundation of the International Style, then recently proclaimed at the eponymous exhibition organized by Henry-Russell Hitchcock and Philip Johnson.[90] For, according to Luckhardt, Moeller's idea of Prussianism as "a principle in the world," when seen in conjunction with "the Gilly concept," contained within it "the fundamental program of a 'world architecture.'"[91]

Luckhardt attempted to bestow a kind of Prussian-Internationalist legitimacy on the politically suspect architecture of Modernism by aligning it with the Moeller-Gilly axis. His hope to give Modernism a future under the new Nazi regime in Germany—a regime with which he was in sympathy—was doomed to failure. Even before 1933 Gilly had been enlisted in the nationalist cause as the hero of an architecture that the poet Hans Schwarz, in his foreword to the new 1931 edition of Moeller's *Der preußische Stil*, called "the eternal Doric of all young and warlike peoples."[92]

Schwarz was probably the uncredited coauthor of the Gilly monograph published by Alfred Rietdorf in 1940—only five years after Oncken's dissertation. In his monograph Rietdorf took Moeller's analysis of 1916 and ran offside with it into the zone of power politics. The book went into a second edition in 1943, a sure sign of the propaganda value that attached to the promotion of heroic cult figures.[93] In his epilogue Rietdorf proudly remarked that he had written on Gilly "from the standpoint of the present, as an avowal of faith in a victorious future." Gilly, as represented in the bust by

Schadow, which transformed him into an eternally youthful hero, had presided over the Olympic Games in 1936; and so, by 1940 it seemed a necessary next move to mobilize him, as Rietdorf did, in the cause of ultimate victory.[94]

Having been commandeered and raped by the Third Reich, the Neoclassical tradition became tainted by association, and in Germany after World War II it was the object of considerable mistrust. An illuminating instance of the disrepute into which the very word *Neoclassicism* (*Klassizismus*) had fallen, and in which it remained for almost two decades, is provided by the title of a book by Hermann Beenken, written between 1940 and 1942 and eventually published in 1952. The author's topic was German architecture in the Neoclassical period, between 1770 and 1820; but in his published title he took refuge in the politically uncontaminated word *Romanticism* (*Romantik*), and it was under that heading that he described the line of evolution that led from Gilly to Schinkel.[95]

It was not until the 1960s that this fear of contagion began to be overcome. The rediscovery of the architecture of the French Revolution prompted a new historical engagement with late eighteenth-century and early nineteenth-century architecture,[96] and Gilly's name was among those that aroused new interest. In 1964 Marlies Lammert published her monograph on David Gilly.[97] In 1965 Wilhelm Salewski republished Friedrich Frick's engravings of Friedrich Gilly's views of Marienburg, which had first appeared between 1799 and 1803.[98] Subsequently in a succession of exhibitions on the theme of Neoclassicism "around 1800," art historians and architects alike took up the topic of Gilly.[99] Finally, as part of the *Internationale Bauausstellung, Berlin, 1987* (International building exhibition, Berlin, 1987), the Berlin Museum in 1984 devoted a separate exhibition to Gilly and the Privatgesellschaft junger Architekten, in which all then-accessible designs and sketches by Gilly were assembled, together with contemporary copies, and set within the context of the current state of scholarly research.[100]

The present publication can thus add to the existing published record only a few, hitherto incompletely researched, archival sources. These include materials held after 1945 in the former Zentralarchiv at Merseburg in the former German Democratic Republic—today the Geheimes Staatsarchiv Preußischer Kulturbesitz. Among these documents is the previously unnoticed catalog of Gilly's personal library,[101] which casts important light on the intellectual context of his understanding of architecture. In the present volume, which seeks to afford new access to Gilly's ideas on architecture through the first English translation of his writings, a facsimile of that catalog is included as Appendix 2.

The catalog was printed, presumably privately, in 1801, after Gilly's death. As a member of the Privatgesellschaft, Gilly had intended to make his library freely accessible to interested persons. It was thus entirely in keeping with Friedrich Gilly's wishes that David Gilly presented his son's books to the library of the Bauakademie. A cabinet order of 30 September 1801, providing for the libraries of the Oberhofbauamt, the Ober-Baudepartment, and the Bauakademie to be combined, reveals that the combined stock was to be supplemented by "the valuable collection of books left by the late Professor Gilly."[102]

The Architect as Writer: Friedrich Gilly's Literary Work

It is certainly an exaggeration to say—as Adler did in his desire to do Gilly justice—that he "devoted himself unremittingly to his literary work."[103] Even so, this particular artistic sideline, which represented the architect's endeavor to explore the theoretical basis of his own actions, was exceptionally important in Gilly's case. He undoubtedly possessed both literary talent and the inclination to exercise it. This still emerges from a reading of Gilly's prose today; it has lost none of its poetic fascination. The sentences seem to have flowed easily from his pen, with lightness and sureness of expression. Schmitz was the first to pay Gilly the compliment of saying that he was "no less of a genius as a writer than as an architect."[104] Schmitz regarded the essays on Bagatelle and Rincy as among "the finest architectural essays in the German language."[105] Oncken was equally full of praise for the lightness of touch, the liveliness, and the gift of acute and palpable expression with which Gilly handled the language; she described his writing as possessing an "almost musical beauty."[106]

    Gilly never lacked for opportunities to write about buildings. From his youth, he was his father's companion and note taker on the latter's professional travels, and Friedrich seems to have been expected to record in words and drawings anything notable that he saw. These note-taking expeditions continued in the course of his later training to become a Prussian building official. In 1790, for instance, he was sent as a draftsman to accompany Senior Architectural Counselor (*Oberbaurat*) Riedel on a journey to study modern water utility buildings in Holland and in the Prussian provinces of Westphalia.

    Oncken, who examined Gilly's report of this journey, listed it in her catalog as consisting of fifty-seven sheets with thirty-six drawings.[107] It is now thought to have been lost in World War II. Also lost during the war were the voluminous notes Gilly took during his journey to France and England; the "written collections" made in preparation for the journey, which according to Levezow filled "a thick quarto volume in themselves"; and the "quantities of handwritten essays, both long and short" that Gilly is said

7. Friedrich Gilly, the stones of Rauen, date unknown, 16.2×25.5 cm. Lost. From Alfred Rietdorf, *Gilly: Wiedergeburt der Architektur* (Berlin: Hans von Hugo, 1940), 15, fig. 7. Santa Monica, The Getty Center for the History of Art and the Humanities.

to have brought back as the literary fruits of his journey.[108] The correspondence between father and son must likewise now be regarded as lost.

The rare, surviving loose leaves from Gilly's travel diaries give no more than a fleeting glimpse of his talent for observing and appropriating noteworthy objects. The earliest of these, transmitted to us by Oncken, consists of a description written on the reverse of an undated drawing of a landscape with prehistoric stone tombs on the Stein-höffel estate (fig. 7), near Berlin. David Gilly had renovated the estate about 1790. The drawing, complemented by a few sentences in which Gilly brings history and landscape together, exemplifies the blend of the literary and the visual within his own imagination.

> It is easy to imagine what extraordinary objects these stones must seem to the local inhabitants, and what tales, spells, and enchanted castles must have sprung from them. The landscape has a rough and wild quality that may perhaps be conducive to this; and the country folk still

send the traveler on his way with the old legends ringing in his ears. The countryside all
around bears traces of the distant past, which arouse echoes of romance. There are many burial
places, often large and curiously arranged, belonging to the ancient Wends, who once lived
here. The wooded and higher parts of the Steinhöffel estate, in particular, are covered with
such gravestones, beneath which one often finds urns containing ashes.

Wandering among the deserted monuments of a numerous and valiant nation,
whose home this once was, one gazes with strange feelings across the peaceful scene to the banks
of the Spree, where a considerable range of hills, that of Rauden, rises into a lovely blue.[109]

A similar mixture of historical empathy and artistic imagination characterized
the first appearance in print of a text by Gilly, namely the article on Marienburg, published in 1796. It was presumably the success of the exhibition of Gilly's drawings the
previous year that prompted the editor of the periodical *Denkwürdigkeiten und Tagesge-*
schichte der Mark Brandenburg to publish an explanatory essay by the artist himself.[110]

Alongside his drawings, the printed word became important to Gilly in its own
right and offered him new areas of opportunity. In 1798 he is said to have written from
Vienna to the scholar Boettiger (who had presumably tried to recruit him as a contributor to "a new journal" during his recent visit to Weimar): "That [too] is what I live for."[111]

Above all, his journalistic ambitions were bound up with the Privatgesellschaft. As its name suggests, this society did not regard itself as a public body, but it did
concern itself with public affairs in the shape of urban building projects. Described—
or might we say disguised—as practice exercises, the members' projects for theaters,
museums, baths, city gates, prisons, government buildings, monuments, and the like
often referred to real projects in ways that were clearly far from coincidental. What is
more, the Privatgesellschaft's declared objective of educating public taste required its
members to publish in order to intervene in the public debate.

Gilly's notes of the outline for a talk to the newly founded Privatgesellschaft,
on a sheet dated 30 January 1799, contain pointers in this direction.[112] In his talk, in
pursuit of the society's policy of keeping up-to-date with developments in architecture
both in Germany and abroad, Gilly introduced his friends to a book published in Paris
in 1798 by the architects Charles Percier and Pierre-François-Léonard Fontaine, *Palais,*
maisons, et autres édifices modernes, dessinés à Rome (Palaces, houses, and other modern buildings, sketched in Rome), which he had probably brought with him, fresh from the press,
on his return from France.

In Gilly's view, this publication on Renaissance palaces in Rome illustrated
perfectly how, long after "the time of the ancients," the architects of "the recent epoch
of art," as represented above all by "Palladio and his contemporaries," had created in
their buildings the "prototypes of a purer, unadulterated style of architecture." And these

buildings, with their reworking of the antique, might in their turn lead "the observant architect" of the present day to a "taste for simplicity and beauty" and thus continue on a higher level the cycle of a perpetual Renaissance.

This message of the educative mission of true art, which was to be pursued not by petty imitation but by timely reappropriation, made the French publication a model of its kind. Innovative even in its graphic presentation, it was the work of "a society of architects in Paris" (as Gilly, surely deliberately, chose to describe them), and he urged the Privatgesellschaft in Berlin to follow the French lead in order to achieve something comparable. Schinkel's *Sammlung architektonischer Entwürfe* (Collection of architectural designs), which appeared in installments between 1819 and 1840,[113] was strongly inspired by the engravings in Percier and Fontaine's work and may be seen as a belated fulfillment of Gilly's ambition.

The fact that Gilly translated the compilers' introduction, "which is of interest in many respects," into German for his Berlin friends underlines the implicit character of its appeal for him. This introduction contained ideas on imitation and on the relation between form and function that Gilly firmly shared. He, too, aspired to realize in contemporary terms the ideals for which Percier and Fontaine praised their Italian predecessors: "Indeed the majority of their works bears the imprint of that rare simplicity that delights us and which, like a truth unveiled, always appears easy to those to whom it is revealed. Picturesque without disorder, symmetrical without monotony, and always meticulous in execution, they often—to use a term of art—combine composition with rendering."[114]

Gilly had no time to realize his various publishing projects. He produced neither a major work of architecture nor a major work of literature. We know from Levezow that his untimely death put an end to preparations for a number of projects. Gilly intended, for instance, to compose a "Lehrbuch der ganzen Perspektive" (Complete manual of perspective), based on his own lectures, which would deal with the fundamentals of draftsmanship and the secrets of painting; he was also said to be working on a treatise on "Theaterperspective und Theatermalerei" (Stage perspective and stage painting).[115] Letters from David Gilly to the publisher Vieweg in Braunschweig, which was bringing out a new edition of David Gilly's own *Handbuch der Land-Bau-Kunst* (Handbook of rural architecture),[116] reveal that Friedrich Gilly had also intended to publish a book on country houses, based on his own studies of villas in France and on the books he had bought there.[117]

None of this happened. Gilly lived to publish only three essays, all probably based on papers read to the Privatgesellschaft. These were descriptions of the villa of Bagatelle and of the country estate of Rincy, both near Paris, and an essay on the changes in architecture caused by the advance of contemporary science. These three pieces were published in the irregular periodical *Sammlung nützlicher Aufsätze und Nachrichten, die Baukunst betreffend*, which appeared from 1797 onward, one of whose editors was David Gilly.

Friedrich Gilly certainly intended to continue with his series of descriptions of exemplary buildings, and in particular of those that he had seen on his travels, for his essay on Rincy ends with the words *"Die Fortsetzung folgt"* (to be continued). But what appeared after his death deserves notice purely for the sake of completeness. Presumably at David Gilly's behest, the volume of the *Sammlung nützlicher Aufsätze* of 1801, which was published only in 1803, includes "Einige ausgehobene Bemerkungen aus dem Reise-Journal des verstorbenen Professors und Ober-Hoff-Bauinspektors Gilly" (Some selected remarks from the travel journals of the late professor and senior building inspector Gilly). These "remarks" consist of an extract from an undated travel diary describing a visit to the cities of Leipzig and Weissenfels and amounting to barely more than a single printed page. This was hardly a fitting posthumous tribute: it simply provided the curt, disjointed, technical details of a water storage installation and a roof construction—themes that were much more in David Gilly's line than in Friedrich's. And, although the words "to be continued" appeared again, no further extracts from Gilly's travel diary ever followed this exiguous first installment.[118]

Marienburg: A Medieval Reverie

Among the sites inspected by David Gilly on his official tour of Pomerania in 1794 was the late thirteenth-century castle of Marienburg, near Danzig. One of the most important of all medieval fortifications, it was built in the course of the colonization of the area that is now Poland by the Prussian Knights of the Teutonic Order. The state official, practical and economically minded as ever, took the view that this ruinous structure would best be demolished. But in the eyes of his son Friedrich, who accompanied him on that tour, the same ruins transformed themselves into a miracle, an architectural revelation.

In words and in pictures Friedrich Gilly's record of what he saw at Marienburg documents far more than a mere generation gap. In his atmospheric view of the castle, historical insight was combined with picturesque sentiment and technical acumen to create a eulogy of the Gothic that was unparalleled in any description of a medieval building since Goethe's celebrated paean of praise for the Strasbourg cathedral and its architect, Erwin von Steinbach, written in 1772.[119] Goethe and his generation had long since turned against the Gothic and all its vagaries, and they now found their ideal of beauty in classical art alone. The architects of the younger generation, in their turn, learned to marvel with Gilly at the ruins of Marienburg.

This response, which was to lead to a reevaluation of the Gothic itself, directly determined the fate of the monument in question, the castle of Marienburg. In 1773 Frederick II had had it converted into an infantry barracks, and in 1795 there were plans for a new program of invasive building works that would have entailed—on David Gilly's recommendation—the demolition of the historic fabric itself. In 1804 the decision was taken to preserve Marienburg as a historic monument, for whose restoration Schinkel subsequently campaigned;[120] it was a decision that would have been inconceivable without Friedrich Gilly's "discovery" of Marienburg and the publication of etchings of his drawings between 1799 and 1803.[121]

A detailed account of the historical events that accompanied the building of Marienburg as part of the forcible "work of conversion" by the Teutonic Order forms the first part of Gilly's essay published in 1796, which is basically a commentary on his drawings shown at the Akademie der bildenden Künste in 1795. After wearying the reader somewhat by expatiating on those "traces of the distant past" that—like the stone tombs of prehistory—"arouse echoes of romance,"[122] he turns to the buildings themselves.

Gilly embarks on the second part of his description for all the world as if it were the true purpose of architecture to create the evocative effect of visual images and to stir the emotions through effects of light—rather as Etienne-Louis Boullée intended when he prefaced his own grandiose architectural ideas with the motto *"Ed io anche sono pittore"* (I, too, am a painter).[123] Gilly devoted this section to the aesthetic and technical causes of the spell cast on the visitor by these "picturesque ruins" with their "colossal and audacious construction": on the outside, "towering walls," and on the inside "soaring vaults" and "spacious passages and halls" that afforded the traveler "a variety of surprising and impressive scenes . . . especially as the effects of light are often extremely fine" (fig. 8).[124] No beholder versed in the arts could pass them by. "The site challenges the draftsman to capture it and the architect to linger and to survey the structure from within."[125]

By identifying this immediacy of sensuous power as the attraction of the building, Gilly signaled a revolution in the viewer's relationship with medieval architecture. The playful use of isolated medieval motifs and forms, as favored by the sentimental contemporary taste for the "Gothick," gave way to the momentous experience of a deeply felt encounter with a real medieval building. The fashion for landscape gardening in the English style, which arose in Germany around 1760, had brought with it a craze for a sham Gothic based more on literary sources than on the form and construction of actual buildings. Among the best-known "architectural" creations in this style in Germany was the Gotisches Haus at Wörlitz, built for the local prince between 1773 and 1793—the house he had really wanted when he built the Wörlitz estate in 1769 (see fig. 1); then, he had yielded to the combined eloquence of Erdmannsdorff

8. Friedrich Gilly, sketch of the vaults in the Middle Castle of Marienburg, 1794, pen and pencil, 14.9 × 22 cm. Staatliche Museen zu Berlin, Preußischer Kulturbesitz, Kunstbibliothek, Hdz 5652.

and Winckelmann and changed his mind. Another example was the castle of Löwenburg at Wilhelmshöhe, near Kassel, built between 1793 and 1798 and incorporating, in addition to the usual apartments, a great hall, a chapel, an armory, and a library with all the trappings familiar from the contemporary Gothic novel.

In his study of late eighteenth-century German art, "Die Erweckung der Gotik" (The awakening of the Gothic), 1928, Alfred Neumeyer pointed out that the Gothic "dabbling" at Löwenburg was still in progress when Gilly's records of Marienburg and Wackenroder's *Herzensergießungen* appeared, both documents of the new turn-of-the-century view of medieval art.[126] Among the architects of the Romantic generation, emotions ran deep; not only did they turn against late Baroque and Rococo travesties of the antique, they also appropriated "their fathers' Gothic trifles,"[127] which they reworked with a new seriousness.

The sentimental thrill that was supposed to be evoked by a picturesque scattering of Gothic ruins on the grounds of a country house or by a building with Gothic ornaments now gave way to a rapt sense of "wonderment" that could be elicited only by the presence of genuine ruins. The effective contrasts of light and shade, the abruptly looming masses of masonry, and the glimpses of subterranean vaults in Gilly's sanguine drawings pointed to the suggestive influence of the imagery of Piranesi; they also bore witness to an emotional encounter with a monument of medieval architecture. The message that there was a "masculine"—one is tempted to say a Doric[128]—magnificence in

Haupt Ansicht des alten Schlosses zu Marienburg.
gebaut um das Jahr 1309. durch die Ritter des teutschen Ordens, unter dem Hochmeister Siegfried von Feuchtwangen.
als Beytrag zur Geschichte der vaterländischen Architectur.

Neumeyer

9. Friedrich Gilly, *View of the Exterior of the Chapter House of Marienburg* (*Hauptansicht des alten Schlosses zu Marienburg*), 1794–1797, engraving by Friedrich Frick, 9.2 × 11.8 cm. From *Sammlung nützlicher Aufsätze und Nachrichten, die Baukunst betreffend* 1, no. 2 (1797), title vignette. Santa Monica, The Getty Center for the History of Art and the Humanities.

medieval architecture is also implicit in Gilly's reference to "the truly grand simplicity" of the style of Marienburg.[129] Here, again, it was not the architectural form or the ornament of the building but the elemental contrast inherent in its structure that made it so "extraordinarily massive," standing "as deeply embedded in the earth as it rises above it," and offering the experience of somber, subterranean vaults as well as light, soaring arcades.[130]

The massive, towering wall piers on the west front of Marienburg (fig. 9) were hollowed out at third-story level and interrupted by slender, twinned pillars. This created a kind of elevated colonnade and a loggia that crossed almost the full width of the building in front of the chapter house. This contrast in the placing of masses, with its Venetian associations that reminded Gilly of the Doges' Palace, produced a sensational effect that was followed by another, when, having "hardly . . . gazed one's fill on the astonishing sight of this aerial rank of columns, suspended high above one's head," one entered the building and stepped under the "magnificent vaults of the former knights' refectory."[131]

These vaults were supported by three monolithic granite piers, and the ribs of the vaults sprang—as Gilly said in a remarkable, poetic image that captures all the grandeur of this triumph over gravity—"like a rocket from each pier."[132] Before his eyes, the spectacle of Gothic rib vault construction transformed itself into a fireworks display, in which the ribs soared like rockets against the night sky of the vault canopy, exploding at the apex of their trajectory, "in alternating points,"[133] into coruscating star patterns.

In a pen-and-pencil drawing (fig. 10), Gilly has shown himself at the moment of this architectural reverie. Deep in thought, he stands against one of the piers of the refectory, as if leaning on a tree; his eyes are raised skyward to the vault, where the imaginary fireworks display of the structural pattern is taking place. His gaze seems to penetrate the vault and lose itself in infinity, as if the vault had no bosses, and as if the building itself—either already ruined or still under construction—existed only in the geometry of its constructional lines.

In the drama of spatial construction that unfolded before Gilly's mind's eye, Gothic architecture finally broke free from its role as stage scenery for an idyll. The romance of ruins was put into reverse, and the Gothic was restored to a life of its own through the image of its construction. The thrill of sublimity that a ruin was supposed to convey to a sensitive soul transformed itself into astonishment at the "truly admirable boldness" of the structure.[134] The image of the bare construction—which, as the part that longest resists the necessary and natural process of decay, defines the "bold" and "colossal" quality of any ruin—here took on a new function as the vehicle of a mood, thus anticipating the "carcass aesthetic" (*Rohbau-Ästhetik*), similarly based on admiration of structural audacity, that bore fruit only in Modernism.[135]

10. Friedrich Gilly, refectory of Marienburg with male figure leaning against a column, 1794, pen and pencil with wash, 25.7×35 cm. Staatliche Museen zu Berlin, Preußischer Kulturbesitz, Kunstbibliothek, Hdz 5651. Photo: Petersen.

11. Friedrich Gilly, vaults in the chapter house of Marienburg, 1794, pen and pencil with watercolor, 24.5 × 28.8 cm. Staatliche Museen zu Berlin, Preußischer Kulturbesitz, Kupferstichkabinett und Sammlung der Zeichnungen, Gilly sz Nr. 20. Photo: Reinhard Saczewski.

By harking back to the principle of the Gothic rib vault, the nineteenth century was able to realize Gilly's vision of the radical dematerialization of structure and the inclusion of infinite space. In the Crystal Palace, built in London in 1851, iron ribs effortlessly supported a glass roof that soared even over full-grown trees and made the building appear weightless, like a "slice of atmosphere."[136] There, an aged Gilly—had he lived, he would have been seventy-nine—might have recaptured in reality the vision that had come to him beneath the vaults of Marienburg: standing inside a building, leaning against a pier (or a tree), and gazing at the sky.

In Gilly's architectural reverie, the Gothic vault (fig. 11) transformed itself into a window open to the sky. The firmament, the cosmos, entered into the construction; in merging with cosmic space, the work of architecture expanded into metaphysics as a bridge between the finite world of humanity and the infinite world of the universe. To fulfill the same purpose that had induced Baroque architects to resort to ceiling painting—namely, to extend the real space of the building into illusionary space—Gilly used the image of structure itself. From structure, he derived a new imagery of freedom, transparency, and weightlessness that was as much of a fiction in terms of contemporary structural technology as the illusionism that had gone before.

In Gilly's account of Marienburg architecture runs the gamut of all its possible states, from heavy to light, from solid to transparent. The moods associated with these states range from subterranean Piranesian gloom to the "grandeur and exhilaration" of the "magnificent vaults" that evoke utopian visions of an aerial architecture, liberated from the weight of earthly existence. Marienburg, which owed part of its fame to the fact that it penetrated as far into the ground as it rose above it, was sunk at one extreme beneath the devouring waves of time while soaring, at the other extreme, into a filigree, almost immaterial structure whose next conceivable stage consisted of light. The momentary architecture of an exploding rocket was an apt image for this extreme state.

It is not far from the architectural antitheses of Marienburg to a painting that Schinkel produced under the title *Gothic Cathedral by the Waterside* (*Gothischer Dom am Wasser*), 1813 (Berlin, Staatliche Museen Preußischer Kulturbesitz, Nationalgalerie, Sammlung Wagener, no. 207). In another Gothic fantasy of vertically arrayed extremes, the cathedral reaches up from the darkness of an enormous rocky massif into an evening sky where it seems to dissolve into light. On the horizontal axis, too, Schinkel's cathedral seems to represent a bridge between antithetical worlds. Flanked by town houses, Gothic on the left and Neoclassical on the right, the cathedral marks the pivotal junction of Gothic and classical: the link between Nuremberg and Rome, Dürer and Raphael, that Gilly's generation attempted to establish in their art.

In Gilly's relationship with the warring styles of the late eighteenth century, the frontier between them had become permeable in both directions. Marienburg, which was historically almost a Venetian building, could be transformed into something almost Roman, combining medieval verticality with the massive force of Rome. As presented by Gilly, the Gothic was indeed no longer "the antithesis of classical architecture" but its "confirmation."[137]

For the sources that might have inspired Gilly's view of the Gothic, it becomes necessary to look beyond the late eighteenth-century German theoreticians, such as Johann Georg Sulzer, who dismissed Gothic architecture wholesale as obsolete.[138] By contrast, French architectural theory in the eighteenth century showed itself to be considerably more open-minded. While condemning contemporary Gothic follies and dismissing the forms of Gothic architecture as defective, French critics could not deny their admiration for the structural audacity and above all the grandeur of spatial effect that they found in the Gothic cathedrals. To bridge this gulf between emotion and reason, between the undoubted aesthetic pleasure and the equally undoubted irregularity of form, they evolved a number of theoretical strategies. Such ideas were certainly well known to Gilly, who came of French Huguenot immigrant stock. The writings of the major French architectural theorists, including Marc-Antoine Laugier, Charles-Etienne Briseux, Jacques-François Blondel, Marie-Joseph Peyre, and Antoine-Chrysostome Quatremère de Quincy, were all in his library.[139]

Blondel had pointed out that the Gothic cathedrals actually revealed the very same proportions as buildings constructed in accordance with the rules of "correct" architecture. Laugier, whose *Essai sur l'architecture* of 1753 (translated into English as *An Essay on Architecture* in 1755) enjoyed a wide circulation throughout Europe, called upon his readers to see the Gothic through classical eyes and to refine it accordingly in order to make it available as a source of inspiration for the architecture of the present day.[140] Like other theoreticians before him, Laugier praised the Gothic for its rationality of construction and its spatial power, but he condemned its forms as illogical and accordingly regarded it as stylistically unacceptable.

In his *Observations* of 1765, which Gilly owned,[141] Laugier praised the Gothic even more highly than he had in the *Essai*. In a description of the magical dynamism of a cathedral interior, he gave way to a positively Romantic enthusiasm. "A captivating arrangement in which the gaze pleasurably traverses several ranks of columns into recessed chapels profusely and unevenly lighted by their stained-glass windows . . . a mingling, a movement, a tumult of openings and masses that interact and contrast to delightful effect."[142]

Laugier's proposal to improve Gothic forms by simplifying them—for instance, by adapting a compound pier to bring it as close as possible to the profile of a column—was by no means unacceptable to Gilly. In a sketch made in Strasbourg of a church interior, Gilly takes his cue from Laugier and converts a slender compound pier

12. Friedrich Gilly, design for a loggia, date unknown, pencil and red ink, 40.5×33.5 cm.
Lost. From Alfred Rietdorf, *Gilly: Wiedergeburt der Architektur* (Berlin: Hans von Hugo,
1940), 47, fig. 30. Santa Monica, The Getty Center for the History of Art and the Humanities.

with its clustered shafts into a plain, tall, Tuscan half-column.[143] In his design for the church of Saint-Germain-l'Auxerrois, Laugier had gone even further by setting pointed arches on a row of massive, fluted columns.

This formulation of a kind of "masculine" Doric medievalism, reinterpreting admired aspects of the Gothic in classical terms, could be reversed to create a "light," slender, as it were Gothic, variety of Doric. For this, all that was needed was a "true" architect (as defined by Blondel): one who was unprejudiced enough to prefer beauty to stylistic purity. Gilly's dreamed reduction of Marienburg to the naked rationality of its construction, outlined against infinite space, was a kind of Gothic answer to the imaginary primeval hut that Laugier had adduced as evidence of the rightness of classical form. Both were predicated on an identity between the abstract, constitutive idea and the architectural form.

Gilly's design for a loggia (fig. 12) is one of the most radical expressions of late eighteenth-century architectural rationalism. It shows a temple, Gothic in its slenderness, in which classical form is pared down—or perhaps we should say dematerialized, as in a dream—to the irreducible minimum of post and lintel. Once more, as in Gilly's vision of the refectory at Marienburg, the naked skeleton of the construction, open to empty space on every side, becomes the architecture. As light as a piered Gothic structure but placed on a massive podium like a classical temple, purged of any trace of history, pure as the primeval hut, Gilly's loggia becomes impossible to assign to any historical age. A plea for a lightweight and transparent monumentality, this imagined building seems timeless, archaic, and utopian, all at once. It evokes associations that stretch back in time to Stonehenge[144] and forward to the modern skeleton constructions of our own century and the steel temples of Mies van der Rohe.[145]

What Gilly looked for at Marienburg was the grandeur created by structure, both above and below ground. However, this longing for the Absolute did not at all mean that such minor, incidental, and comparatively unspectacular features as technical installations, water supplies and drains, or the castle's ingenious hypocaust system escaped his curiosity. This is most vividly illustrated by the episode of the revolving chair, which Gilly described at the end of his Marienburg essay as a unique technological curiosity. This chair, placed opposite the altar, was reserved for the grand master of the Teutonic Order; he could take his seat on it inside his own apartment and then have himself swiveled round "on this suspended framework" in order to appear "quite effortlessly among the knights gathered in worship" in the adjoining church "and later return in the same manner."[146]

Gilly's closing remark, "Such was the progress, even at that early date, of ingenuity in the pursuit of comfort,"[147] seems to have struck a number of his readers as irreverent, if not downright improper. There must have been some complaints, or else

13. Friedrich Gilly, Marienburg, view of the entrance with bridge, 1794, pen and pencil with brown India ink wash, 27.8 × 24.2 cm. Staatliche Museen zu Berlin, Preußischer Kulturbesitz, Kupferstichkabinett und Sammlung der Zeichnungen, Gilly sz Nr. 6. Photo: Reinhard Saczewski.

why would the editor have published an additional text by Gilly, with a preamble of his own? In this rider, Gilly supplied the curious contrivance with an explanation to set it in a rather more serious light, which he hoped would "not be unwelcome to attentive readers and to antiquarians in particular."[148]

The favorable public response to Gilly's Marienburg drawings (figs. 13, 14) prompted their publication in a suite of copper engravings by Friedrich Frick. In 1799 the *Journal des Luxus und der Moden* (Journal of luxury and fashion) announced their publication and urged its readers to subscribe.[149] Whether the publication was a success is another matter. According to Adler, the first subscription list contained only thirty-eight names.[150] Gilly only lived to see the completion and issue of the first few plates. In the rest of the series, which was completed only in 1803, the engraver took liberties with Gilly's drawings.

14. Friedrich Gilly, the Teutonic Knights entering the chapter house of Marienburg, 1794, pen and pencil with wash, 18.3×26.5 cm. Staatliche Museen zu Berlin, Preußischer Kulturbesitz, Kunstbibliothek, Hdz 5661. Photo: Petersen.

The introduction to the series, in which Gilly had no say, was printed after his death; it revealed some new priorities. Frick had rewritten Gilly's history of Marien-burg, aiming at completeness and exactitude in detail, but without the climactic mo-ments that marked Gilly's atmospheric view of medieval architecture. It had also been necessary to have new studies made of Marienburg, because—as Frick explained in his introduction—Gilly's drawings were "not only sketched but also assembled out of his imagination."[151] Gilly's tinge of emotion would no longer do in face of the editor's con-cern for "historical correctness" and the increasing interest in archaeological accuracy.[152]

Frick's engraving of the refectory is a striking illustration of this increased lit-eralism. In Gilly's original drawing (see fig. 10) he showed himself in the solitary figure of the architect in a hat and a long cloak, leaning against a pier and lost in reverie. In Frick's engraving (see fig. vii, p. 124), by contrast, the same figure has moved one pace forward without greatly changing his pose; but now, instead of listening only to his own dreams, he attends to the words of a guide who assumes a didactic pose, with one arm outstretched to point into the interior and direct his companion's attention, a pose in which Frick has clearly inserted himself into the picture.

The same concern with scientific accuracy speaks from the composite plates of patterns and details, which Frick lays out before the viewer with didactic precision, almost like the parts of a kit. With the help of these, an industrious craftsman might one day come along and reassemble Marienburg as a work of architecture.

The Friedrichsdenkmal: Temple in an Urban Landscape

In the summer of 1796 the Akademie der bildenden Künste announced, for the second time, a competition to design a monument to Frederick II of Prussia, who had died in his palace at Potsdam in 1786. (The first, inconclusive, competition had been held in 1791.)

Immediately after the king's death a number of individual artists worked independently on the idea of a memorial. From the German artists' colony in Rome, Schadow and Alexander Trippel sent proposals for a monument that would show the king in the traditional "Marcus Aurelius pose"—as a Roman emperor on a pacing horse. Others, such as the historiographer and philosopher Jean Henri Samuel Formey, proposed a plain pyramid adorned only with the Latin inscription "Friderico." Even a celestial monument was suggested: the royal astronomer, Johann Elert Bode, assembled seventy-six small stars recently discovered by himself into a constellation under the name of *Gloire de Fréderic* (Frederick's Glory).[153] Still in 1786, and again from the German artists' colony in Rome, came the idea of a monument in the form of a temple. Hans Christian Genelli proposed a plain Doric prostyle structure containing a sarcophagus on which the figure of the king would recline, a design that was to gain wide currency as the virtual prototype of the Neoclassical mausoleum.

In his project for the monument, Gilly took up the idea of a temple, but he went far beyond any solution envisaged by the authors of the competition in 1796. He handled his brief with positively regal assurance, disregarding the competition's stipulations even in the choice of a site. More than any previous design, Gilly's project reflected the awareness that this king had been known as "the Great": in sheer size, this Friedrichsdenkmal dwarfed all its predecessors.

To erect a fitting memorial to a Prussian king who had become a national hero—and on whom the *epitheton ornans* of "the Great" had been bestowed by no less a person than Voltaire—was an undertaking that clearly carried with it its own ideas of scale. One consequence of this, in Gilly's eyes, was that an architectural memorial to Frederick should be seen in the context of the planning of the city as a whole. This being so, it seemed to him that the site stipulated in the competition—on the street Unter den Linden, near the Opera and the Zeughaus (armory)—was inadequate. As a worthier site for his memorial, Gilly chose Leipziger Platz, the city square just inside the Potsdam Gate. The memorial itself comprised not only a temple on a podium in the center of the square but also the context that the temple required in order to assert its significance, for Gilly's grand urban gesture embraced the design of the surrounding buildings.

In an accompanying text, which has come down to us in two versions, different in wording but virtually identical in substance,[154] Gilly justified his decisions by explaining the factors that governed this unusual project. Inside the Potsdam Gate, at the southwestern entrance to the walled city, the octagonal Leipziger Platz was ideal in a number of ways as a site for the monument. The Potsdam Gate marked the end of Leipziger Straße, "one of the longest and finest streets in the city," which offered the visitor who entered the city at this point a long vista that conveyed "the most stately and favorable impression of the beauty of the capital."[155] Located on the edge of the city, at the threshold between Friedrichstadt—the quarter laid out on a Baroque plan under Frederick I and developed under Frederick II—and the Tiergarten, just outside the city walls, Leipziger Platz was part of "the finest section of the city . . . that district that owes its present elegance to the late king himself."[156] From outside the city, this was also the termination of the high road from Potsdam, "one of the most-traveled and most convenient military roads between the two royal residences";[157] through this square Frederick II had often passed on his way to his palace at Potsdam, and this added a direct personal relevance to the urban context of the monument.

This urbanistic interpretation of the brief, which breached the conditions of the competition and caused something of a stir in Berlin, is a further indication of the horizons against which Gilly's architectural ideas took shape. Here, too, quite obviously, French ideas were involved, although Gilly made no mention of this in his explanatory text. At the back of his mind must have been the celebrated competition to find a suitable site for a statue of Louis XIV in Paris, which provoked a long-lasting public debate on urban planning and commemorative architecture. While some architects tied their memorial projects to the completion of the facade of the Louvre, others set out, by placing the memorial in a specially designed context, to promote the improvement of a whole district.

In Paris the most radical opponent of the building of a new city square to accommodate the king's statue was none other than Voltaire. In his essay "Des embellissemens de Paris" (On the improvements of Paris), 1749, Voltaire took the view that Paris required to be improved not so much by new squares as—far more urgently—by new fountains, marketplaces, and orderly streets in the many neglected parts of the city. Gilly similarly saw his project for a memorial as a contribution to the development of the urban fabric. In it he undertook to give shape to one of the entrances into the city rather than add a final touch to the space on Unter den Linden known as the Forum Fridericianum, which was created under Frederick II by the building of the Opera, the Bibliothek, and the Hedwigskirche.

Writing on urban planning and garden design in his *Essai*, Laugier had emphasized the importance of the design of city gates for the beautification of cities and had made recommendations that Gilly obviously took to heart. According to Laugier—and to Gilly's explanatory text—long avenues lined with two or three rows of trees should lead to the city gate, which, as in Gilly's design, should take the form of a triumphal arch. Immediately inside the gate should be an extensive square from which, as far as possible, the streets should radiate in a fan formation, as from the Piazza del Popolo in Rome; Potsdamer Platz followed this model.

Gilly had also drawn ideas on the layout of monumental squares from the celebrated work by Pierre Patte, *Monumens érigés en France* (Monuments built in France), 1765, which contained a map of Paris with all the various projects for a memorial to Louis XV inserted in their places, thus supplying a typological inventory of urban squares.[158]

In Berlin itself, moreover, there was a direct precedent for the commemorative use of a city gate as a monument. When the Brandenburg Gate was rebuilt as the first major architectural project after the death of Frederick II, the Akademie der Wissenschaften (Academy of sciences) proposed that it should be renamed Porta Fridericiana. Carl Gotthard Langhans's structure marked the Tiergarten end of the great avenue Unter den Linden, which offered an imposing perspective to the traveler who entered the city through the gate; its urban functions were thus very similar to those defined by Gilly. The Brandenburg Gate gave definitive form to the square-shaped Pariser Platz, one of the three great Friedrichstadt plazas that marked a quadrant around the city center. At the next gate southward, the octagon of Leipziger Platz (unlike the *Rondell*, or circus, of the third plaza, Belle-Alliance-Platz, now Mehring-Platz) had yet to acquire its architectural framework in 1796; and so this afforded the opportunity to complete the whole ambitious urban scheme in accordance with new principles.

Winckelmann's remark, made in 1752, that in Potsdam he had seen both "Athens and Sparta"[159] must still have been ringing in the ears of contemporaries when construction of the Brandenburg Gate began; its solemn inauguration in 1789 would have been a momentous event in the life of Friedrich Gilly, who had then just moved to Berlin. The Brandenburg Gate was well calculated to encourage talk of Berlin as "Athens on the Spree," for Langhans had taken the Propylaeum in Athens, as recorded in the publications of Julien-David Le Roy and of James Stuart and Nicholas Revett, as his model. In 1797 Langhans's student Gilly saw his chance to follow in his master's footsteps with a design for Leipziger Platz and its Potsdam Gate and thus to endow the Prussian Athens with the Parthenon that it still lacked. The note "Athens is a model. Acropolis. Not so

Rome"[160] that Gilly wrote on one of his sheets of sketches for the Friedrichsdenkmal (see fig. iii, p. 134) was about more than the abstract form of his temple for Frederick: it announced an intended urban dimension.

As Gilly explained in his text, the chosen site on Leipziger Platz was "spacious enough for the monument to be seen in its entirety."[161] This detached view, which permitted the building to be seen to full effect without competing with other, existing monuments, would enhance its spatial presence. "To place the memorial in the center of the city, surrounded by a host of buildings, would render that impression weaker and more short-lived."[162] Conversely, as Gilly added in further justification of his choice of site, the memorial would not put other, existing buildings at a disadvantage through its size.

This desire for detachment, based on the urban ideal of a long-range relationship between independent structures, meant that a suitable location would necessarily lie at the edge of the city. Only this would provide the dialectic of simultaneous closeness and remoteness—in terms of space and in terms of the quality of life in public—that would enable the monument to breathe. Leipziger Platz was "not out of the way"; it was "much frequented by citizens and travelers alike," and it thus possessed the "particular distinction" of being "much frequented in itself" but "nevertheless remote from the bustle of affairs," so that there was no danger of "scenes of profanity and scandal" that would have "desecrated the atmosphere of this shrine."[163] It was here, on the threshold between city and country, in a location that possessed the delightful property of being "animated without being clamorous,"[164] that the monument found its artistic niche in the urban topography.

Like the site, the monument itself was full of antitheses. The acropolis of Frederick II rose like an artificial island in the center of Leipziger Platz (see figs. i, ii, p. 128). On a dark, massive podium, high above the street and the surrounding buildings, stood a white temple "in a simple, ancient Doric form."[165] The synthesis of temple and city gate meant that, despite its outward look of quasi-Egyptian massiveness, the substructure had to be pierced by two wide vaults at right angles to each other: "Vaulted passages open up the view through this podium."[166] It was simultaneously forbidding and inviting, a massive bulwark and an open shell. In the domed central space at the intersection of the vaults, Gilly planned to install the sarcophagus containing Frederick's remains.

As at Marienburg, massiveness and openness interacted to delight the eye with a series of perspectival views. In Gilly's colored rendering of the Friedrichsdenkmal, the evening light rakes through the full length of the dark podium. It shines brightly, even on the soffit of the vault at the Leipziger Straße end, as if the building had collected light within it like a lantern. Attracted by this light-filled subterranean world, the visitor entered the memorial precinct, which with its four great external stairways was an invitation to an extraordinary perambulation or promenade in three dimensions.

The Friedrichsdenkmal was designed to be walked around and climbed. The perambulation that began with the visitor's entry to the square was intended to transform itself on the way "around the monument . . . into a veritable promenade"[167] and to lead through the interior, up to the temple, and through the "open colonnades of the porticoes"[168] into the *cella*. Here a statue was erected in a niche, lit from above through an opening in the roof of the temple: in Gilly's words, "the most beautiful of all forms of lighting."[169]

The climax of this ritual peregrination through enclosed and open space, which was also a *promenade architecturale* offering unaccustomed views of the anatomy of architecture, was "the view that meets the eye on leaving the temple,"[170] which Gilly called "a prospect unique of its kind."[171] The monument served to set the scene for the true spectacle, which was the panorama of the city. "The view that meets the eye on leaving the temple—the whole of Friedrichstadt at the visitor's feet—is so grand and so singular that no other [location] affords its equal."[172]

A tour of the majestic staircases and external steps of the podium of Gilly's Friedrichsdenkmal would indeed have offered a "veritable promenade," in accordance with all the rules of the late eighteenth-century literature on the "art of taking a walk." The bourgeois family stroll, or promenade, customarily led outside the city gates to a hill with a view back across the city from which one had come. The artificial architectural landscape of Gilly's monument was the urbanized form of this promenade, now offering a comparable experience *inside* the city walls.

Karl Gottlob Schelle—a disciple of the Leipzig philosopher Karl Heinrich Heydenreich, whom Gilly admired, and of whom we shall have occasion to speak in connection with Gilly's essay on the relationship between art and science—discussed the ingredients of the art of promenading and the relationship between nature, landscape, and sensibility in his book *Spaziergänge; oder, Die Kunst, Spatzieren zu gehen* (Promenades; or, The art of taking a walk), published in 1802.[173] In terms of Schelle's theory of the walk as an art form, Gilly's Friedrichsdenkmal fulfilled the requirements of a perfect promenade, including its specific spatial conception. By virtue of its position, this monument combined "both kinds of promenade," amid nature and in the city; through the changes of direction involved in climbing its steps, the monument offered the opportunity "to embrace the horizon by a slight turn of the body"; and, finally, the monument offered something "that no outing in a carriage or on horseback can offer," namely "the full and tranquil enjoyment of the view," possible only from the summit of a hill "that is accessible only to pedestrians."[174] On the plaza that Gilly had praised as "animated without being clamorous,"[175] the walker might experience the state of inward and outward attentiveness, the "free play of the forces of sensibility," that Schelle captured in the happy phrase "floating, as it were, lightly above the objects in view."[176]

To walk up and down in an open portico was a habit characteristic of the philosopher. In 1798 Goethe deliberately chose the title *Propyläen* (Propylaea) for a periodical he was publishing in order to suggest that "knowledge," even "after lengthy wanderings," was "still in the forecourts."[177] (Gilly took note of the journal, as we know from his essay "Einige Gedanken über die Notwendigkeit, die verschiedenen Theile der Baukunst, in wissenschaftlicher und praktischer Hinsicht, möglichst zu vereinen" [Some thoughts on the necessity of endeavoring to unify the various departments of architecture in both theory and practice], published in 1799 and translated in this volume.)[178] For Goethe, the architecture of the ones who realized they were still in the forecourts was a metaphor for knowledge itself: "Step, gate, entrance, portico, the space between inside and outside, between the sacred and the profane: such alone can be the space in which we shall linger with our friends."[179]

The peripatetic observer and collector of impressions was a standard feature in representations of the Greek temple, as seen around 1800. The people Schinkel chose to populate the scenery in his perspectival drawing of the upper staircase landing in the Altes Museum—which can be regarded as an homage to Gilly's Friedrichsdenkmal—speak volumes for this. As enshrined in Gilly's temple for Frederick II, the same idea clearly informs Hegel's description of the Greek temple as a place for spontaneous encounters and unconstrained dialogue. "And so the impression conveyed by these temples remains simple and grand, but at the same time cheerful, open, and comfortable; for the whole edifice is designed for lingering, for walking to and fro, for coming and going, rather than for the inward concentration of a gathering enclosed and divorced from the world outside."[180]

Gilly's design was appropriate for the commemoration of a monarch who was celebrated for his love of philosophy and music, and who regarded his palace of Sans Souci as a hermitage, high above the terraced vineyards in his park at Potsdam. In 1769, in his personal testament, Frederick himself wrote: "I have lived like a philosopher and desire to be buried as one, without ostentatious mourning and funerary pomp. . . . I am to be buried at Sans Souci, at the top of the terraces, in a tomb that I have caused to be built."[181]

Gilly, whose declared intention was to give tangible form to "the idea of Potsdam," also led the visitor to the top of an array of terraces; there, free of superfluous wants, removed from everyday life but still bound by fellowship, one might experience that state of sociable unsociability—"being sufficient unto oneself"—that Immanuel Kant described as close to the sublime.[182] And so, symbolically, Gilly had brought back to the city the spirit of the hermit of Sans Souci, who in his last years had so contemptuously turned his back on the world. Like an urban version of Rousseau's Island, which became a common feature of eighteenth-century parks in the guise of a Philosopher's Grave, the monument offered itself as a setting for the "reveries of a solitary walker" (*Les rêveries du promeneur solitaire*)—to borrow the title of a book that Rousseau began in 1776[183]—who from the heights of this urban belvedere might enjoy an unobstructed view across the regular blocks of the Friedrichstadt and the open spaces of the Tiergarten.

Gilly's temple precinct brought a new expansiveness into the urban space and its plan. The Berlin of compact blocks and corridorlike streets was expanded into new spatial dimensions by this projection of an ideal urban nucleus. The idea of the city monument as the source of a sense of community gave rise to a Neoclassical vision that set out to transform the confined urban space of the Baroque into an open townscape of cuboid forms. The motif of the elevated temple was central to this vision. Schinkel's major buildings in Berlin continue the tradition of urban architecture in precisely the same spirit.

The fact that Gilly designed the Friedrichsdenkmal with his Palladio open on the desk beside him—as is proved by notes containing page references on one sheet of sketches—permits further conclusions as to the urban dimension of his architectural concept. Palladio was unique in the degree to which he used the motif of the temple on a podium as a defining landmark in the creation of urban space. The facades of his Venetian churches, such as Il Redentore and San Giorgio Maggiore, use the formula of a temple on a high podium to project an ideal image of a city center, opening up the narrow, medieval horizons of the urban fabric and expanding it beyond the Bacino di San Marco.

Freed of the homogenizing force of the centralized perspective that feudal potentates of the Baroque had employed to assert their authority, the late eighteenth-century temple in the open countryside was an embodiment of the ideals of the new age. The rise of bourgeois individualism, pleading natural rights as an argument for social and political emancipation from the Baroque caste system, was matched by the emergence of an antihierarchical conception of space; and this found significant expression in the English landscape garden. A temple in parkland was more than just a picturesque motif. As a freestanding piece of architectural sculpture, it made space accessible to consciousness because the building could be experienced and explored; it thus played its part in the restoration of a spatial continuum that was no longer frontal and centralized but panoramic. The total visibility of the structure in its setting—as demanded by Gilly within the urban fabric—played its part in the reinterpretation of urban space as a landscape sequence.

The new aesthetic and philosophical sense of space that went with the early Neoclassical love of monuments entailed a new relationship with the Absolute: that is to say, above all, a new relationship between building, earth, and sky. According to ideal-

15. Friedrich Gilly, Temple of Solitude (*Der Tempel der Einsamkeit*), about 1799/1800, pen and brush with wash, 11.8×23.5 cm. Staatliche Museen zu Berlin, Preußischer Kulturbesitz, Kupferstichkabinett, KdZ 7234. Photo: Jörg P. Anders.

istic philosophy, only the incorporation of the infinite in the finite, of the ideal in the real could endow architecture with the threshold quality that would introduce the Absolute, through the aesthetic experience, into the earthly world. Many of Gilly's designs are about creating this dialog with the Absolute by architectural means. This is as true of the tiny Temple of Solitude in its parkland setting as it is of the vast, urban "Temple of Solitude" that was the Friedrichsdenkmal.

Gilly's Temple of Solitude (fig. 15) is a small, circular structure incorporating the antithesis discovered at Marienburg. Built over a subterranean vault, it is open to the sky. It is intended as a place of solemn stillness where the tired and solitary wayfarer may find solace in contemplation. There he can add his voice to Hölderlin's or Schiller's lament for the lost totality of existence,[184] turn his gaze skyward, and undergo an aesthetic experience that ushers him into the presence of the Absolute.

In the Friedrichsdenkmal architecture similarly acts to grant the observer a part in a greater whole. The open *cella* of the temple, with its window toward the sky, completes the "veritable promenade"[185] and adds a metaphorical dimension to the visitor's perambulation through space. The typically early Romantic, aesthetico-religious longing for subjective identification with the Absolute finds striking expression in one of Gilly's notes on the Friedrichsdenkmal (in words that might already have been spoken

16. *Elevation of a Temple Thought to Have Been Dedicated to Jupiter Serapis at Pozzuoli, near Naples* (*Elevation d'un Temple que l'on pense avoir été dédié a Jupiter Serapis a Pouzzols près de Naples*), engraving, 23 × 34.3 cm. From Jean-Claude-Richard de Saint-Non, *Voyage pittoresque; ou, Description des royaumes de Naples et de Sicile* (Paris: Imprimerie de Clousier, 1781–1786), 1: part 2, page 173. Santa Monica, The Getty Center for the History of Art and the Humanities.

by the Gilly who stood in reverie in the refectory of Marienburg). "I know of no more beautiful effect than that of being enclosed on all sides—cut off, as it were, from the tumult of the world—and seeing the sky over one's head, free, entirely free. At evening."[186]

It is a sentence that vividly recalls the celebrated words at the end of Kant's *Kritik der praktischen Vernunft* (Critique of practical reason) of 1788. "Two things inspire new and ever-growing feelings of wonderment and awe, whenever contemplation turns toward them: the starry sky above me and the moral law within me."[187] To capture this emotion, Gilly turned for inspiration, as his notes show, to the Temple of Jupiter-Serapis at Pozzuoli, near Naples (fig. 16), which is set within a colonnaded court.[188] He needed to devise an architecture that would encourage retirement and reflection, an architecture that would make it possible to gaze undistractedly at the sky in order to bring the moral order down from it and into the human heart. The "monastic" seclusion that Gilly's poet friend Wackenroder considered appropriate for aesthetic contemplation reflected the same emotional model of religious reverie. Wackenroder likened the encounter with a work of art to a prayer, a dialog with God. It was an act in which, as in Gilly's Temple of Solitude, the viewer knelt in "humble longing" and "bared his breast in silent ecstasy to the light of heaven."[189] In Schinkel's earliest project for a museum, designed under the influence of Gilly as one of the "brethren" of the Privatgesellschaft, this same vision found its appropriate expression in a building with a classical portico and two monastic-looking cloisters.

Bagatelle and Rincy: Exemplary House and Garden

In his essays on the villa of Bagatelle and the country house of Rincy, near Paris, Gilly described two of the places that he had visited on his study tour of France. They formed an antithetical pair, very much in the spirit of the idealist principle to which Gilly subscribed that perfection is to be attained by way of complementary opposites. Bagatelle sprang from a whim on the part of Louis XVI's brother, the comte d'Artois, who in 1777 made a bet with Queen Marie-Antoinette that he could build a villa during the few weeks that the court was at Fontainebleau. This manifestation of sheer high spirits—Bagatelle was run up in just sixty-four days with no expense spared—was matched by a splendid pendant, as Gilly put it, in the shape of the country house of Rincy with its estate, the product of centuries of slow growth. Not courtly ceremonial but "the most varied view of rural activities and customs" complemented the picturesque aspect of the property as a whole, in which "labor and utility" were "everywhere allied with pleasure and grace."[190]

What suggested a "comparison" between these two princely residences, for all the difference in their purpose and character, was the "simplicity and charm" that each displayed in its own way: "exaggerated pomp" had been "cunningly avoided," and "spontaneous charm" was nowhere oppressed by luxury. A certain inner balance between art and function made both Bagatelle and Rincy appear equally exemplary. "Undistracted by gratuitous artifice, we survey well-considered arrangements that might serve as patterns for any similar undertaking elsewhere: patterns that are rightly held to be among the best of their kind."[191]

The way to the villa of Bagatelle was a "splendid and much-frequented walk" from the Tuileries "by way of the delightful Champs-Elysées, through the *barrière*" and into the Bois de Boulogne.[192] To judge from his description, Gilly paid no attention to the buildings of the *barrière* at l'Etoile, one of the important city gates of Paris that had been built in the mid-1780s to designs by Claude-Nicolas Ledoux: he had not one word to say about the buildings or about their architect. As his travel sketches from Paris confirm, however, he certainly had taken note of Ledoux's work. He made sketches of a number of the *barrières* and also of the celebrated Hôtel Thélusson built by Ledoux around 1780.[193]

The reader learns nothing of the modern architecture that lay on the way to Bagatelle—even though, at the end of his essay, Gilly laments the prevalent German ignorance of modern French architecture. His reference to "the narrative of one recent traveler, in which French architecture and architects are treated at some length," confuses matters still more;[194] for here Gilly is referring to an article in the *Journal des Luxus und der Moden* by Wilhelm von Wolzogen, who, under the title "Über die Barrieren von Paris" (On the *barrières* of Paris), which Gilly does not give in his note, devoted himself almost exclusively to Ledoux's *barrières*.[195] In Wolzogen's article Ledoux's structures, with their "so-called Paestum columns" and their "stamp of strength and simplicity," were praised as a triumph of architecture and urban design. "In the *barrières* I see architecture in its infancy and simplicity; in the colonnade of the Louvre, by comparison, I see its cultivation and refinement. When I depart from Paris, these grand and beautiful forms grant me repose from the fatigue inflicted by the excessive refinement and tangle of so many ornaments, tasteful in detail but frequently tasteless in their relation to the whole."[196] As far as I know, this is the first published reference in German to an architect whom twentieth-century art historians have hailed as a leading representative of "revolutionary architecture."

In the context of Gilly's discussion of Bagatelle and Rincy, the controversial architecture of Ledoux was clearly irrelevant. Perhaps, too, Gilly's own opinion of such buildings was neutral or even hostile, in spite of the interest that his sketches of the newest urban architecture—Parisian theaters, places of assembly, architecture for festivals on the Champ de Mars, shopping arcades, and apartment buildings—seemed to demonstrate.

Although he demanded a renewal of architecture, Gilly did not give his approval to the innovator Ledoux, who broke with convention, but to an architect who cautiously refined what was given to him. François-Joseph Bélanger, the most elegant and best-known architect of the Louis XVI style—which marked the transition from Baroque to Neoclassicism—was singled out by Gilly as "one of the few artists to have given an entirely new direction to French architecture . . . exalting it far above the prevailing frivolity of the age."[197]

A student of Le Roy, Bélanger made his name in 1777 with his masterpiece, the villa of Bagatelle, which contained the most celebrated "English garden" of the period. Gilly regarded this house and its gardens, twenty years old when he saw them, as "incontestably one of the finest works of recent French architecture." Bagatelle presented an "excellent model" of taste and arrangement and also displayed the highest degree of perfection in the "neatness and care" of its execution. This last was all the more remarkable in view of the "well-nigh incredible rapidity" with which the construction had been done.[198] Bélanger's plan had been drawn up and approved in forty-eight hours; materials and transportation intended for other building projects had been requisitioned as far as possible and diverted to Bagatelle. There, from late September to late November 1777, some nine hundred workmen went into action, and the villa, together with its terraces and garden walls, sprang from the earth virtually overnight.[199]

The idea of the almost magical speed of construction and of the military order involved in the planning of this "almost inconceivable creation" aroused Gilly to a state of high enthusiasm.[200] At the very beginning of his article he pictured the scene with a sense of wonder vividly reminiscent of his response to Marienburg. Here, however, instead of the bare bones of architecture lit up by the magical pyrotechnics of the constructional scheme, he saw a real picture of a building under construction that by daylight and by torchlight appeared as "an architectural miracle."[201]

The construction work passed before his mind's eye in an immaculate sequence of operations that reminds us of the division of labor in industrial production. So incredible did the process seem, that Gilly predicted Bagatelle would become renowned for "the miraculous speed of its making, which will be passed down in anecdote and one day, perhaps, lost in legend."[202] The historical scene in Gilly's drawing of Marienburg had been peopled by knights returning from the crusades; in this modern drama, the stage was filled with a swarm of workers on a torchlit battlefield waging nocturnal war against the clock.

To a modern reader Gilly's description of the construction process seems to anticipate the pace and the techniques of mass production in the age of Henry Ford. The organic coherence of traditional methods is disrupted, and the construction process itself seems to be turned on its head. There is no sequence of related operations that would be intelligible in craft terms. Nor does work seem to be tied to the site, for all the component parts can be produced independently of each other. While work proceeds on the foundations, the ashlar walls are "completed almost to the point of laying the stones." The keyword is simultaneity. The furniture and fittings are commissioned at the same time as the foundation stone is laid, and the paneling of the rooms is made up "in distant workshops." Work is soon "proceeding on the base and the cornice concurrently" in Gilly's mental picture of the process, which takes on a positively futuristic logic. As he says, "the painters were already at work on decorations for walls that had yet to be built."[203]

Bagatelle presented itself to Gilly as a monument to "artistic effort" of the first

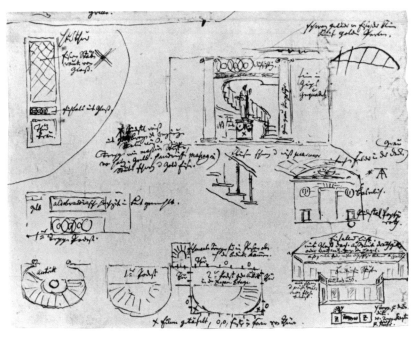

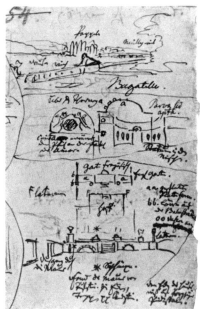

17. and 18. Friedrich Gilly, details of sketches with annotations concerning "Bagatelle,"
1798–1799. Lost. From Alfred Rietdorf, *Gilly: Wiedergeburt der Architektur* (Berlin: Hans von
Hugo, 1940), figs. 161 and 157. Santa Monica, The Getty Center for the History of Art and the
Humanities.

19. Friedrich Gilly, view of French country houses: Floriette, Montreuil, Trianon, Retraite,
Bagatelle, Union, 1798–1799, pen drawing. Lost. From Alfred Rietdorf, *Gilly: Wiedergeburt
der Architektur* (Berlin: Hans von Hugo, 1940), 155, fig. 156. Santa Monica, The Getty Center
for the History of Art and the Humanities.

order. Technical expertise and art combined magnificently, enlisting all their powers to enmesh in "common activity," like the gears of a mechanism whose workings the individual was unable to apprehend. The workers concentrated on their individual tasks and contributed to the "grand design without ever grasping the interconnection of all the parts. That was visible, perfect in every detail, only to the ordering imagination of its deviser."[204] This demiurgic mental feat of anticipating the whole of an organized process, down to the minutest detail, was the prerogative of the modern architect as the organizer of the construction industry. His ingenuity liberated objects from their isolated existence and organized them into a cosmos in which every part had its preordained place.

After evoking this scene of feverish activity, Gilly embarked on a leisurely and comprehensive description of the villa, as also recorded in numerous little sketches. To visit the building, the art-loving traveler took a walk. Arriving at the park gate, he crossed the grounds, passed the kitchen gardens and outbuildings, and approached the house by way of the terrace (fig. 17). The simple, centralized plan of the house, the nature and decor of the individual rooms, the furnishings, the mural paintings by Hubert Robert, and the construction of the flying stair (fig. 18), down to the detail of its unusual handrail, all met with Gilly's entire approval. His words reveal the pleasure he must have felt in surveying the whole building once more in his mind's eye.

Of all the villas in the neighborhood of Paris, some of which Gilly sketched (fig. 19), Bagatelle was his favorite. His own design for Villa Mölter (fig. 20), on Tiergartenstraße in Berlin, which was probably roughly contemporaneous with his article on Bagatelle, clearly reveals the latter's influence, both in plan and in structural makeup.[205] Schinkel must have witnessed Gilly's enthusiasm firsthand, for as Schinkel's biographer, Waagen, tells us, "the first piece of work" that Gilly set for his student was to copy the plan of Bagatelle.[206]

Gilly's guided tour of Bagatelle, a spatial itinerary that "delights the eye at every turn,"[207] ends—like the commentary on the Friedrichsdenkmal—with a view of the surroundings as seen from within. The account of Bagatelle begins with the image of architecture picturesquely set off by nature; it ends with nature again, but this time it is nature as seen in the gardens, set off by architecture.

Gilly had his reservations about this "natural" aspect of the artistic synthesis that was Bagatelle. In his account of Rincy, which also ends by panning across the landscape, he gives full rein to his enthusiasm; here, by contrast, he contents himself with a curt reference to the view. At Rincy the spatial itinerary expands into a genuine "promenade" because the visitor looks out into "an unconstrained and smiling landscape, in which one longs to lose oneself."[208] The relationship between interior and exterior produces the pleasurable state of being enticed first this way then that by a number of

Landhaus des Herrn Geheimen Rath Mölter.
entworfen von Fr. Gilly

20. Friedrich Gilly, *Sketch of Villa Mölter, Berlin. Plan and garden view (Entwurf zum
Mölterschen Landhaus, Berlin. Grundriß und Gartenseite),* 1799, drawing by Friedrich
Schinkel, engraving by A.[nton] Wachsmann, 23.6 × 18.6 cm. From *Sammlung nützlicher
Aufsätze und Nachrichten, die Baukunst betreffend* 4, no. 1 (1800), title vignette. Santa
Monica, The Getty Center for the History of Art and the Humanities.

competing attractions. The interplay of forces is such that one is compelled to tear oneself away from each successive object if any progress is to be made at all. On entering
the gates, the visitor is "encompassed" by views that make him hesitate, wondering
"whether to stop here or to follow the path that leads on."[209] It is no different on later
walking outside the dairy building: "One is finally tempted to forsake this lovely room
only in order better to enjoy the magnificent landscape, and one is carried away by new
delights."[210]

   In contrast, Gilly was unable to summon up any enthusiasm for the garden of
Bagatelle, "laid out in the modern manner, which the French, too, have adopted under
the name of the English style, in order to free themselves of the monotonously scrupulous regularity of their older style of garden design."[211] How much, if anything, he
knew about the genesis of this major French garden must remain an open question. In
spite of his predilection for history, he did not discuss the matter in his essay.

   The first design for the garden of Bagatelle had been drawn up in 1777 by the
celebrated Scottish landscape gardener Thomas Blaikie, who had been in the service of
the French crown since 1776. Blaikie's original design was conceived as more of a landscape than a garden. It fell to Bélanger to bring it more into line with French taste.
Bélanger had visited England in 1766 and had worked for Lord Shelburne at Bowood

in Wiltshire; in the early 1770s he had made a name for himself as a garden designer in the picturesque Anglo-Chinese style with his designs for the prince de Ligne's gardens of Beloeil in Belgium. He reworked Blaikie's design, essentially simplifying it, without changing the character of the garden with its invitation to marvel at exotic trees and plants grown from seeds supposedly collected in Hawaii by Captain Cook on his last voyage to the South Seas. After the Revolution and the flight of the comte d'Artois, the park was opened to the public; the entrance tickets issued to visitors such as Gilly were designed by Bélanger.[212]

Gilly was clearly less interested in the historical background than in the question of what had been gained or lost by this "transformation" of the "trimmed and imprisoned" Baroque garden.[213] But before voicing his own criticisms of the "current taste in the art of the landscape" and of the crimes committed in the name of the picturesque,[214] Gilly paused to cite two contemporary authorities: the abbé Delille and the marquis de Girardin. The abbé was the author of the popular poem *Les Jardins* (The gardens), 1782, and also a celebrated prose writer and translator of Virgil. The marquis was the author of a treatise on gardening published in 1777; he was also the owner and creator of the celebrated gardens of Ermenonville, where Jean-Jacques Rousseau, who benefited from the patronage of the marquis, was to spend the last weeks of his life. Only after this literary digression did Gilly come out with his own opinion.

As in Germany, so in France, he wrote, people had latterly been following the "shop-bought books that contain only the gleanings of English garden design," with the result that gardens had degenerated into "diminutive, artificial models of gardens," where nothing any longer had a settled place of its own, and where nature was "merely bedizened" and "pretentious." The "artificial mounds" dignified by the name of hills or the brooks "set in masonry and yet still made to meander" were proof enough of this. And so the art of landscape gardening in France had lost more than it had gained, had "fallen far short of the ideal," and, "in moving toward picturesque freedom and the seeming absence of constraint," had "been marked more by pettiness than by grandeur." The hint that even in the Baroque garden "there is a way of preserving nature in all her grandeur and delightful freedom"[215] was a pointer to that ideal coexistence of opposites that was the touchstone of true art—and that Gilly found wanting in the imitators of the English garden.

Gilly was by no means alone in this criticism. From the 1770s onward the debate in Germany on the English garden was conducted with increasing vehemence. The accusation of "Gallomania," which Sulzer hurled at the devotees of the Baroque garden in his *Allgemeine Theorie der schönen Künste* (General theory of the fine arts), 1771, was swiftly countered by the historian Justus Möser, who coined the phrase "the English gardening disease."[216] A literary battle erupted, with a torrent of publications on the art of landscape gardening;[217] only a few of these found their way into Gilly's library, which was, however, well supplied with such authorities as Christian Cai Laurenz Hirschfeld and Friedrich-August Krubsacius.[218]

There was, at all events, no lack of bitter polemics on the subject of fashions in garden design. Gilly may well have been confirmed in his own view by meeting Boettiger, who had struck a very similar note in his *Reise nach Wörlitz, 1797* (Journey to Wörlitz, 1797), 1798, describing landscape gardening as "a kind of painting" whose accumulation of "expensive apparatus" was too little to be serious yet too much to be a joke.[219] Goethe, who published his own sharp criticism of contemporary garden fashions in 1787 under the ironic title *Triumph der Empfindsamkeit* (The triumph of sensibility), dismissed the whole debate on the sensory and aesthetic proprieties of garden design with the laconic suggestion that anyone who wanted to see a real park should go on a four-week tour of Switzerland and that anyone who wanted to look at real architecture should go to Rome.

Gilly regarded the whole idyllic business of temples and huts of all kinds, miniature bridges, and other "accumulated frivolities" as "childish and wearisome in the extreme"[220]—a reproach from which the Bagatelle garden was by no means free. Here "the abandonment of rule" in favor of "playfully trivial" taste had caused the charming contrast between the "beauty of Nature" and the "building proper" to be "mitigated, if not erased."[221]

In the article on Rincy, which appeared six months later than that on Bagatelle, Gilly began by referring briefly to the latter villa; and here he actually revoked the criticisms that his distaste for fashions in "English" landscape gardening had perhaps led him to express somewhat too strongly. Now he spoke of Bagatelle as "a most delightful country villa, adorned with decoration of the most refined sort, which unites Art with Nature in the happiest conceivable manner."[222]

The layout of Rincy supplied an example of a world ordered in accordance with altogether happier principles. In it there was no "gratuitous artifice" but the "judicious combination of utility with beauty."[223] There was no need, in this case, to supply a simulacrum of Nature for the sake of picturesqueness; for Rincy combined agriculture, animal husbandry, and hunting, and with its living quarters and outbuildings, pavilions and huts, the estate formed a pastoral ensemble in its own right.

On an artistic tour of Rincy, the visitor might rediscover "the entirely rural." Here Gilly was not describing a pleasure villa but a modest, functional structure, the dairy. Its simple construction embodied the virtues of solidity, order, and cleanliness, down to the forms of the utensils and the bowls in which milk was laid by (see fig. i, p. 160). From this simple structure one might learn that pure and pleasing form might be achieved "without great expense," and that "simplicity . . . serves to adorn and ennoble even the most commonplace implements, vessels, and other objects": a maxim of the functional aesthetic that anticipated twentieth-century "product design" by many years.[224]

At the very end of his discussion of Rincy, Gilly turned his attention to "an unpretentious structure" in a meadow, a building of the type known as a Swiss chalet, with space for cattle and with living quarters for the herdspeople (see fig. ii, p. 162). Built "entirely from timber studs and wattle and daub" and roofed with clapboard and shingles, this chalet made a telling contrast to the architectural quotations and the follies of the English landscape garden. "Located in a distant, quiet corner of the park, this entirely natural construction, in its picturesque setting, presents a surprising and pleasing prospect. A chalet of this kind is indeed worth more than all the modish overelaboration of temples and gaudy pavilions."[225]

Thoughts on the Reunion of Art and Science:
The Necessity of Poetry

In the sequence of their publication in the volume from 1799 of the *Sammlung nützlicher Aufsätze und Nachrichten, die Baukunst betreffend,* Gilly's three essays form a symmetrical composition in their own right. The descriptions of Bagatelle and Rincy appear on either side of a third essay that deals not with built architecture but with the conditions that govern architecture in general and the training of architects in particular. The burden of Gilly's argument in that essay was his dislike—which also found expression in his accounts of French buildings and gardens—of what he saw as a certain prevalent one-sidedness, both in theory and in practice.

In itself, the title, "Einige Gedanken über die Notwendigkeit, die verschiedenen Theile der Baukunst, in wissenschaftlicher und praktischer Hinsicht, möglichst zu vereinen" (Some thoughts on the necessity of endeavoring to unify the various departments of architecture in both theory and practice), implied that something was wrong with contemporary architecture, and the target of the criticism was not hard to identify. Gilly's introductory remark, that reflections like these might not "seem entirely out of place" in a periodical whose purpose it was to collect and pass on "experience in the entire realm of architecture,"[226] was nothing if not plain: he was taking the editors of the periodical at their word.

A number of members of the Supreme Prussian Building Administration, including David Gilly, had in January 1797 launched the *Sammlung,* with its subtitle *Für angehende Baumeister und Freunde der Architektur* (For aspiring architects and friends of architecture). It was an architectural journal of a new kind in that it was not directed to the interested and educated general reader but to an explicitly professional audience, with original contributions by specialists in the most varied departments of architecture and construction. The founding of this, the first professional journal of architecture in Germany, reflected a number of changes that had overtaken the profession in the second half of the eighteenth century.

The only previous German architectural periodical had been the *Allgemeines Magazin für die bürgerliche Baukunst* (General magazine for civil architecture) founded in Weimar in 1789 with the intention of disseminating general knowledge about architecture to a cultivated bourgeois readership, whose taste it sought to educate through book reviews, extracts from books, and translations. It ceased publication in 1796, a fact that in itself casts light on the increasing tendency toward specialization.

From the editorial preamble to the first volume of the *Sammlung* we learn that it was launched in response to the pressure of events. The editors had, it seems, been brought together by their common awareness of the need to bring art and science closer together with a view to giving "scientific guidance" to the artist and "artistic feeling" to the scientist; it had not been their initial intention to found a periodical but rather to compose a basic "manual" of architecture. As things were, however, no such work could "yet"—or rather, no such work could any longer—be written. It would necessarily have to contain "nothing but acknowledged truths"; and, "in relation to architecture as a whole," there were as yet no such truths. It was this predicament that had led to the publication of the *Sammlung* as a periodical collection of essays, in the implicit hope that, out of the specialist contributions published therein, "a complete manual of architecture for our time might one day be compiled."[227]

In "Einige Gedanken" Gilly did not, however, address the editorial collective as such but rather the newly opened Bauakademie, whose prospectus and aims were published in the same volume of the *Sammlung* as his essay.[228] In his text, Gilly made no direct mention of this new institution. It was hardly for him to criticize it openly as he was employed there as a professor. However, the most influential of the *Sammlung*'s editors and contributors also represented a majority of the professors at the Bauakademie, so Gilly's critique of architectural education could not miss its mark.

Modeled on the Ecole centrale des travaux publics in Paris (which would later become the Ecole polytechnique)—the school of engineering established by the Convention on 11 March 1794—the Bauakademie was oriented not so much toward "great" architecture as toward the practical and technical problems associated with training civil engineers and architects for government service. This bias prompted Gilly to make a number of fundamental observations.

Clearly, it was not enough for the young architect to accumulate knowledge in the hope that one day he might be able to put it together into something appropriate. What he wanted was to supply in practice what his age needed and to find principles that would enable him to hold his own in the face of an ever-growing range of expectations and demands. The compression of existing knowledge into a single encyclopedic work comprising "an outline of the entire education of an architect would" (much virtue in Gilly's subjunctive *would*) "unarguably be of the greatest importance and interest"; but this must—and could—be postponed indefinitely. A number of highly unsatisfactory contemporary publications, such as the *Encyclopädie der bürgerlichen Baukunst* (Encyclopedia of civil architecture) by Christian Ludwig Stieglitz, published 1792–1798, can only have confirmed Gilly in this view.[229] Such a comprehensive conspectus of knowledge might "perhaps in time be expected from the pen of some knowledgeable writer";[230] but as things were at present this typically eighteenth-century form of compilation bore little relevance to the young architect's concerns.

What was far more important, in Gilly's view, was to gain a clear idea of what it was that fundamentally defined the art of architecture; and for this it was necessary to gain an insight into its "general features" and "essential relations." Even those specialists who, "mindful of their own limitations, must for their own sakes restrict themselves to one or another aspect of their chosen subject," stood to benefit from such reflections in order to adopt "on occasion . . . a more elevated vantage point and survey the whole."[231]

A view from such a vantage point seemed an urgent necessity given the inconsistency and imprecision that prevailed in the definition of even the simplest terms. As Gilly wrote, "No term has been more variously and loosely applied than 'construction' [*Bauen*]." Equally vague, he went on, was the notion of the "science of construction [*Baukunde*]," which was supposed to stand for the architect's necessary theoretical equipment.[232] Either *Baukunde* was defined by farfetched and fortuitous associations, or it consisted at best of a superficial "initial application of certain common principles," whereby "highly disparate subjects" had been "associated as if they were closely akin."[233] Gilly does not seem to have been unduly shocked by this more or less casual definition of the scope of architecture. What on earth, apart from the practical "advantages inherent in the traditional union between them" and the "initial coincidence of their general principles," did "river engineering . . . hydraulics . . . mechanical engineering . . . mining," or "the making of roads, which also goes by the name of construction," have in common with each other or, finally, with "the art of erecting monumental edifices, or cities, or houses?"[234]

Seen in terms of "direct or intrinsic relevance," the "art of architecture itself [*die eigentliche Baukunst*]" was a world apart from the disciplines of civil engineering, as enumerated by Gilly. "In its own proper domain," the art of architecture was distinguished by an "extraordinary multiplicity" of reference, and to master this was a major undertaking in itself. By contrast with the syllabus of the Bauakademie, which was almost entirely taken up with engineering subjects, architecture needed to be considered "from distinct points of view," "not only in the individual topics with which it deals but also in its associated purposes, wants, and inquiries."[235]

The elaborate argumentation deployed by Gilly did little to clarify the basis for these "distinct points of view." That would emerge, he said, as soon as one looked for the "points of contact" whereby "the purposes and wants themselves necessarily form connections," as required by the "practice" of architecture.[236] In order to discover the purposes and to establish the laws that governed his work, the architect had to operate on many levels. "Now we see him exercising his artistic talent in the realm of taste. . . . Now, as the purpose that determines his plan grows more rigorous, all the requirements inherent to that purpose unite to present a rule, to which his art must be applied. Now it is purpose alone, the dictate of necessity, that becomes the prime law of his work and determines its nature and its form."[237]

Only one person was qualified to be the arbiter of this interaction: the architect who had trodden the thorny path of a "various . . . course of instruction."[238] This demanded of him a breadth of study, both in the arts and in the sciences, that—as Gilly was at pains to emphasize—deserved more respect than it had hitherto received. This artist was required to understand the practical demands of a whole universe of constructional tasks; to translate them into functional, useful "arrangements"; to give them artistic form; and, not least, to go down to the construction site and turn them into workmanlike and inexpensive buildings. The minutest demands of domesticity; the planning of cities, streets, and squares; buildings for transit and for commerce; factories and workshops; and "countless public needs": all these were his concern. In addition, he would be required to provide for "rural economy, husbandry, and the bonds of trade and traffic in the shape of canals, bridges, and roads."[239]

No end to the scope of his work seemed to be in sight. The "objects of the most varied nature" that offered themselves to the architect "on that great stage that is architecture" proliferated, in line with social changes, at a speed that "brought with it a daily increase in the mass of essential knowledge that any architect—however rich he may be in experience—is required to master."[240]

Under the impact of social and technological changes that represented both a stimulus and a threat to the architect, the gulf between the artist and the technician became wider, a gulf that posed a challenge to the architect's self-image as both a specialist and a generalist. The impact of technological and social progress on architecture had raised the fundamental issue of the architect's true role. Gilly had used the example of Bagatelle to describe the fascination of a modern production process based on the division of labor; now he warned of the dangers of an overemphasis on science and of its inherent tendency to lead to the modern cult of specialization.

The evolution toward a "pernicious one-sidedness, not to say division"[241] of architecture between art and science could be countered only by a "comparative view of the entire realm of construction."[242] Even if universal development was reserved for the "exceptional talent" only and it therefore was unfair to demand everything "of any individual architect," all the more care should and must be taken in the training process "to place no limitations of any kind" on the aspiring architect's "training or studies." Everyone should acquire "sound judgment, at least in those parts of the profession most closely related to his own." Without this, the result would be "a degree of one-sidedness that frequently proves pernicious for the individual and for society."[243]

This was the predicament in which—"especially of late"—architecture found itself. It was a predicament influenced, and indeed "necessarily affected," by "the way in which it has been regarded and treated."[244] Gilly ascribed some of the responsibility for this to the "critiques of art and theoretical formulas" that the prolific eighteenth century had turned out in its efforts to find a scientific basis for architecture. To be convinced of this, his contemporaries had only to recall "the futile feuds and controversies between the academic architects and their various adversaries in France and England, with all the dire consequences that ensued."[245]

In theory and practice alike, this "pernicious one-sidedness" was damaging. After first sinking to "the level of mere craftsmanship . . . from which it then had to be rescued," architecture went to the opposite extreme and became the preserve of abstract theorists and antiquarians with no artistic knowledge. "With the spread of learning, architecture came to be treated as a largely scholarly pursuit. The age of the manuals now dawned. Mathematics, in particular, took architecture in hand and even presumed . . . to solve the problem of taste."[246]

Here Gilly was probably alluding to the mathematical argumentation of such writers as Christian Wolff and Leonhard Christoph Sturm, who treated architecture as a branch of applied mathematics and categorized it in a typically eighteenth-century, systematic, strictly rationalist spirit.[247] The champions of this school of thought would have been classed by the poet Wackenroder among those "theorists and systematizers" and "overly ingenious writers of modern times," whom he accused of having "sinned against the *ideals* of the fine arts" with their "futile words."[248]

The examination of "architecture in antiquity," which Gilly knew from many engravings and treatises, old and new, seemed to hold out little promise of a future impulse that might serve to counteract the one-sided orientation of architecture. What was more, the "scientific" study of ancient architecture was subject to the fundamental difficulty that this was "too remote" for any possible "comparison"; even "any attempt to describe it" was attended by "many difficulties."[249] In this view, Gilly had the support of no less an authority than Goethe. In his essay "Über Lehranstalten zu Gunsten der bildenden Künste" (On institutions for the teaching of the fine arts), from which Gilly quoted a passage at the end of "Einige Gedanken," Goethe remarked that nature had isolated every age with, "as it were, walls of brass that no man may overleap."[250]

The vital truth that the architecture of antiquity had to offer to the present was plain for all to see, with no need to delve deep into matters of theory. "Whatever may have been its status or its connection with the sciences, it was then, more than at any other time, that architecture naturally enjoyed a close alliance with *the arts*." As if to confirm the rightness of his demand that the architect's studies should not be limited to technical concerns, Gilly added: "Yet only an unequaled combination of knowledge and talent could have produced the perfection of the works of that age."[251]

The relationship with art marked the critical point in all architectural activity. Here lay the parting of the ways between the artist and the craftsman, the technician and the theoretician. The dictates of modern rationalism and functional thinking had threatened to banish art from the whole field of construction, and architecture was threatened by a functionalist takeover.

> *Architecture had long since been admitted as a true companion of the fine arts; but few now came forward to defend this right or even its right to the name of art. Some conceded it half a vote in the congress of the arts, but others struck it entirely from the list, citing its ignominious subservience to necessity and utility. And so architecture came to be considered merely a mechanical pursuit, and it was subordinated first to one superior authority and then to another: its task was to serve and be useful.*[252]

An age in which—as the poet Schiller put it in his letters of 1795 *Über die ästhetische Erziehung des Menschen* (On the aesthetic education of man)—utility had become the "great idol to which all powers must submit, and all talents pay tribute," such an age stood in need of a new definition of architecture, a definition that would obey "the necessity of the mind, not the exigency of matter."[253] It would be a redefinition that would owe nothing either to the pure theoretician—such as the art historian—or to the technologically oriented engineer-architect. The crisis would be resolved not by the modern specialist but by a man whose concern was with the things of the spirit. "One philosopher, by advancing an entirely new conception, has shown that—on certain conditions—architecture can still be recalled from exile and restored to its ancient rights."[254]

Who was this philosopher who could sit at his desk and help to liberate architecture from its exiled state? Gilly revealed his identity to his readers only indirectly, in a footnote reference to an article in the issue from October 1798 of the *Deutsche Monatsschrift* (edited since 1795 by his journalist brother-in-law, Friedrich Gentz). Gilly gave the title of the piece in question, "Neuer Begriff der Baukunst als schönen Kunst" (A new concept of architecture as a fine art), but omitted its author's name. Only the reader who took the trouble to look up the periodical itself would have discovered that the article bore the name of Karl Heinrich Heydenreich, poet, philosopher, and professor at University of Leipzig.

Heydenreich, who had given Schelle the idea of writing a treatise on the "art of taking a walk,"[255] had first come to prominence in 1790 with *System der Ästhetik* (System of aesthetics), in which he took issue with the rival literary theories of the day.[256] His book claimed to embody a "theory of the fine arts" that might be "read and appreciated" by anyone who had received from Nature both "the beautiful gift of sensibility and the spirit of reflection."[257] However, there was no discussion of architecture in Heydenreich's book, of which Gilly owned a copy. Heydenreich's system of aesthetics differentiated between the "mechanical" and the "fine" arts, and, as one of the mechanical arts that serve a "physical" and not a "spiritual need," architecture was entirely dismissed from consideration. Only through ornamental embellishment could mechanical art approach the state of fine art. Architecture was, of course, "highly susceptible to embellishment," but by its very nature it remained a mechanical art and could never aspire to the status of poetry, music, fine art, or landscape gardening.[258]

As its title suggests, the essay cited by Gilly marked a shift in Heydenreich's position. He now rejected his own former distinction between architecture and the other arts as "hairsplitting" and set up a dialectic of function and idea that Gilly found persuasive. This new Heydenreichian dialectic distinguished between a higher and a lower purpose. A building that had no "higher purpose" beyond its "natural purpose" of keeping out the weather remained—however it might be adorned and ornamented— "a work of common architecture." But for buildings in which "the physical purpose was a means to a higher and intrinsically nobler purpose," such as "churches, buildings intended for deliberation on matters of state, arsenals, buildings for the cultivation of science and of art, rural villas, and the like," the architect must put into his design "the beautiful expression of the higher purpose." It then followed that the work on which he was engaged was a work of "fine" art. The architect remained "bound" by the physical purpose but not to such an extent "as to hinder his genius from finding liberal scope for invention, within which he may choose his forms in accordance with his own feeling."[259]

Using the building of a rural villa as his example, Heydenreich so vividly evoked the process whereby art transcends necessity that one is tempted to imagine that he had before him one of those pen-and-wash perspective renderings in which Gilly transformed his own villa designs, both in mood and in character, into images of a pastoral idyll. "If it is to be a work of fine architecture, on seeing it in its setting (which in itself is part of its invention), we must breathe an atmosphere of rural repose, gentle stillness, and simplicity; these sensations must emerge from the form itself; we must become poets, momentarily caught up in a vision of patriarchal peace and idyllic innocence."[260]

Only the imaginative power that could interpret and present the work's purposes in poetic terms, with a tight, symbolic interlocking of type and metaphor, function and form, could raise construction from the realm of necessity to the realm of art and transform the architect, in Heydenreich's words, into a poet.

> *When the artist succeeds in endowing his buildings with such forms that the idea of the physical purpose entirely disappears, and the beholder is elevated at once to the higher purpose and to the free interplay of images associated with that purpose: then his work is a work of fine architecture. It stands to reason that it must also satisfy all the laws of fitness for purpose, as well as those of proportion. . . . Every work of fine architecture may be seen as* a poetic rendering of the higher purpose of the building, couched in beautiful architectural forms that at once banish all merely physical considerations.
>
> *The most enthusiastic champion of fine architecture could scarcely attach to it a loftier or a nobler conception than this. It emerges as a true* Fine Art. *Its works are the sole fruits of genius; and the mental state of the inventive architect is closely allied to that of the inventive figurative artist or poet. His design is not so much forced on him by the* physical *purpose of the work as created by his* poetic conception of its higher *purpose.*[261]

This "loftier or nobler conception," directed toward what Schinkel was to call the "fundamental principle of all construction," namely "the clearest possible presentation of the ideal of fitness for purpose,"[262] was the central concern of Gilly's essay. The artist stood on the philosopher's shoulders in order to see the world with new eyes and to join him in seeking beauty in the realm of Truth and Necessity. Philosophy and aesthetics combined to point the way for an art that "is as useful as it is pleasurable."[263] Only through such "reciprocal influence" could there be "any general advance toward perfection, especially as things are at present; and for this," wrote Gilly, with an eye to the shortcomings of the training of architects, "the ground cannot be laid too soon."[264]

The principle of a "general advance toward perfection" through "reciprocal influence" was not only a means to an artistic end, it held good for the union of art and science and indeed for the identity of thought and feeling in general. "Einige Gedanken" formed part of a mood of thinking that was characteristic of the philosophical language of the age. A glance at the most important textual document of the period, the so-called "Älteste Systemprogramm des deutschen Idealismus" (Earliest system-program of

German idealism), will make this clear; for this was the document that set out the new preconditions for a reunion of poetry and philosophy, art and science.

The "Systemprogramm" was drawn up, probably in the winter of 1796–1797, by the youthful Friedrich Wilhelm Schelling, Hölderlin, and Hegel; it encapsulates the thought and feeling of Gilly's generation. Against the prevalent one-sidedness caused by a "monotheism of reason and heart," these young philosophers of Sturm und Drang raised a new rallying cry: "A polytheism of imagination and art: that is what we need!"[265] In "Einige Gedanken" Gilly was no less eager than these "architects" of a new art of the mind to "give back wings" to "laboriously plodding" science, so that it might "satisfy a creative spirit, such as ours is, or is to be."[266]

Science must be made sensuous, and poetry must be made scientific, in opposition to those "literal-minded philosophers [*Buchstabenphilosophen*]," the technicians of thought and the purist theoreticians of art, who, as Goethe put it, "would like to turn everything to prose, in architecture as elsewhere."[267] Even before Heydenreich, Goethe had emphasized the importance of poetry to architecture in his essay on architecture of 1795. "It is the poetic part, the fiction, that turns a building into a true work of art."[268]

Philosophy and art now joined hands. Philosophy must become poetry; poetry must become philosophy. The "Systemprogramm" demanded of the philosopher what Gilly expected of the architect. He must venerate art with a sacred enthusiasm.

The philosopher must possess as much aesthetic power as the poet. The only people without an aesthetic sense are our literal-minded philosophers. The philosophy of intelligence is an aesthetic philosophy. It is impossible to be intelligent about anything—even in history, no intelligent reasoning is possible—without an aesthetic sense. This is what is lacking in those who do not understand ideas: those who confess, honestly enough, that anything beyond tables and indexes is a mystery to them.[269]

Only "the idea of Beauty" was capable of building the necessary bridge between reason and emotion; for this alone embodied "the idea that unites all ideas." In the "Systemprogramm" the poet and the philosopher in unison made their profession of faith in a new religion of art: "I am now convinced that the highest act of reason—given that reason embraces all ideas—is an aesthetic act, and that Truth and Goodness are akin only in Beauty."[270]

The ideal beholder of art was the "philosophical critic," one who, in Heydenreich's words, possessed a spark of "artistic genius" of his own, and who was capable not only of appreciation and enthusiasm but also of reflecting, as a philosopher, on the sources and the value of his enjoyments.[271] Heydenreich's poetic philosophy marked a paradigm shift that chimed perfectly with Gilly's mistrust of the popular French and

English theories that were so well represented in his own library. To release architecture from its exile, Gilly looked not to the architectural theoretician but to the poetic philosopher or the philosophic poet—to one who could unite truth with poetic invention in the idea of beauty.

Other poet-philosophers besides Heydenreich gained an audience by proclaiming the identity between Mind and Nature, art and knowledge, which became the foundation of a new religion of art based on the longing for a reconciliation between science and the senses. One of these important thinkers was the writer Karl Philipp Moritz, one of the most contradictory and at the same time one of the most noteworthy figures in late eighteenth-century German literature.

With eight titles, Moritz was the author best represented in the catalog of Gilly's library (aside, that is, from the eleven editions of Vitruvius);[272] Winckelmann was next, with seven titles.[273] All such "numbers games" should be treated with due caution; even so, these statistics may possibly tell us something about the contradictions within Gilly's personal view of art.

Moritz criticized Winckelmann's method with very much the same arguments that Gilly employed against the "one-sided" view of architecture. Winckelmann's celebrated description of the Apollo Belvedere seemed to Moritz "far too conglomerate and too contrived," dismembering the artistic whole into "a composition of fragments." This kind of description had, he wrote, "done far more harm than good" to the visual response to the work of art, for it concentrated too narrowly on specifics instead of "affording us a closer understanding of the whole and of the necessity of its parts."[274]

Like Gilly, a Freemason, Moritz was thus a man who owed a special allegiance to the principles of toleration, freedom of thought, and love of mankind. He had acquired a considerable literary reputation, and his writings veer between literature and aesthetics, between psychology and mythology, between Enlightenment and sensibility. In February 1789, on the recommendation of Goethe (a close friend ever since the two men had first met in Rome), Moritz was appointed professor of the theory of the fine arts at the Akademie der bildenden Künste in Berlin. There, from the spring of that year onward, he gave courses on art theory, classical antiquity, and mythology, which were attended by Gilly's friends Wackenroder and Tieck and by Alexander von Humboldt, who was a frequent visitor to the Gilly household.[275]

Moritz's audience probably also included Gilly himself, then a student at the Akademie working under Erdmannsdorff, an architect who was in personal contact with Winckelmann and had therefore strongly stimulated Gilly's interest in classical antiquity. It may be that Moritz had something to do with Gilly's intensive study of the "history of antiquity, and principally the Egyptians, Greeks, and Romans," of which we hear from Levezow.[276] These studies went beyond the artistic concerns of Winckelmann to embrace a holistic view of the mythology, art, and literature of these peoples, which was entirely in the spirit of Moritz (as represented in the works by Moritz that formed part of Gilly's library).

Moritz's writings had many kinds of inspiration to offer. In his "Versuch einer Vereinigung aller schönen Künste und Wissenschaften unter dem Begriff des sich selbst Vollendeten" (Attempt to unite all the fine arts and sciences under the concept of self-perfection),[277] Moritz anticipated the central ideas of Gilly's "Einige Gedanken" on the union of art and science in architecture. Moritz's reflections on "Abwechslung und Einheit in der Landschaft" (Variety and unity in the landscape), the fruits of his walks in the gardens of Villa Borghese and of Raphael's villa, might well have served as direct models even for the style of description in Gilly's accounts of Rincy and Bagatelle.[278] In *Vorbegriffe zu einer Theorie der Ornamente* (Prolegomena to a theory of ornament), intended as a provisional surrogate for the "complete theory of the fine arts" that was the ultimate goal of his teaching in Berlin, Moritz expressed ideas on architecture to which Gilly could have given wholehearted assent. The following is an example: "Man desires not only to dwell in a building with pleasure but also to look at it with pleasure, and almost as many hands are at work for the nourishment of the eye as for the feeding of the body."[279]

In according primacy to the poetic, in legitimizing the aesthetic act as the highest act of reason, an entire late eighteenth-century generation was drawing its own historical conclusions from its experience of the Age of Reason. The Enlightenment had redefined the central issue of philosophy, replacing the traditional God / World / Man equation with a modern equation: Universal Knowledge / Nature as Unifier / Cognitive Subject. By an act of reason, the Enlightenment had broken the spell of the ancient myths; and the emotional reaction, when it came, took the form of poetic protest. Shaken by the collapse of libertarian ideals in the revolutionary Terror, the avant-garde of the generation born around 1770 embarked on a critique of the Enlightenment that employed the tools of the Enlightenment itself.[280] The shipwreck of reason amid the excesses of the Revolution had made it brutally clear that no rational, political action could ever establish liberty once the means to that end took on a life of their own. "What has always made the State into a hell has been man's desire to make it into his heaven." With these words, Hölderlin's Hyperion laid his finger on the sore point in the Enlightenment dialectic. He went on to lay down his own indictment of "pure reason": "Nothing intelligent has ever come out of mere intellect; nothing reasonable has ever come out of mere reason."[281]

Through poetry, humanity must recover its sensibility. For Gilly's generation, this became a political program. The urgent need for a reunion of knowledge and feeling had been expressed in the "Systemprogramm" in one sentence that conveyed the crucial gist of the new mentality: "We must have a new mythology, but a mythology that stands in the service of ideas; it must be a mythology of *reason*."[282]

This call for the remythologization of reason was an acknowledgment that reason needed to be complemented by something else. This did not imply a rejection of reason as such. Once science was no longer the sole ruler of knowledge, it would become possible to regain a new wholeness and to ensure that the means to an end would never again run out of control: that reason would never again—as had so recently been the case—obliterate humanity.

This is the wider mental context of Gilly's call for the renewal of architecture through the reunion of art and technology. Gilly's "remythologization" of the art of construction under the primacy of poetry was intended to restore art to its "ancient"— that is, mythologically warranted—"rights." Art, and not science, embodied the true language of humanity; the idealists believed that the poetry of every people and every age had something in common. This universality was the source of the social authority of the poetic, and the philosopher and the artist saw themselves (and each other) as the emissaries and vice-regents of that authority. Firm in their faith in eternal recurrence they set out—as described in the "Systemprogramm"—to restore poetry to its higher dignity. "In the end it will become what it was in the beginning: *the teacher of humankind*."[283]

Only poetry could teach human beings how to put into successful practice the new age's ideals of liberty and equality. The aesthetic revolution must come before the political revolution: beauty before liberty, idea before purpose. Only then could political and practical action be rescued from the certain failure to which purposive (or functional) thinking and the loss of control over means—the sources of that "pernicious one-sidedness"—ineluctably led. To solve the problems of society "in the world of experience," it was necessary to proceed—to quote a celebrated sentence from Schiller's *Über die ästhetische Erziehung des Menschen*—"by way of aesthetics . . . for the path to liberty leads through beauty."[284]

At the end of that path lay the vision of liberty as a social condition, as outlined in the closing words of the "Systemprogramm":

> *The enlightened and the unenlightened must at last join hands: Mythology must become philo-sophical, and the people rational; philosophy must become mythological, that philosophers may become sensory beings. Then eternal concord will reign among us. There will be no contempt in anyone's eye; never again will a blind populace tremble in the presence of its wise men and priests. . . . Only then can we hope for an equal development of all human abilities, those of the individual and those of all individuals. Strength will never again be oppressed; and all minds will be free and equal!*[285]

Gilly's program for the redemption of architecture kept very close to this image, which he made into an Oath of the Horatii in which the architect joined hands with the scientist:

> *For everywhere the architect must learn to value the scientist, and the scientist to value the architect; architects, each with particular talents and native gifts, must work together in mutual respect; and no vain pride must mark out the supposed "artist"* [Baukünstler] *among them. Each must extend a hand to all in the interests of mutual aid—all the more so as the goal to which all aspire grows ever more distant and more manifold.*[286]

But for the enlightened and the unenlightened to join hands—or so the "Systemprogramm" reasoned—ideas must become "aesthetic, that is to say, mythological," for otherwise the people would take no interest in them. By the same token, mythology must become "rational" if the philosopher, as the champion of reason, was not to feel ashamed of it. The hope that art would exert a formative influence on the individual and on the great mass of the population was founded on the idea of its educative mission. The development and schooling of the individual must be pursued in the spirit of a new unity of science and art.

Gilly saw architecture as an art conceived to apply a "judicious combination of utility with beauty";[287] and as such it was particularly dependent on "the interest and the response—and thus on the level of education—of the public at large."[288] Only as the object of the "most attentive public support" could architecture thrive; and, wherever it flourished, it was "itself a sign of a cultivated society," and thus an expression of a "more general interest." It might therefore be seen as "a gratifying example" when—as with the founding of the Bauakademie—a state gave "its practical patronage to architecture as an important agent of the common good." By the same token, it was the particular duty of all concerned to promote not only the cultivation of the public at large but "its receptivity to excellence, grandeur, and beauty."[289]

In support of this last demand Gilly cited "the judicious words of a universally revered author," giving the last word in his essay to Goethe. In 1799, in the second volume of his periodical *Propyläen*, Goethe had written the essay "Über Lehranstalten zu Gunsten der bildenden Künste," which Gilly found extremely useful in articulating his own views on the training of the architect. In this, Goethe declared:

> *If art be controlled and subdued, if it be made to conform to the dictates of its age, it will wither and perish.* . . . . If the arts are to flourish and advance, there must be a universal and active love of art, with a predisposition toward greatness. . . . . *It is vain to expect that elegance, taste, and fitness for purpose will spread their influence through every*

craft; for this can never happen until a feeling for art has become general and until those qualities are in demand.[290]

The youthful architect thus enlisted the support of an authority whose competence in matters artistic was beyond all doubt. With a modest call to "the ablest men" in architecture to support the "principles of breadth of view, mutual association, and social utility," Gilly brought to an end "Einige Gedanken."[291]

Painterly Perspectives: Cubes in the Sand

Gilly's espousal of the reunion of art and science, as proclaimed in "Einige Gedanken," prompts the question as to how far he lived up to his aspirations in his own teaching at the Bauakademie, where he held professorial responsibility for "instruction in optics and perspective . . . also in architectural and mechanical draftsmanship."[292]

According to the course outline submitted by Gilly on 17 May 1799, the teaching of optics and perspective embraced architectural draftsmanship over a range that extended from pure geometrical construction, by way of the rendering of historical works of architecture, to the treatment of artistic and painterly effects.[293]

According to Leon Battista Alberti the arts of painting and mathematics are as indispensable to the architect as are voice and syllables to the poet;[294] so, according to this, Gilly was providing instruction in the very elements of architecture. Levezow wrote of the "affectionate satisfaction" that was the response of Gilly's "numerous listeners," and he praised above all "the new connection" that Gilly made, "in accordance with his method, between mathematical and strictly painterly perspective," a connection that may very well stand for that link between poetry and science that was central to idealist thinking.[295]

In the outline of May 1799, Gilly went on to propose that for the sake of economy, duplicate copies of books with engravings be transferred from the royal libraries to the Bauakademie for teaching purposes, and that "a number of highly necessary recent works" be acquired.[296] In September 1799, before embarking on his first winter semester, Gilly submitted to the director of the Bauakademie a provisional outline of his lecture course on optics and perspective and appended a "Verzeichnis einer Auswahl, der auf der hiesigen Königlichen Bibliothek vorhandenen Doubletten" (List of a selection of duplicates present in the royal library of this city), compiled by himself, in order to suggest to the "esteemed Director . . . which books might be purchased, whether for now or for later, or else transferred to the Akademie on loan."[297]

The selection of eleven books that Gilly listed as "highly important for instruction in architecture and in draftsmanship" together with his course outline on "Optik und Perspektive als Grundlage einer theoretisch artistischen Anweisung zur Zeichenkunst besonders für Architekten" (Optics and perspective as the basis of a theoretical artistic instruction in the art of draftsmanship, for architects in particular)[298] can be seen as a clear reflection of Gilly's view of both the precise (or constructional) and the poetic (painterly or picturesque) aspects of his subject.

He divided his material into three sections. The first was "linear draftsmanship in theory and practice," subdivided into the theory of projection and laws of geometric construction; handling of the artistic effect of perspective ("with reference to picturesque effect"); and the optical impression made on the human eye ("apparent effects and foreshortening of architectural masses and their parts"). The second was "lessons in light and shade"; and the third was "lessons in color."[299]

This progression of draftsmanship from construction through artistic considerations to painterly effect, which led "to a particular gratification for the eye through the nature of the colors and harmony," was also reflected in the book list submitted by Gilly. The list began with Antoine Desgodets, *Les édifices antiques de Rome*, 1682 (translated into English as *The Ancient Buildings of Rome* in 1795), the principal work of an architect who had methodically surveyed the buildings of Rome and who prided himself on the accuracy of his measurements, pointing out errors in the work of such predecessors as Serlio and Palladio (which soon led to accusations of pedantry).[300] The list ended with the extravagant vision of the fictive archaeology of Piranesi, whose *Opere varie di architettura, prospettive, grotteschi, antichità sul gusto degli antichi Romani* (Various works on architecture, perspectives, grotesques, antiquities, according to the taste of the ancient Romans), 1750, was listed under a short title.

The yawning gulf between these two views of antiquity was bridged by other works selected by Gilly. They included modern classics, such as Claude Perrault's edition from 1673 of Vitruvius;[301] standard works on the remains of antiquity, such as the engraved work on the monuments of Athens published in 1758 by Le Roy,[302] whose acquaintance Gilly had made in Paris; Thomas Major's account of the temples of Paestum, published in 1768;[303] the celebrated albums of engravings of the monuments of Rome by Antonio Labacco, 1552,[304] and Jean Barbault, 1761;[305] and volumes of plates on the antiquities of Baalbek and Palmyra. The selection was rounded off by a *Voyage pittoresque; ou, Description des royaumes de Naples et Sicile* (Picturesque journey; or, Description of the kingdoms of Naples and Sicily), 1781–1786, for which—as also for the accompanying works on perspective and geometry—Gilly could refer to his well-stocked personal library.[306]

The list of duplicates was supplemented by a further list of books that, in Gilly's view, "would not be indispensable acquisitions, or urgently required for specific

21. Friedrich Gilly, perspectival drawing, date unknown, pen and watercolor. (Estate of Martin Friedrich von Alten.) Staatliche Museen zu Berlin, Preußischer Kulturbesitz, Kunstbibliothek, Hdz 7718, Kasten 3085a. Photo: Petersen.

teaching purposes, but might be purchased on readily acceptable terms, at *very low prices*, to become the foundation of a future library solely dedicated to the use of the Akademie."[307] Among the authors recommended here were such well-known names as Vincenzo Scamozzi, Wendel Dietterlin, Carlo Fontana, Giovanni Pietro Bellori, Winckelmann, and Bonaventur van Overbeke.

Among the papers of Martin Friedrich von Alten, a friend of David Gilly, there are two perspective studies (figs. 21, 22) that probably derive directly from Friedrich Gilly's teaching at the Bauakademie and may even be by his own hand.[308] Both are pen-and-wash drawings, no doubt meant for one of the volumes of teaching materials that Gilly intended to publish. Identical in logic and structure, they show arrangements of geometric solids in a landscape setting. Both vividly underscore how, for Gilly, the learning of techniques of draftsmanship went hand in hand with the "study of grand effects" that alone could lead to perfection.[309]

One of these two perspective studies (see fig. 22)—so concentrated in its architectural and landscape forms that no one but Gilly could have created it—is a visual manifesto for the rebirth of the art of architecture that he, in the spirit of idealism, had espoused as his sacred duty.

22. Friedrich Gilly, cubes in the sand: perspectival study with landscape, date unknown, pen and watercolor, 23×30.5 cm. (Estate of Martin Friedrich von Alten.) Staatliche Museen zu Berlin, Preußischer Kulturbesitz, Kunstbibliothek, Hdz 7719. Photo: Petersen.

It is one of the most remarkable architectural drawings of the later eighteenth century. Bare, stereometric blocks, entirely original in conception and arrangement, are assembled into a group of abstract solids, embedded in the expanse of a Mediterranean coastal landscape and bathed in its warm light. The inclined ramps of the nearest block recall the steps of the Friedrichsdenkmal, which transmutes under these southern skies into an abstract sculpture of reason. Entirely without decorative detail, these cubes on a south Italian shore proclaim the utopian vision of an architecture cleansed of superfluity, a naked architecture that gains its three-dimensional suggestiveness only through the effect of abstract solids.

Like Gilly's design for a loggia, this world of pure form has an air of timelessness that evokes associations with the abstract Neoclassicism of the twentieth century. One is reminded of the stage designs of Adolphe Appia; of Mies van der Rohe's apartment blocks on Afrikanische Straße in Berlin; of the free-floating "architectons" of a Kazimir Malevich; or of the Mediterranean definition of architecture as the exact and wise interplay of solids in light that was a prime article of faith for Le Corbusier.

But whereas twentieth-century Modernism with its love of suspended forms sets out to free solids from the effects of earthly gravity, Gilly's "architectons" bear down on the earth with all the weight of naked, hewn blocks, immovable as a pyramid. These abstract volumes are set down in epic terrain: a classical landscape shaped by the reading of Ovid, which supplies an interpretative context for the cubic compositions of reason. The picturesque charm of this landscape, with its deep shadows, dramatic clouds, and distant volcanoes, points to a coastal landscape in the south of Italy, like that of the Bay of Naples or the Gulf of Salerno. The horizon of this landscape of the mind—a surrogate for Greece, the home of myths and of art itself—is the coordinate to which the sculpture of reason is referred. An exhilarating sense of freedom prevails in this space in which Reason and Nature conduct a dialog. We are aware of the infinite and all-embracing cycle of Nature, the necessity that gently overarches all existence. Given this mythologically warranted continuity, the stereometric block initiates and proclaims a coming style: a style that contributes to the rebirth of architecture, just as reason enshrined in poetry contributes to the attainment of the idea of liberty.

The cubes in the sand are attended by the same magical and mythical aura that surrounds the ruins of antiquity in the paintings of the same period. We sense the intended symbolic affinity with the antique in a landscape in which—on our own *voyage pittoresque* through the remains of the ancient world—we might expect to find Greek temples, just as, south of Naples, we find the temples of Paestum.

In his article on art schools, cited by Gilly, Goethe had criticized the "Egyptian ponderousness" and the "Paestum columns" that were becoming prevalent in contemporary architecture at a time when "we had hardly yet escaped from the Gothic and Chinese aberrations." We shall never know whether Goethe had Gilly, among others, in mind when he went on to express the desire for a man of "proven taste," a "teacher and a master . . . who will earnestly warn his students against such errors from the very outset and will direct them onto the better path."[310]

Simultaneously archaic and utopian, those cubes in the sand bear witness to a Paestum style of a very different kind, both abstract and modernistic; they open up the prospect of an architecture that is both classical and modern, an architecture entirely liberated from stylistic imitation. If Gilly was indeed their creator, then we are entitled to regard him as the "benefactor of his age" who, in Goethe's words, "has the good fortune to achieve the introduction of a purer taste."[311]

Notes

Bracketed numbers following page numbers in the bibliographic citations below refer the reader to the translation of the cited text that appears in the present volume.

Insofar as possible, references to books in the catalog of Gilly's library (see Appendix 2) are given complete bibliographic citations.

1. Friedrich Carl Wittichen, ed., *Briefe von und an Friedrich von Gentz* (Munich: R. Oldenbourg, 1909), 1: 226–27, quoted from Alste Oncken, *Friedrich Gilly, 1772–1800* (Berlin: Deutscher Verein für Kunstwissenschaft, 1935; reprint, Berlin: Mann, 1981), 101: "*Daß er ein Mensch von großer Wißbegierde und von nicht gemeinen Kenntnissen in seinem Fache, daß er überdies ein liebenswürdiger Mensch im besten Sinne des Wortes ist, das alles könnte ich ganz mit Stillschweigen übergehen, weil ich dreist darauf rechnen darf, daß Sie es sehr bald, auch wenn er Ihnen durch niemand empfohlen wäre, bemerkt haben würden. Aber was ich Ihnen sagen muß, weil dies in eine Sphäre gehört, die außerhalb der Grenzen eines vorübergehenden Umgangs liegt, und was mich nicht etwa bloß persönliche Liebe sagen heißt, ist, daß in diesem jungen Mann eines der ersten Kunstgenies wohnt, die unser Vaterland in diesem Zeitalter hervorgebracht hat. Es bezeichnet den Umfang seiner Talente noch lange nicht genug, ob es gleich immer schon viel für ihn sagt, daß alle Sachverständigen ohne Ausnahme ihm in seinem vierundzwanzigsten Jahre den unstreitigen Rang des ersten Architekten im Preußischen Staat einräumten; so wie man ihm überhaupt keine Gerechtigkeit widerfahren läßt, wenn man ihn, dem in jeder bildenden Kunst in höchste Stufe zu erreichen bestimmt war, bloß als einen Architekten betrachtet.*"

2. Wilhelm Heinrich Wackenroder, *Werke und Briefe*, ed. Friedrich von der Leyen (Jena: E. Diederich, 1910), 2: 108, quoted from Oncken (see note 1), 29: "*Ich habe eine Bekanntschaft gemacht, die mir nicht erfreulicher sein konnte: mit einem jungen Architekten Gilly, den Bernhardi kennt. Aber jede Schilderung ist zu schwach! Das ist ein Künstler! So ein verzehrender Enthusiasmus für alte griechische Simplizität! Ich habe einige sehr glückliche Stunden ästhetischer Unterhaltung mit ihm gehabt. Ein göttlicher Mensch!*"

3. Oncken (see note 1), 29.

4. [Wilhelm Heinrich Wackenroder], *Herzensergießungen eines kunstliebenden Klosterbruders* (Berlin: Johann Friedrich Unger, 1797); rev. ed., with epilogue by Richard Benz (Stuttgart: Philipp Reclam, 1987).

5. See Appendix 2, p. 16, no. 75.

6. Alfred Neumeyer, "Die Erweckung der Gotik in der deutschen Kunst des späten 18. Jahrhunderts: Ein Beitrag zur Vorgeschichte der Romantik," *Repertorium für Kunstwissenschaft* 49 (1928): 75–123, 159–85, esp. 118, assessed Gilly and Wackenroder—who also died young—as parallel phenomena and attributed to Gilly a role in architecture similar to that played by Wackenroder in literature. The relationship between Gilly and Wackenroder remains undefined and can merely be inferred from their Berlin circle of acquaintances. See also Oncken (note 1), esp. 29.

7. Marlies Lammert, *David Gilly: Ein Baumeister des deutschen Klassizismus* (Berlin, 1964; reprint, Berlin: Mann, 1981).

8. *"Die Dächer sind in der Natur etwas zu hoch."*

9. On the public and critical response to the Brandenburg Gate, see *Schlesische Provinzialblätter* for 1789, as quoted by Rolf Bothe, "Antikenrezeption in Bauten und Entwürfen Berliner Architekten zwischen 1790 und 1870," in Willmuth Arenhövel, ed., *Berlin und die Antike: Architektur, Kunstgewerbe, Malerei, Skulptur, Theater und Wissenschaft vom 16. Jahrhundert bis heute*, exh. cat. (Berlin: Deutsches Archäologisches Institut, 1979), 1: 299.

10. Mentioned anonymously in the Akademie catalog for 1791, p. 55, no. 128. See Helmut Börsch-Supan, ed., *Die Kataloge der Berliner Akademie-Ausstellungen, 1786–1850*, vol. 1, Quellen und Schriften zur bildenden Kunst, ed. Otto Lehmann-Brockhaus and Stephan Waetzoldt, no. 4 (Berlin: Bruno Hessling, 1971).

11. Konrad Levezow, *Denkschrift auf Friedrich Gilly, königlichen Architekten und Professor der Academie der Baukunst zu Berlin* (Berlin: Georg Reimer, 1801); all subsequent references to this text are to the version published in Internationale Bauausstellung Berlin 1987, *Friedrich Gilly, 1772–1800, und die Privatgesellschaft junger Architekten*, exh. cat. (Berlin: Willmuth Arenhövel, 1984), 217–42, esp. 232. Levezow gives the subject of this drawing as "Entrance to the Chapter House." Drawings are not listed individually in the catalog of the Akademie exhibition of 1795. The reference is presumably to the drawing reproduced in plate X of Frick and Gilly's published Marienburg series. See Wilhelm Salewski, ed., *Schloß Marienburg in Preußen: Das Ansichtswerk von Friedrich Gilly und Friedrich Frick: In Lieferungen erschienen von 1799 bis 1803* (Düsseldorf: Galtgarben, 1965).

12. Geheimes Staatsarchiv Preußischer Kulturbesitz, Abteilung Merseburg (hereafter GStA Merseburg), Geheimes Zivilkabinett, Rep. 96 A Tit. 12 A, fol. 8; copy of letter from Frederick William III, 28 November 1795.

13. Friedrich Gilly, "Über die vom Herrn Oberhof-Bauamts-Kondukteur Gilly im Jahr 1794 aufgenommenen Ansichten des Schlosses der deutschen Ritter zu Marienburg in Westpreußen," in J. W. A. Kosmann and Th. Heinsius, eds., *Denkwürdigkeiten und Tagesgeschichte der Mark Brandenburg* (June 1796): 667–76; idem, "Zusatz zu dem Aufsatz des Herrn Oberhof-Bauamts-Kondukteurs Gilly über Marienburg," *Denkwürdigkeiten und Tagesgeschichte der Mark Brandenburg* (August 1796): 892.

14. In a letter from David Gilly to the king, dated 8 September 1798, we read: *"Mein Sohn der Hofbau-Inspector hat nunmehr den größten Theil seiner Reisen zurückgelegt; er hat Holland, Frankreich, Engelland und zuletzt noch den zünftigen Schleswigschen Kanal besucht und ist jetzt, da die Umstände die Reise nach Italien so sehr widerrathen, entschloßen nur noch einen Theil von Ober-Deutschland zu bereisen und gegen Winter in sein Vaterland zurückzukehren"* (My son, the royal building inspector, has now completed the greater part of his travels; he has visited Holland, France, England, and latterly also the state-of-the-art Schleswig Canal; and now, since circumstances render a visit to Italy so inadvisable, he has resolved merely to tour a part of southern Germany and to return to his native country at the onset of winter). GStA Merseburg (see note 12), Rep. 96 A Tit. 12 A, fol. 8.

15. Gustav Friedrich Waagen, "Karl Friedrich Schinkel als Mensch und Künstler," *Berliner Kalender auf das Gemein Jahr 1844* (Berlin, 1844), 317; this has been reprinted with an introduction by Werner Gabler (Düsseldorf: Werner, 1980).

16. Friedrich Gilly, ms. of paper read to the Privatgesellschaft on 30 January 1799, in Internationale Bauausstellung Berlin 1987 (see note 11), 178.

17. Hella Reelfs, "Friedrich und David Gilly in neuer Sicht," *Sitzungsberichte der Kunstgeschichtlichen Gesellschaft zu Berlin,* n.s., 28/29 (1981): 18–23.

18. Internationale Bauausstellung Berlin 1987 (see note 11), 174ff.

19. Levezow (see note 11), 234: " . . . *zur Aufmunterung des Genies durch gemeinschaftlichen Wetteifer, zur Erholung nach den gewöhnlichen Geschäftsarbeiten, durch Veranlassung zu Arbeiten genialischer Art.*" A noteworthy early sign of recognition was the inclusion of Gilly in the *Dictionnaire universel, historique, critique et bibliographique,* ed. Louis Mayeul Chaudon (Paris: De l'impr. de Mame frères, 1810–1812), 7: 436. See Werner Oechslin, "Friedrich Gillys kurzes Leben, sein 'Friedrichsdenkmal' und die Philosophie der Architektur," in Internationale Bauausstellung Berlin 1987 (see note 11), 22–40.

20. Levezow (see note 11), 234: "*Außerdem theilte man sich durch Vorlesungen historische Nachrichten über den Fortgang der Baukunst und die neuesten größeren Bauunternehmungen des In- und Auslandes mit, so wie auch gesammelte biographische Nachrichten von verstorbenen berühmten Architekten. Zuweilen hielt ein Mitglied der Gesellschaft eine Vorlesung über irgend einen wichtigen Gegenstand der schönen Architektur.*" It is likely that Gilly's descriptions of the villa of Bagatelle and of the Rincy farm estate were originally written as papers of this kind.

21. GStA Merseburg (see note 12), Rep. 76 alt IV, Kuratorium der Bauakademie, Nr. 25. Other instructors at the Bauakademie included David Gilly, "country house architecture and general structural theory, bridge and hydraulic engineering, and economics of construction"; Carl Gotthard Langhans, "mathematics and drawing"; Friedrich Becherer, "architectural draftsmanship"; Alois Hirt, "history of architecture"; Heinrich Karl Riedel, "agricultural architecture"; Johann Albert Eytelwein, "mathematics, statics, river engineering, and dike building." On the curriculum of the Bauakademie, see Johann Albert Eytelwein, "Nachricht von der Errichtung der königlichen Bauakademie zu Berlin," *Sammlung nützlicher Aufsätze und Nachrichten, die Baukunst betreffend* 3, no. 2 (1799): 28–40.

22. Copy of letter in GStA Merseburg (see note 12).

23. GStA Merseburg (see note 12), Gen. Directorium, Bau-Akademie Deput. Tit. VI, Nr. 8, Acta wegen des Unterrichts in der Optik und Perspective: Professor Gilly, Simon: 1799–1809, fol. 10: "*Die langwierige Kränklichkeit, woran ich leider nun schon seit Jahren leide, ist von der Art, daß mehrere Ärtze mir den Gebrauch des Karlsbades jetzt als ein nothwendiges Heilmittel verschreiben, und ich kann, um mir selbst nicht Vorwürfe zuzuziehen, dieser Vorschrift nicht entgegen seyn, so unangenehm vieles dabey ist, und besonders, daß ich mich zu einer gänzlichen Unterbrechung meiner Dienst-Verhältniße entschließen muß. Ich bin aber nun schon nothwendig zu einer Reise gezwungen, und lege deshalb abschriftlich das Attest, welches ich dieserhalb vom Artzt erhalten habe, bey.*

Ich sehe mich nun genötigt hierzu bey seinem königlichen hochlöblichen Directoris der Bau-Akademie ganz gehorsamst um einen Urlaub von ohngefähr 6 bis 8 Wochen, als solange etwa die Kur und Reise dauern möchte, nachzusehen, und bin der Hoffnung, daß sein hochlöbliches Direktorium meine ganz gehorsamste Bitte gütigst unter-

stützen werde. Zudem ich den glücklichen Gewinn der wiederhergestellten Gesundheit sehnlich erwarte, bin ich von dem Wunsche durchdrungen der mir anvertrauten Geschäfte künftig desto fleißiger vorzustehen, wobey ich keine Mühe scheuen werde."

24. GStA Merseburg (see note 12), Rep. 76 alt IV, Kuratorium der Bauakademie, Nr. 25, fol. 5, letter from Bauakademie directorate (*Directorium*) to board of trustees (*Curatorium*), 14 July 1800: *"Wir haben allen Grund zu wünschen, daß dieser schätzbare Lehrer bey der Akademie wieder hergestellt werde, und haben uns daher veranlaßt gefunden Ew. Exzellenz und dem kgl. hohen Curatorium der Bau-Akademie diesen seinen Wunsch gehorsamst vorzutragen und dabey zu erklären, daß wir um so mehr auf die gnädige Erfahrung desselben, ganz gehorsamst antragen, da wir bereits die Einleitung getroffen haben, daß durch seine Abwesenheit nichts versäumt werde. [Marginal annotation: 'Bey diesen Umständen wird der Urlaub bewilligt. 19. July 1800.'] Derselbe hat seiner übrigen Verhältnisse wegen auch bereits bey der Kgl. Majestät um die allerhöchste Erlaubniß nachgesucht und hofft diese bald zu erhalten. Berlin den 14. July 1800. Riedel"* (We have every reason to wish to see this estimable instructor restored to the Akademie, and this prompts us respectfully to forward this request from him to Your Excellency and to the distinguished Royal Board of Trustees of the Bauakademie, and to declare that we feel all the more able to make respectful application for a favorable consideration of the same in that we have already taken steps to ensure that no work will suffer as a result of his absence. [Marginal note: "This being so, leave of absence is granted. 19 July 1800."] In respect of his other duties, he has already made application to His Majesty for leave of absence and hopes to receive this shortly. Berlin, 14 July 1800, Riedel).

25. Oncken (see note 1), 77. Walther Th. Hinrichs, *Carl Gotthard Langhans: Ein Schlesischer Baumeister, 1733–1808* (Strasbourg: Heitz & Mündel, 1909), 77.

26. Oncken (see note 1), 60. The correspondence on this subject between the building authority (*Baubehörde*) of the city of Königsberg and the Oberbaudepartment (Building administration) in Berlin is in GStA Merseburg (see note 12), Generaldirection Oberbau-Department, Tit. XXXIV, Nr. 24, Bd. IV, 78ff.

27. Friedrich Rabe, "Beschreibung des zu Paretz über der Eisgrube erbaueten Lusthauses," *Sammlung nützlicher Aufsätze und Nachrichten, die Baukunst betreffend* 4, no. 2 (1800): 123–24.

28. Autobiography of Karl Friedrich Schinkel (1825), in idem, *Briefe, Tagebücher, Gedanken,* ed. Hans Mackowsky (Berlin: Propyläen, 1922), 26.

29. Rolf Bothe, "Die Bewertung Gillys in der kunst- und bauhistorischen Forschung," in Internationale Bauausstellung Berlin 1987 (see note 11), 12–19. The present account enlarges upon Bothe's outline of the critical and art-historical response to Gilly, with some corrections in matters of detail.

30. Franz Kugler, *Karl Friedrich Schinkel: Eine Charakteristik seiner künstlerischen Wirksamkeit* (Berlin: George Gropius, 1842), 15: *"Die Ideen, zu denen sich Gilly in der kurzen Spanne seines künstlerischen Wirkens emporgearbeitet hatte, sollten durch seinen Schüler, der ihm weder an lebendigen Sinne für den Ernst der Schönheit, noch an Energie des Willens und ausgebreitetem Talente nachstand, erfüllt werden"* (The ideas to which Gilly had worked his way in the brief span of his artistic career were to find fulfillment in his disciple,

who was his inferior neither in his lively sense of the earnestness of beauty nor in his energy of will and breadth of talent).

31. The phrase is *"Naturwiederholung seines Meisters":* see Johann Gottfried Schadow, *Kunst-Werke und Kunst-Ansichten* (Berlin: Verlag der Deckerschen Geheimen Ober-Hofbuchdruckerei, 1849), 61. On the comparison between Gilly and Schinkel, see also Oncken (note 1), 106f.

32. This is the message of the footnote that Theodor Fontane devotes to Gilly in his account of the Schinkel drawings of the Steinhöffel estate, in the second part of his *Wanderungen durch die Mark Brandenburg* (Berlin: W. Hertz, 1863), vol. 2, *Das Oderland.* Gilly is also mentioned in the chapter on Schinkel in the first part: *Wanderungen durch die Mark Brandenburg* (Berlin: W. Hertz, 1862), vol. 1, *Die Grafschaft Ruppin.* See the reprint, Michael Ruetz, ed., *Fontanes Wanderungen durch die Mark Brandenburg* (Berlin: Aufbau-Verlag, 1987), 475, 476, 113, 114.

33. Alfred Woltmann, *Die Baugeschichte Berlins bis auf die Gegenwart* (Berlin: Gebr. Paetel, 1872), 150.

34. George Galland, "Ein früh Verstorbener: Friedrich Gilly," *Baugewerks-Zeitung* 10 (October 1878): 114–15: *"Groß und bedeutend ist der Ruf jenes Künstlers nicht, dessen Andenken wir durch die folgenden Zeilen auffrischen und für den wir bei den Lesern Mitgefühl erwecken wollen."*

35. Richard Schöne, "Schinkels Bedeutung für die Architektur und über das künstlerische Wirken von Heinrich Strack und Martin Gropius," in Julius Posener, ed., *Festreden Schinkel zu Ehren, 1846–1980* (Berlin: Fröhlich & Kaufmann [1981?]).

36. Friedrich Adler, "Friedrich Gilly—Schinkels Lehrer," *Zentralblatt der Bauverwaltung* 1, no. 1 (1881): 8–10; 1, no. 2 (1881): 17–19; 1, no. 3 (1881): 22–24; reprinted in idem, *Zur Kunstgeschichte: Vorträge, Abhandlungen und Festreden* (Berlin: Mittler, 1906), 141–57.

37. In this connection there is a useful report of Adler's address in *Deutsche Bauzeitung* 16, no. 27 (1881): 160–61, from which it unmistakably emerges that this was not, as Bothe (see note 29) assumes, the speech given at the *Schinkelfest: "Als vor wenigen Tagen in den weitesten Kreisen der Fachgenossenschaft den Manen des größten Architekten Berlins ein seltenes Fest der Huldigung und hingebenden Verehrung bereitet wurde, da war es selbstverständlich, daß innerhalb des Rahmens der zahlreichen Ovationen in Wort, Schrift und Bild derjenigen Faktoren und Elemente nur flüchtig gedacht werden konnte, welche für das Leben und Wirken des gefeierten Meisters epochemachend wurden, bevor er sich dem Höhepunkt seines künstlerischen Könnens näherte. Es muß daher dankbar anerkannt werden, daß, noch unter dem Eindruck der eben erst verrauschten Festlichkeiten, welche von neuem urbi et orbi den unverlöschlichen Ruhm Schinkel's verkündet haben, auch dem Namen seines unvergeßlichen, der Baukunst leider zu frühzeitig entrissenen Lehrers, Friedrich Gilly, ein Tribut dankbarer Verehrung dargebracht wurde. In der Sitzung des Berliner Architekten-Vereins vom 28. März cr. entrollte der Geh.[eime] B[au]r[a]th., Herr Prof. Adler mit gewohnter schwungvoller Beredtsamkeit ein Bild des Lebens, der Entwicklung und der künstlerischen Leistungen jenes hochbegabten Architekten, welcher mit seltener Genialität und mit glücklichem Erfolge gegen die verdorbene Geschmacksrichtung des 18. Jahrhunderts angekämpft und die Reinheit und Würde der griechischen Kunst als Grundlage des höheren architektonischen Studiums hingestellt hat. . . . Er war ein Phänomen, welches wie ein Meteor vorüber gegangen ist"* (A few days ago, when in the widest professional circles a

rare and festive tribute of veneration was paid to the *manes* [spirit] of Berlin's greatest architect, it was natural that amid the numerous verbal, written, and pictorial tributes it was impossible to do more than touch fleetingly upon those individuals and influences that were crucial in the Master's life and work before the time when he approached the height of his powers. Grateful acknowledgment is accordingly due to the tribute of gratitude and veneration that was also paid—in the wake of those recent festivities that proclaimed anew, *urbi et orbi*, the imperishable fame of Schinkel—to the name of his unforgettable teacher, Friedrich Gilly, whose early death was such a loss to the art of architecture. At the meeting of the Berliner Architekten-Verein on 28 March, the state architect Professor Adler, with his customary eloquence and vigor, unfolded an image of the life, development, and artistic achievement of that supremely gifted architect, who fought with rare genius and happy success against the corrupted taste of the eighteenth century and established the purity and dignity of Greek art as the basis of advanced architectural study. . . . He was a phenomenon that passed like a meteor).

38. Adler, 1906 (see note 36), 142, 149f.

39. Fontane, 1987 (see note 32), 2: 476.

40. Adler, 1906 (see note 36), 156: "*Wo ist ein deutscher Architekt, von dem gleiches nachgewiesen werden kann?*"

41. Adler, 1906 (see note 36), 154: "*Aus seinen architektonischen Zeichnungen hebe ich folgende hervor: Zunächst eine in meinem Besitze befindliche, auf braunem Papier in Aquarell gemalte Perspektive*" (Of his architectural drawings, I single out the following: firstly a perspective rendering in my possession, in watercolor on brown paper). Another reference exists to Gilly drawings in Adler's collection, ibid., 155.

42. Adler, 1906 (see note 36), 157: "*Gillys bedeutendste Leistung für die Baukunst ist und bleibt die Wiederentdeckung der Marienburg und ihre Einführung in die kunstwissenschaftliche Literatur. Denn hier sind die starken Quellen entsprungen, welche durch Schinkels Genius die Baukunst der Gegenwart so wohltätig befruchtet haben.*"

43. Friedrich Adler, "Die Bauschule zu Berlin von C. F. Schinkel," in Posener (see note 35), 90f.

44. On Adler's architectural ideals, see Eva Börsch-Supan, *Berliner Baukunst nach Schinkel, 1840–1870* (Munich: Prestel, 1977), 547; Peter Lemberg, "Leben und Werk des gelehrten Berliner Architekten Friedrich Adler, 1827–1908" (Ph.D. diss., Freie Universität Berlin, 1989).

45. Paul Mebes, *Um 1800: Architektur und Handwerk im letzten Jahrhundert ihrer traditionellen Entwicklung* (Munich, 1908; 3rd ed., rev. Walter Curt Behrendt, Munich: F. Bruckmann, 1920).

46. Carl Zetzsche, *Zopf und Empire* (Berlin: Kanter & Mohr, 1906), part 1, *Fassaden aus der Empire-Zeit*; part 2, *Türen, Tore und Fenster*; part 3, *Architektonische Details und Einzelheiten des innern Aufbaus*.

47. The title-page vignette for part 1, "Idea for a Country Villa," was taken from the title vignette in *Sammlung nützlicher Aufsätze und Nachrichten, die Baukunst betreffend* 5, no. 1 (1803); and that for part 3, "Signpost in the Form of a Seat," was taken from the title vignette from ibid. 3, no. 3 (1799).

48. Hinrichs (see note 25); David Joseph, *Der Frühhellenismus der Berliner Schule* (Berlin, 1911);

Paul Klopfer, *Von Palladio bis Schinkel* (Esslingen: Paul Neff, 1911); Erich Paul Riesenfeld, *Erdmanns-dorff: Der Baumeister des Herzogs Leopold Friedrich Franz von Anhalt-Dessau* (Berlin: Bruno Cassirer, 1913); Adolph Doebber, *Heinrich Gentz: Ein Berliner Baumeister um 1800* (Berlin: C. Heymann, 1916); Arthur Moeller van den Bruck, *Der preußische Stil* (Munich: R. Piper, 1916; Breslau: Wilhelm Gottlieb Korn, 1931).

49. On this see Fritz Neumeyer, "Klassizismus als Problem: Berliner Architektur im 20. Jahrhundert," in Arenhövel (see note 9), 395–419.

50. "Zum neuen Jahrgang: Modernes und Modisches," *Berliner Architekturwelt* 16 (1914): 3: *"Gilly ist Mode und wird, Gott sei's geklagt, nicht sinnvoller 'gekupfert', als wie man vor zwanzig Jahren den Hirtschen Formenschatz—nachempfand—."* The quotation continues: *"Jetzt liegt schon wieder der Schinkel in den Ateliers von 'Meistern' als Vorbild, ja, zur Ausnutzung aus, die einst als Sterne der Traditionslosigkeit galten! Und so werden wir Schinkeliden von zweitem Aufguß haben, die nur das sicher beweisen, daß sie keine Schinkel sind"* (Now, once again, Schinkel is on display as a model, indeed as a quarry for exploitation, in the studios of those very masters who once were known as the stars of traditionlessness. And so we shall have warmed-over Schinkelites who can demonstrate only that they certainly are no Schinkels).

51. Paul Zucker, "Ein vergessener Berliner Künstler: Friedrich Gilly," *Neudeutsche Bauzeitung* 9 (September 1913): 696.

52. Hermann Schmitz, "Friedrich Gilly," *Kunst und Künstler* 7 (1909): 201–6; idem, "Die Ent-würfe für das Denkmal Friedrichs des Großen und die Berliner Architektur um das Jahr 1800," *Zeitschrift für bildende Kunst,* n.s., 20 (1909): 206–14; idem, "Die Baumeister David und Friedrich Gilly in ihren Beziehungen zu Pommern," *Monatsblätter der Gesellschaft für Pommersche Geschichte und Altertümer* (June 1909): 81–87, 108–11.

53. No article devoted to Gilly is found in the literature of the intervening period. There is only a brief mention of the Friedrichsdenkmal in an exhibition review in 1886: Schäfer, "Die Ju-biläumsausstellung der bildenden Künste in Berlin," *Zentralblatt der Bauverwaltung* 6 (1886): 388.

54. Hermann Schmitz, *Berliner Baumeister vom Ausgang des 18. Jahrhunderts* (Berlin: Verlag für Kunstwissenschaft, 1914), "Vorwort."

55. Late in life—in a conversation with Dirk Lohan preserved in the Mies van der Rohe Ar-chive, The Museum of Modern Art, New York—Mies recalled having attended classes at the Kunstgewerbemuseum school in 1908 conducted by the school's director, Bruno Paul, in whose practice Mies worked until his transfer to the office of Peter Behrens in that year. It was probably thanks to Paul's love of Neoclassicism that Schmitz was invited to give his course of lectures, which in the prevalent atmosphere of interest in Neoclassicism would certainly not have escaped Mies's attention. There may possibly be a connection here with Mies's high opinion of Schloß Paretz, the house remodeled in 1797 by David Gilly, to which Mies took Bauhaus students on excursions as late as May 1933. See a letter from Hans Kessler, dated 12 May 1933, in Peter Hahn, ed., *Bauhaus Berlin: Auflösung Dessau 1932, Schliessung 1933, Bauhäusler und Drittes Reich* (Weingarten: Künstlerverlag Weingarten, 1985), 177. Paretz was the subject of another publication by Hermann Schmitz,

Schloß Paretz: Ein königlicher Landsitz um das Jahr 1800 (Berlin: Verlag für Kunstwissenschaft [1919]).

56. Schmitz, "Friedrich Gilly" (see note 52): 203ff.

57. Schmitz, "Die Baumeister David und Friedrich Gilly" (see note 52): 81.

58. Schmitz (see note 54), 40: *"So wertvoll und von so schönen architektonischen Ideen erfüllt die hinterlassenen Blätter Gillys erscheinen, so müssen wir doch anerkennen, daß sie eine allerdings höchst geschmackvolle und originelle Verarbeitung der zeitgenössischen, besonders der in Paris kultivierten klassischen Formen sind, daß aber eine geniale Neuschöpfung eines architektonischen Organismus nicht darin enthalten ist."*

59. Hermann Schmitz, *Die Gotik im deutschen Kunst- und Geistesleben* (Berlin: Verlag für Kunstwissenschaft, 1921), 203. See also idem, *Die Kunst des frühen und hohen Mittelalters in Deutschland* (Munich: F. Bruckmann, 1924).

60. Hermann Schmitz, *Kunst und Kultur des 18. Jahrhunderts in Deutschland* (Munich: F. Bruckmann, 1922), 367f.

61. Wilhelm Niemeyer, "Friedrich Gilly, Friedrich Schinkel und der Formbegriff des deutschen Klassizismus in der Baukunst," *Mitteilungen des Kunstvereins zu Hamburg* 7 (1912): 7: *"Das Lebensbild des Künstlers zeichneten Friedrich Adler 1881, neuerlich Hermann Schmitz* [Kunst und Künstler, *Jahr VIII (1908)*], *veranlaßt durch einen Hinweis und Wunsch des Verfassers dieser Betrachtung, dem die wichtige Materialsammlung von Zetzsche* Zopf und Empire *die Bedeutung Gillys erschlossen hatte"* (The artist's life story was recounted by Hermann Adler in 1881 and more recently by Hermann Schmitz (*Kunst und Künstler* 8 [1908] [Probably Schmitz's article on Gilly in *Kunst und Künstler* 7 (1909), see note 52]), at the suggestion and wish of the present writer, who had been made aware of Gilly's significance by Zetzsche's important collection of materials, *Zopf und Empire*).

62. C[arl] Z[etzsche], review of Niemeyer, "Friedrich Gilly . . . und der Formbegriff" (see note 61), *Der Baumeister* 11 (January 1913): B91, B92.

63. Wilhelm Niemeyer, *Der Formwandel der Gotik als das Werden der Renaissance: Eine Betrachtung der Architektur des ausgehenden Mittelalters in Deutschland* (Munich: F. Bruckmann, 1904).

64. Wilhelm Niemeyer, "Peter Behrens und die Raumästhetik seiner Kunst," *Dekorative Kunst* 10 (1907): 137–65; idem, "Ein Bau Alfred Messels (Rathaus in Ballenstädt)," *Form: Eine Wochenschrift für Baukunst und Kunstgewerbe* 1 (1908): 3–6; idem, "Messel: Fassade, Berlin Bendlerstraße 6," *Form: Eine Wochenschrift für Baukunst und Kunstgewerb* 2 (1908): 3–8.

65. See advertisement in Fritz Hoeber, *Peter Behrens* (Munich: G. Mueller & E. Rentsch, 1913), after page 249. The volume on Behrens was the only one in the promised series that actually appeared.

66. Niemeyer (see note 61), 13ff. The quotations that follow are from the same source.

67. Paul Zucker, *Raumdarstellung und Bildarchitektur im Florentiner Quattrocento* (Leipzig: Klinkhardt & Biermann, 1913).

68. Zucker (see note 51), 703.

69. Zucker (see note 51), 703.

70. After Alfred Messel's death in 1909, the journal *Berliner Architekturwelt* brought out a

commemorative issue: Fritz Stahl, *Alfred Messel* (Berlin: E. Wasmuth, 1910). There followed a study of Messel's life and work by Walter Curt Behrendt, *Alfred Messel*, with an introduction by Karl Scheffler (Berlin: Bruno Cassirer, 1911).

71. See Hans Mackowsky, "Heinrich Gentz: Ein Berliner Baumeister um 1800," *Zeitschrift für bildende Kunst*, n.s., 52 (1917): 58. Messel's drawings were published with an accompanying text by Richard Borrmann, "Das Fürstenhaus und die alte Münze am Werderschen Markt in Berlin," *Zeitschrift für Bauwesen* 38 (1888): 287–98, and later in Doebber (see note 48), pl. 18.

72. Niemeyer (see note 61), 10: "*Bis vor kurzem noch ein edelster Besitz Berlins, hat das Haus zum lebhaften Schmerz Alfred Messels dessen Nationalbank Platz machen müssen*" (Until recently a precious part of Berlin's heritage, the house has had to make way, to the grief of Alfred Messel, for his new Nationalbank building).

73. Fritz Neumeyer, "Die Portalnische: Ein Motiv des Berliner Frühklassizismus und sein Weg ins 20. Jahrhundert," in Arenhövel (see note 9), 523–31.

74. Stahl (see note 70), 2.

75. Karl Scheffler, "Die Bedeutung Messels," in Behrendt (see note 70), 17f.; reprinted in Karl Scheffler, *Die Architektur der Großstadt* (Berlin: Bruno Cassirer, 1913), chapter on Messel, 144f.

76. Karl Scheffler, "Die Bedeutung Messels," in Behrendt (see note 70), 15: "*Trotzdem Schinkel der Letzte und Messel wieder der Erste in der Reihe sind, trotzdem dieser also als Schinkels Erbe in gewisser Weise bezeichnet werden muß, weisen seine besten und tiefsten Bauten doch nicht auf das Alte Museum oder auf die Neue Wache zurück, sondern auf Langhansens Brandenburger Tor, auf Gentzens Alte Münze, auf Gillys Bauten und auf die alten Stadthäuser aus der Zeit um 1800. Frei und selbständig weisen sie darauf zurück*" (Schinkel was the last in his line, and Messel was the first in his; in a sense, therefore, Messel must be regarded as Schinkel's heir. But his best and most profound buildings do not hark back to the Altes Museum, or to the Neue Wache, but to Langhans's Brandenburg Gate, to Gentz's Alte Münze, to the buildings of Gilly, and to the old town houses of the years around 1800. Free and autonomous though they are, that is the direction in which they point).

77. Karl Scheffler, "Die Bedeutung Messels," in Behrendt (see note 70), 20.

78. Peter Behrens, "Alfred Messel: Ein Nachruf," *Frankfurter Zeitung*, 6 April 1909, morning edition; an extract in Hoeber (see note 65), 225. Also significant in this context is the obituary by the Jugendstil artist August Endell, "Zu Alfred Messels Gedächtnis," *Kunst und Künstler* 7 (1909): 331f., in which Messel is hailed as "the perfecter of eclecticism" and "liberator and redeemer": "*Die Hoffnung auf eine lebendige Architektur ist wiedergekehrt. Das danken wir Alfred Messel*" (The hope of a living architecture has returned. For this we have Alfred Messel to thank).

79. Fritz Neumeyer, *The Artless Word: Mies van der Rohe on the Building Art*, trans. Mark Jarzombek (Cambridge: MIT Press, 1991), 354 n. 44; Tilmann Buddensieg, "Mies und Messel: Zu einem fehlenden Kapitel in der frühen Biographie von Mies van der Rohe," in Christian Beutler, Peter-Klaus Schuster, and Martin Warnke, eds., *Kunst um 1800 und die Folgen: Werner Hofmann zu Ehren* (Munich: Prestel, 1988), 346–51.

80. Moeller van den Bruck, 1931 (see note 48), 15.

81. Moeller van den Bruck, 1931 (see note 48), 147.

82. Peter Behrens, "Das Ethos und die Umlagerung der künstlerischen Probleme," in *Der Leuchter: Jahrbuch 1920 der Schule der Weisheit*, ed. Hermann Graf von Keyserling (Darmstadt: Otto Reichl, 1920), 324.

83. *Kündung: Eine Zeitschrift für Kunst* (Hamburg, 1921). The periodical ceased publication after the first year.

84. Le Corbusier, *Vers une architecture* (Paris: G. Crès et cie, 1924).

85. Sigfried Giedion, *Spätbarocker und romantischer Klassizismus* (Munich: F. Bruckmann, 1922); August Grisebach, *Carl Friedrich Schinkel* (Leipzig: Insel, 1924); Gustav Pauli, *Die Kunst des Klassizismus und der Romantik*, Propyläen Kunstgeschichte, vol. 14 (Berlin: Propyläen, 1925); Siegfried Graf Pückler-Limpurg, *Der Klassizismus in der deutschen Kunst* (Munich: Mueller & Koeniger, 1929); Franz Landsberger, *Die Kunst der Goethezeit: Kunst und Kunstanschauung von 1750 bis 1830* (Leipzig: Insel, 1931).

86. Horst Riemer, *Friedrich Gilly's Verhältnis zum Theaterbau, unter besonderer Berücksichtigung seiner Skizzen nach französischen Theatern und seines Entwurfes für das Nationaltheater in Berlin* (Ph.D. diss., Berlin, Friedrich-Wilhelms-Universität; Bochum: n.p., 1931).

87. Wolfgang Herrmann, *Deutsche Baukunst des 19. und 20. Jahrhunderts* (Breslau: Ferdinand Hirt, 1932), part 1, *Von 1770 bis 1840;* reprinted together with part 2, which was suppressed in 1933 (Basel and Stuttgart: E. Birkhäuser, 1977).

88. Oncken (see note 1).

89. Wassili Luckhardt, "Vom preußischen Stil zur neuen Baukunst," *Deutsche Allgemeine Zeitung,* 23 March 1933; reprinted, with revisions, in *Die Kunst* 70 (September 1934): 273–76, and in *Das schöne Heim* 5 (1934): 357–60. Reprinted in *Brüder Luckhardt und Alfons Anker: Berliner Architekten der Moderne*, Schriftenreihe der Akademie der Künste, vol. 21 (Berlin: Akademie der Künste, 1990), 125–30. The quotations that follow are from the publication of 1933.

90. Henry-Russell Hitchcock and Philip Johnson, *The International Style* (New York: W. W. Norton, 1932).

91. Luckhardt, 1933 (see note 89): 125.

92. Hans Schwarz, preface to Moeller van den Bruck, 1931 (see note 48), 11.

93. Alfred Rietdorf, *Gilly: Wiedergeburt der Architektur* (Berlin: Hans von Hugo, 1940; reprint, Berlin: Hans von Hugo, 1943). On Schwarz's coauthorship of this, see Reelfs (note 17), 18.

94. Rietdorf (see note 93), 178–79: *"Die Olympischen Spiele von 1936 zeigten die Gilly-Büste von Schadow an weithin sichtbarer Stelle. Ihre Wiedergabe im Plakat feierte in Gilly einen Heroen, in dem sich edelster Wettkampf der Künste verkörpert hatte. Der kriegerische Ernst von 1939 und 1940 bedarf nicht weniger solcher Gestalten, die mit innerem Feuer das Schicksal durchglühen und bis an das Ende durchhalten. Fast immer sind es die Frühvollendeten, die von diesem Feuer besessen sind. Sie kämpfen und sterben, aber ihr Tod verpflichtet. . . . So gehen sie in die ewige Jugend der Völker ein. Durch sie verliert der Tod seine dürre Knochengestalt und nimmt das Gesicht eines Jünglings an. Ihre Tragik wird zur Verklärung und trägt sie in die Zukunft hinein. Das Wesen Gillys hat an solcher*

Verklärung teil. . . . Es gesellt sich dem Wesen derer hinzu, die auf den Schlachtfeldern des Ostens, Nordens und Westens für den Frieden fallen. . . . So ist dieses Buch über Gilly geschrieben worden, vom Standpunkt der Gegenwart und als Bekenntnis zu einer sieghaften Zukunft. Das mag den Mann der reinen Wissenschaft befremden, aber es erklärt seine Form" (At the Olympic Games of 1936, Schadow's bust of Gilly was visible from afar. Its reproduction on the poster honored, in Gilly, a hero who had himself been the embodiment of the noblest artistic emulation. The warlike solemnity of 1939 and 1940 stands in no less need of such figures: those whose inner flame lights up their destinies and endures to the end. They fight and die, but their death lays a duty on others. . . . Thus they go forth, into the eternal youth of nations. In them, Death himself sheds his wizened, bony features and assumes the countenance of a youth. Their tragic fate becomes their transfiguration and carries them forward into the future. Gilly's innermost being partakes of that transfiguration. . . . It joins with the essence of all those who die for the cause of peace on the battlefields of the East, the North, and the West. . . . And so this book on Gilly has been written, from the standpoint of the present, as an avowal of faith in a victorious future. This may offend the man of pure science, but it explains the form that the book has taken).

It is also symptomatic of the Gilly cult that in 1942, on the orders of Albert Speer, the design for the Friedrichsdenkmal was executed in the form of a scale model. On this, see Rudolf Wolters, "Das Berliner Friedrichsdenkmal," *Die Kunst im Deutschen Reich*, ed. B (August/September 1942): 154–57, and in the same journal see Heinrich Johannes, "Das Denkmal Friedrichs des Großen von Gilly," 157–61.

95. Hermann Beenken, *Schöpferische Bauideen der deutschen Romantik* (Mainz: Matthias Gruenewald, 1952).

96. As, for instance, in the exhibition organized by the Bibliothèque Nationale in Paris, *Les architectes visionnaires de la fin du XVIIIᵉ siècle* (Geneva: Musée d'Art et d'Histoire, 1965), which toured the world. On the history of the reputation of French Revolutionary architecture, see Winfried Nerdinger, Klaus Jan Philip, and Hans-Peter Schwarz, eds., *Revolutionsarchitektur: Ein Aspekt der europäischen Architektur um 1800*, exh. cat. (Munich: Hirmer, 1990), esp. 13ff.

97. Lammert (see note 7).

98. Salewski (see note 11).

99. Manfred Klinkott, "Friedrich Gilly, 1772–1800," in *Dortmunder Architekturausstellung 1977: Fünf Architekten des Klassizismus in Deutschland*, exh. cat., Dortmunder Architekturhefte, no. 4 (Darmstadt: n.p., 1977), 11–13; Julius Posener, "Friedrich Gilly, 1772–1800," in Sonja Günther, ed., *Berlin zwischen 1789 und 1848: Facetten einer Epoche*, exh. cat. (Berlin: Akademie der Künste, 1981), 105–22; Nerdinger, Philip, and Schwarz (see note 96), 72–99.

100. Internationale Bauausstellung Berlin 1987 (see note 11).

101. See Appendix 2.

102. See Appendix 2, fol. 147.

103. Adler, 1906 (see note 36), 147.

104. Schmitz, "Friedrich Gilly" (see note 52): 205: *"Als Schriftsteller ist Gilly nicht weniger genial, wie als Baumeister."*

105. Schmitz (see note 54), 332. Schmitz was equally flattering in his *Schloß Paretz* (see note 55), 19, where he described the essays on Bagatelle and Rincy as "among the most delectable descriptions of architecture in the German language." Further praise of Gilly's literary achievement is found in Zucker (see note 51), 689, and in Moeller van den Bruck, 1931 (see note 48), 139.

106. Oncken (see note 1), 96f.

107. Oncken (see note 1), 132. Presented by David Gilly in memory of his son; present whereabouts unknown.

108. Levezow (see note 11), 230, 234.

109. Oncken (see note 1), 97: *"Es läßt sich wohl begreifen, wie diese Steine den Bewohnern der Gegend als außerordentliche Gegenstände erscheinen und Anlaß zu Dichtungen und Verzauberungen und verwünschten Schlössern geben konnten. Etwas Rauhes und Ödes in der Gegend, wo sie liegen, befördert dies vielleicht, und die Sagen werden dem Wanderer noch jetzt von dem Landmann mit auf die Reise gegeben. Überhaupt trägt das Land umher Spuren des grauen Altertums, die das Romanhafte erwecken. Man sieht viele, mitunter sehr große und recht merkwürdig angelegte Grabstätten der alten Wenden, welche ehemals hier hausten. Besonders die Waldung und Höhe des Gutes Steinhöffel ist bedeckt mit solchen Begräbnissteinen, darunter häufig Urnen mit Asche pp. gefunden werden.—Man wandert unter diesen verödeten Denkmälern eines sonst hier hausenden, zahlreichen und tapferen Volkes und blickt mit einer sonderbaren Stimmung über die stille Gegend bis zu den Ufern der Spree hin, wo sich am Horizont die ansehnlich hohe Bergkette von Rauden in ein schönes Blau erhebet."*

110. Gilly, "Über die . . . Ansichten" (see note 13).

111. *"[auch] dafür lebe ich."* Quoted in Nerdinger, Philip, and Schwarz (see note 96), 336, without any indication of a source for the letter written by Friedrich Gilly from Vienna.

112. Friedrich Gilly, notes for a paper read to the Privatgesellschaft on 30 January 1799, in Internationale Bauausstellung Berlin 1987 (see note 11), 178, cat. no. 97: *"Die älteren ital. Baumeister, Palladio und seine Zeitgenoßen besonders, haben den Ruhm, nach den Zeiten der Alten, vorzüglich gewonnen ([Einschub vom linken Rand:] Vorbilder einer reinern unverfälschten Bauart in ihren Werken hinterlaßen zu haben, Vorbilder die—) die ganz besonders zu näherer Anwendung dieser Kunst auch unsere Bedürfniße leiten, und zu einem einfachen schönen Geschmack den beobachtenden Archit. anführen werden.—Italien hat tausend Schätze dieser Art für den Studierenden, auch aus der neuern Periode der Kunst, neben dem herrlichen Alterthum—und ist es ein Wunder daß hir, wo alle Kunst so fruchtbringend gedieh, auch diese immer vorzüglich blühte?*

Wir können nicht genug wünschen, daß jene Werke durch die Auswahl geschichter Künstler, in treuen geschmackvollen Abbildungen möglichst bekannt gemacht und ausgebreitet werden mögen. Wie sehr müßen es besonders die wünschen, denen das Glück noch nicht zu Theil ward, den Anblick jener Meisterwerke und die Wärme des heiligen Landes selbst zu genießen. Der Vortheil den das Studium der Baukunst aus einer Samlung und Bekandtmachung jener Schönheiten ziehen wird, das hervorstechende Verdienst jener genievollen Künstler hat die Herausgabe eines neuen Werks veranlaßt, welches eine Gesellschaft von Archit. in Paris unter dem Titel: Maisons et Palais der Rom pp herausgiebt. Ich lege es Ihnen hiebey vor, mit einer Übersetzung der dazu gehörigen Einleitung, welche in vieler Hinsicht interessant ist" (The older Italian architects, Palladio and his contemporaries in particular, enjoy the reputation of having, after the time of the ancients ([Insert from left margin:] left in their works prototypes of a purer, unadulterated style of architecture: prototypes that—) that direct our needs toward a closer application of that art and that will conduct the observant architect toward a taste for simplicity and beauty. Italy has a thousand treasures of this kind for the student, stemming from the recent epoch of art as well as from antiquity—and is it any wonder that in that country, where all the arts have borne such plentiful fruit, this art, too, has always flourished so magnificently?

We cannot too fervently desire to have those works selected by able artists and made known and disseminated as widely as possible in accurate and tasteful illustrations. How keenly, in particular, must this be desired by those who have never enjoyed the happiness of seeing those masterpieces for themselves and of enjoying the warmth of that sacred land! The benefit that the study of architecture must derive from the collection and dissemination of those beauties and the eminent merit of those artists of genius have occasioned the publication of a new work, which a society of architects in Paris publishes under the title of *Maisons et palais de Rome*. I hereby present to you a translation of the introduction, which is of interest in many respects).

113. Karl Friedrich Schinkel, *Sammlung architektonischer Entwürfe* (Berlin: L. W. Wittich, 1819–1840).

114. Charles Percier and Pierre-François-Léonard Fontaine, *Palais, maisons, et autres édifices modernes, dessinés à Rome* (Paris, 1798; reprint, Hildesheim: Georg Olms, 1980), "Préface," 5: *"En effet, la plupart de leurs ouvrages portent l'empreinte de cette simplicité rare qui enchante, et qui, comme une vérité dévoilée, paroît toujours facile à ceux auxquels on la découvre. Pittoresques sans désordre, symétriques sans monotonie, et toujours soigneux dans l'exécution, ils réunissent souvent, pour s'exprimer en termes d'art, la composition au rendu."*

115. Levezow (see note 11), 235f.

116. David Gilly, *Handbuch der Land-Bau-Kunst vorzüglich in Rücksicht auf die Construction der Wohn- und Wirtschaftsgebäude für angehende Cameral-Baumeister und Oeconomen*, 2 vols. (Berlin, 1797–1798; 2nd ed., Braunschweig: F. Vieweg, 1800).

117. See Reelfs (note 17), 19.

118. *Sammlung nützlicher Aufsätze und Nachrichten, die Baukunst betreffend* 5, no. 1 (1803): 127. For the reasons given here, it has been decided not to include this text in the present publication.

119. Johann Wolfgang Goethe, "Von deutscher Baukunst" (1772), in idem, *Werke* (Weimar: Hermann Böhlaus Nachf., 1896), 37: 139–51. On this see Harald Keller, *Goethes Hymnus auf das Straßburger Münster und die Wiedererweckung der Gotik im 18. Jahrhundert 1772/1972*, Sitzungsberichte der Bayerischen Akademie der Wissenschaften, philosophisch-historische Klasse, no. 4 (1974).

120. See Schinkel's report to the state chancellor, Fürst von Hardenberg, on 11 November 1819, in Alfred Freiherr von Wolzogen, *Aus Schinkel's Nachlaß* (Berlin: Kgl. geh. Ober-Hofbuchdruckerei, 1863), 3: 208–16.

121. Salewski (see note 11).

122. See Gilly's description of the prehistoric landscape around the Steinhöffel estate (note 109).

123. See Etienne-Louis Boullée, *Architektur: Abhandlung über die Kunst* (Zurich and Munich: Artemis Verlag für Architektur, 1987), 44.

124. Gilly, "Über die . . . Ansichten" (see note 13): 671 [108].

125. Gilly, "Über die . . . Ansichten" (see note 13): 671 [108]: *"Der Zeichner wird gezwungen diese Situation zu ergreifen und der Baumeister muß verweilen um das Werk in seinem Innern zu betrachten."*

126. Neumeyer (see note 6).

127. Neumeyer (see note 6), 111: *". . . der gotischen Spielereien der Väter."*

128. In this context Neumeyer (see note 6), 77, coined the expression *"der männliche Mittelalter"* (the masculine Middle Ages) to describe "Gothic seen monumentally for the first time."

129. Gilly, "Über die . . . Ansichten" (see note 13): 668 [105].

130. Gilly, "Über die . . . Ansichten" (see note 13): 673 [108].

131. Gilly, "Über die . . . Ansichten" (see note 13): 674 [109].

132. Gilly, "Über die . . . Ansichten" (see note 13): 674–75 [109–10].

133. Gilly, "Über die . . . Ansichten" (see note 13): 675 [110].

134. Gilly, "Über die . . . Ansichten" (see note 13): 674 [109].

135. When Mies van der Rohe explained his legendary glass skyscraper design (1921) for the Friedrichstraße Railroad Station in Berlin, he did so entirely in terms of this same sense of wonderment in an article published without a title in *Frühlicht* 1, no. 4 (1922): 122: *"Nur im Bau befindliche Wolkenkratzer zeigen die kühnen konstruktiven Gedanken, und überwältigend ist dann der Eindruck der hochragenden Stahlskelette"* (Only skyscrapers under construction reveal the bold constructive thoughts, and then the impression of the high-reaching steel skeletons is overpowering). See my own account of "Construction as Promise of Art," in Neumeyer (note 79), 110f.

136. Richard Lucae, "Über die Macht des Raumes in der Baukunst," *Zeitschrift für Bauwesen* 19 (1869): 293–306.

137. Niemeyer (see note 61): 7, 8.

138. As in Johann Georg Sulzer, *Allgemeine Theorie der schönen Künste in einzeln, nach alphabetischer Ordnung der Kunstwörter auf einander folgenden, Artikeln abgehandelt,* 2 vols. (Leipzig: M. G. Weidemanns Erben & Reich, 1771 and 1774; pirate eds., 1773 and 1779); an edition in four volumes from 1786 is listed in the catalog of Gilly's books, p. 14, nos. 37–40 (see Appendix 2).

139. See catalog of Gilly's books, Appendix 2, p. 9, nos. 1–2, Charles-Etienne Briseux, *Traité du beau essentiel dans les arts* (Paris: Author, 1752); p. 22, no. 229, *Catalogue des livres de la bibliothèque de feu citoyen Blondel* (Paris: year IV [1796]); p. 23, no. 240, Jacques-François Blondel, *De l'utilité de joindre à l'étude de l'architecture celle des sciences et des arts qui lui sont rélatifs* (Paris: La Veuve Desaint, 1771); p. 6, nos. 66–67, Marie-Joseph Peyre, *Oeuvres d'architecture,* 2 vols. (Paris, year IV [1796]); p. 6, no. 77, Marie-Joseph Peyre, *Oeuvres d'architecture* (Paris: Prault & Jombert, 1765); p. 16, no. 66, Antoine-Chrysostome Quatremère de Quincy, *Considérations sur les arts du dessin en France* (Paris: Desenne, 1791).

140. The fundamental account of this is Wolfgang Herrmann, *Laugier and Eighteenth-Century*

French Theory (London: A. Zwemmer, 1962), esp. the chapters "Gothic through Classical Eyes" and "Embellished Gothic."

141. In the catalog of Gilly's books, p. 23, no. 250, Marc-Antoine Laugier, *Observations sur l'architecture* (The Hague: Desaint, 1765); Laugier's celebrated *Essai sur l'architecture* (Paris: Duchesne, 1753) is not listed.

142. Laugier, *Observations* (see note 141), 130: "*Une distribution charmante, où l'oeil plonge délicieusement à travers plusieurs files de colonnes dans des Chapelles en enfoncement, dont les vitraux répandent la lumière avec profusion & inégalité; . . . un mélange, un mouvement, une tumulte de percés & de massifs, qui jouent, qui contrastent, & dont l'effet entier est ravissant.*"

143. It remains an unanswered question which church in Strasbourg is meant. In her list of Gilly drawings, under B 144 and B 145, Oncken (see note 1) suggests the church of Saint Thomas with a question mark. Rietdorf entitles the sketch "Strasbourg cathedral." Gilly may also have visited the church of the Capuchins (1774), which the architect J. B. Kléber supplied with columns instead of compound piers, very much in the spirit of Laugier.

144. In the catalog of Gilly's books, p. 20, no. 171, *A Description of Stonehenge, near Salisbury* (Salisbury, 1795) [perhaps, *A Description of Stonehenge; Extracted, etc.* (Salisbury: J. Easton, 1795)].

145. See my article, "Eine neue Welt entschleiert sich: Von Friedrich Gilly zu Mies van der Rohe," in Internationale Bauausstellung Berlin 1987 (note 11), 49f. See also my interpretation (ibid., fig. 24) of Gilly's sketch of the rue de Chartres, in which he converts a Paris house into a skeleton structure that comes astonishingly close to the twentieth-century apartment building type.

146. Gilly, "Zusatz zu dem Aufsatz" (see note 13): 892 [112].

147. Gilly, "Über die . . . Ansichten" (see note 13): 676 [110]: "*So weit war man also schon damals in Erfindungen für die Bequemlichkeit gediehen.*"

148. Gilly, "Zusatz zu dem Aufsatz" (see note 13): 892 [112].

149. "Prospekte von Marienburg an der Nogat in Preußen," in *Journal des Luxus und der Moden* (January 1799): 16–18: "*Berlin im December 1798.—Unser Hofinspector Hr. Gilly, der vor kurzem von einer gewinnreichen Reise durch Frankreich, England und Teutschland zurückgekommen ist, von welchen wir die schönsten Früchte besonders in Absicht auf Theaterarchitektur zu erwarten haben, fand bey Gelegenheit eines künstlerischen Streifzuges durch Preußen im Jahre 1794 besonders die Ansichten des Schlosses Marienburg an der Nogat, dem ehemaligen Sitz des Hochmeisters des deutschen Ordens in Preußen, sehr merkwürdig. Die pittoresken Partien, die dieß größtentheils noch erhaltene Denkmal aus der Baukunst des Mittelalters von außen und innen darbietet, die Größe und Einfachheit des Styls, in welchen es sich dem besten in der sogenannten Gothischen Baukunst näherte, bewegen den Reisenden, auf der Stelle mehrere genaue perspectivische Zeichnungen davon zu entwerfen, und sie dann bey seiner Rückkehr nach Berlin mit der ihm eigenthümlichen Kunst zu vollenden. Sie fanden bey den öffentlichen Ausstellungen in den Sälen der Akademie den uneingeschränkten Beyfall der Kenner*" (Berlin, December 1798. Our Royal [Building] Inspector, Mr. Gilly—who has recently returned from a rewarding tour of France, England, and Germany, which we must expect to bear the richest fruit, particularly in respect of

theatrical architecture—was on an artistic tour of Prussia in 1794 when he was profoundly impressed by the view of the castle of Marienburg on the Nogat, the former seat of the grand master of the Teutonic Order in Prussia. The picturesque parts, both within and without, that this still largely intact monument of medieval architecture has to offer, and the grandeur and simplicity of its style, in which it resembles all that is best in so-called Gothic architecture, prompted the traveler to make a number of accurate perspectival sketches on the spot, which he then worked up, on his return to Berlin, with all his characteristic artistry. At the public exhibitions in the halls of the Akademie, they won the unqualified approval of the connoisseurs).

150. Adler, 1906 (see note 36), 144.

151. Salewski (see note 11), "Vorbericht," 1.

152. Salewski (see note 11), "Vorbericht," 1.

153. Jutta von Simson, *Das Berliner Denkmal für Friedrich den Großen* (Berlin: Propyläen, 1976), 9ff.

154. Version 1 is a "brief description" of the project, appended by Gilly to his letter to the king of 21 April. The text, signed by Gilly, is preserved in GStA Merseburg (see note 12), Rep. 76 alt III, Kuratorium der Akademie der bildenden Künste und mechanischen Wissenschaften, Nr. 382, fol. 18ff.

The somewhat longer Version 2 is transcribed and published by Rietdorf (see note 93), 57–61. Rietdorf gives as his source a transcript by "Moser" of a holograph by Gilly. Very little is known about J. C. F. Moser. He was a Berlin architect and contemporary of Gilly's. In 1793 both men exhibited their proposals for a large school in the annual exhibition of the Akademie der bildenden Künste. At the time, they were both supervisors at the Royal Building Administration (*Oberhofbauamts-Kondukteur*) (Börsch-Supan [see note 10], 1793, cols. 50–51). In April 1800 Moser, by then promoted to senior architectural counselor (*Oberbaurat*), together with Gilly supervised the construction of the National Theater in Berlin, which was being built to designs by Carl Gotthard Langhans.

Oncken (see note 1), 43 n. 195, refers to the same transcript, which she ascribes to volume 1 of the (now-lost) sketchbooks of Gilly's drawings at the Technische Hochschule. Oncken also, erroneously, cites an earlier publication of Gilly's text in *Berliner Blätter*, 18 October 1797. See below, p. 136.

155. Version 2, Moser transcript (see note 154), [131].

156. Version 2, Moser transcript (see note 154), [131].

157. Version 2, Moser transcript (see note 154), [131].

158. The catalog of Gilly's books (Appendix 2, p. 10, no. 13) cites only one of Pierre Patte's works: *Etudes d'architecture, contenant les proportions générales, entrecolonnemens, portes . . . et détails choisis des meilleurs édifices de France et d'Italie* (Paris: Author, 1755).

159. See Landsberger (note 85), 48.

160. *"Athen ist ein Muster. Acropolis. Rom nicht so."*

161. Version 1 (see note 154), fol. 19 [130].

162. Version 2, Moser transcript (see note 154), [132]: *"Mitten in der Stadt würde schon eben diese Lage des Momumentes, wo es von vielen Gebäuden umgeben ist, diesen Eindruck vorübergehender, schwächer machen."*

163. Version 2, Moser transcript (see note 154), [131].

164. Version 1 (see note 154), fol. 19 [130].

165. Version 1 (see note 154), fol. 19 [129].

166. Version 1 (see note 154), fol. 19 [129]: *"Gewölbte Bogengänge öffnen die Durchsicht durch diesen Unterbau."*

167. Version 1 (see note 154), fol. 19 [130].

168. Version 2, Moser transcript (see note 154), [133].

169. Version 2, Moser transcript (see note 154), [133].

170. Version 1 (see note 154), fol. 19 [130].

171. Version 2, Moser transcript (see note 154), [133].

172. Version 1 (see note 154), fol. 18f. [130]: *"Der Anblick, welcher dem Auge beim Austritt aus dem Tempel gewährt wird,—die ganze Friedrichstadt zu Füßen des Wanderers—ist so groß und einzig, daß sich auf keinem anderen [Platz] ein völlig gleicher erwarten läßt."*

173. Karl Gottlob Schelle, *Spatziergänge; oder, Die Kunst spatzieren zu gehen* (Leipzig, 1802); ed. with an epilogue by Markus Fauser (Hildesheim: Olms-Weidmann, 1990).

174. Ibid., 64, 111f.

175. Version 1 (see note 154), fol. 18f. [130].

176. Schelle (see note 173), 52, 43.

177. Johann Wolfgang Goethe, "Einleitung," *Propyläen* 1, no. 1 (1798): iii: " . . . *nach langem Umherwandeln . . . sich noch immer in den Vorhöfen befinde."*

178. For this, see section below, "Thoughts on the Reunion of Art and Science: The Necessity of Poetry," pp. 165–73.

179. Goethe (see note 177): iii: *"Stufe, Thor, Eingang, Vorhalle, der Raum zwischen Innern und Aeussern, zwischen dem Heiligen und Gemeinen kann nur die Stelle seyn, auf der wir uns mit unsern Freunden gewöhnlich aufhalten werden."*

180. Georg Wilhelm Friedrich Hegel, *Ästhetik* (1830; Frankfurt: Europäische Verlagsanstalt, 1966), 1: 64: *"Und so bleibt denn auch der Eindruck dieser Tempel zwar einfach und großartig, zugleich aber heiter, offen und behaglich, indem der ganze Bau mehr auf ein Umherstehen, Hin- und Herwandeln, Kommen und Gehen als auf die konzentrierte innere Sammlung einer ringsum eingeschlossenen, von Äußeren losgelösten Versammlung einge-richtet ist."*

181. Friedrich II der Große, *Das Testament des Königs*, ed. Friedrich von Oppeln-Bronikowski (Berlin: Volksverband der Bücherfreunde, 1925), 16: *"Ich habe wie ein Philosoph gelebt und will als ein solcher begraben werden, ohne Trauergepränge und Leichenpomp. . . . Man bestatte mich in Sanssouci auf der Höhe der Terrassen in einer Gruft, die ich habe herrichten lassen."*

182. Immanuel Kant, *Kritik der Urteilskraft*, in idem, *Werke*, ed. Wilhelm Weischedel, 10 vols. (Darmstadt: Wissenschaftliche Buchgesellschaft, 1983), 8: 367.

183. Jean-Jacques Rousseau, *Les rêveries du promeneur solitaire*, ed. Henri Roddier (1782; Paris: Garnier, 1960).

184. Adler, 1906 (see note 36), 153, was the first to point to the literary parallel: Gilly's Temple of Solitude reminded him of Friedrich Hölderlin, Jean Paul, and Friedrich Mathisson. The parallel with Hölderlin was later taken up most notably by Moeller van den Bruck, 1931 (see note 48), 136: *"Er selbst war wie Hölderlin: Schwelle und Tempel"* (He himself was like Hölderlin: threshold and temple), and by Rietdorf (see note 93).

185. Version 1 (see note 154), fol. 18f. [130].

186. Sheet of sketches showing the Friedrichsdenkmal, reproduced by Oncken (see note 1), plate 27 [135]: *"Ich kenne keinen schöneren Effekt, als von den Seiten umschlossen, gleichsam vom Weltgetümmel abgeschnitten zu sein und über sich frei, ganz frei den Himmel zu sehen. Abends."*

187. Immanuel Kant, *Kritik der praktischen Vernunft*, in idem, *Werke in acht Büchern*, ed. Hugo Renner (Berlin: A. Weichert, 1921), 5: 229: *"Zwei Dinge erfüllen das Gemüt mit immer neuer und zunehmender Bewunderung und Ehrfurcht, je öfter und anhaltender sich das Nachdenken damit beschäftigt: Der bestirnte Himmel über mir und das moralische Gesetz in mir."*

188. Note on Friedrichsdenkmal sketch: *"Kein Beispiel außer in Puzzuoli"* (No example except at Pozzuoli). Gilly would have been able to see illustrations of this temple in two engraved works in his own library: Giulio Cesare Capaccio, *La vera antichità di Pozzuolo* (Rome: Filippo de Rossi, 1652), and Jean-Claude-Richard de Saint-Non, *Voyage pittoresque; ou, Description des royaumes de Naples et de Sicile*, 4 vols. (Paris: Imprimerie de Clousier, 1781–1786), 2: 173.

189. Wackenroder (see note 4), 72. On the significance of Wackenroder's text for late eighteenth-century art, see Neumeyer (note 6), 111, 117f.

190. Friedrich Gilly, "Beschreibung des Landsitzes Rincy unweit von Paris," *Sammlung nützlicher Aufsätze und Nachrichten, die Baukunst betreffend* 3, no. 2 (1799): 116–22, esp. 118, 117 [157, 156].

191. Ibid., 116 [155].

192. Friedrich Gilly, "Beschreibung des Landhauses Bagatelle bey Paris," *Sammlung nützlicher Aufsätze und Nachrichten, die Baukunst betreffend* 3, no. 3 (1799): 106–15, esp. 108 [142].

193. Oncken (see note 1), 127, lists among the now-lost drawings in Gilly's artistic estate: "No. 200: Paris, architectural studies, guardhouses at the *barrières*, including Saint-Denis, Saint-Martin, Ecole Militaire, etc." and "No. 205: Paris, architectural studies, including Hôtel Thélusson."

194. Gilly (see note 192): 115 [147].

195. Wilhelm von Wolzogen, "Über die Barrieren von Paris," *Journal des Luxus und der Moden* 13 (February 1798): 76–82.

196. Ibid.: 79: *"An den Barrieren sehe ich die Baukunst in ihrer Kindheit und Einfalt; an der Colonnade vom Louvre vergleiche ich ihre Ausbildung und Verfeinerung. Gehe ich aus Paris heraus, so ruhe ich hier an jenen großen schönen Formen wieder aus von der Ermattung, so die übergroße Verfeinerung und das Gewirre so vieler Verzierungen, die geschmackvoll in den Details, zum Theil geschmacklos zum Ganzen sind, in mir erregten."*

197. Gilly (see note 192): 114f. [147].

198. Gilly (see note 192): 106 [139].

199. For more detail on the building history, see Barbara Scott, "Bagatelle: Folie of the Comte d'Artois," *Apollo* 95 (June 1972): 476–85; Béatrice de Andia, Franck Folliot, et al., eds., *De Bagatelle à Monceau, 1778–1978: Les folies du XVIIIᵉ siècle à Paris*, exh. cat. (Paris: Musée Carnavalet, 1978). On Bélanger, see Jean Stern, *A l'ombre de Sophie Arnould: François-Joseph Bélanger, architecte des Menus-Plaisirs* (Paris: Librairie Plon, 1930).

200. Gilly (see note 192): 107 [141].

201. Gilly (see note 192): 107 [139].

202. Gilly (see note 192): 108 [141].

203. Gilly (see note 192): 107 [141].

204. Gilly (see note 192): 108 [141].

205. See Oncken (note 1), 84.

206. Waagen (see note 15), 317.

207. Gilly (see note 192): 114 [147].

208. Gilly (see note 190): 122 [161–62].

209. Gilly (see note 190): 121 [159].

210. Gilly (see note 190): 121, 122 [161]: "*Nur um den Anblick der herrlichen Gegend mehr zu genießen, verläßt man endlich dieses liebliche Zimmer, und wird von neuen Schönheiten fortgezogen.*"

211. Gilly (see note 192): 108 [142].

212. Scott (see note 199), 478f.

213. Gilly (see note 192): 109 [142].

214. Gilly (see note 192): 109 [143].

215. Gilly (see note 192): 109 [143–44].

216. See Justus Möser's satiric letter "Das englische Gärtgen" (1775), in *Justus Mösers Sämtliche Werke*, vol. 5, *Patriotische Phantasien und Zugehöriges* (Berlin: Gerhard Stalling, 1945), part 2, 281–83, signed "Anglomania Domen."

217. See note 138. The anonymous author of an essay on the latest in landscape gardening, "Garten Kunst: Neueste Werke in derselben," *Journal des Luxus und der Moden* (June 1798): 358, tells us: "*Einer meiner Freunde, der alles hierher gehörige sammelt, hat über 150 Schriften in seiner Gartenbibliothek, die bloß seit Hirschfeld in Teutschland geschrieben wurden*" (One of my friends, who collects everything relevant to this subject, has in his garden library over 150 works written since Hirschfeld in Germany alone). Another who inveighed against the indiscriminate imitation of the English garden was Christian Cai Laurenz Hirschfeld, professor of philosophy in Kiel, whose celebrated *Theorie der Gartenkunst* was published in two volumes in 1775 (Leipzig: M. G. Weidmanns Erben & Reich) and expanded to five in 1779–1785 (Leipzig: M. G. Weidmanns Erben & Reich).

218. Garden literature in the catalog of Gilly's library: p. 8, no. 107, *Ansichten der vorzüglichsten Partien im Garten zu Machern*, 1799, 1. Heft; p. 8, no. 120, Johann Gottfried Klinsky, *Versuch über die Harmonie der Gebäude zu den Landschaften* (Dresden: In dem Museum von Arnold & Pinther, 1799); p.

11, no. 41, Antoine-Joseph Dezallier D'Argenville, *La théorie et la pratique du jardinage*, 4th rev. ed. (Paris: Pierre-Jean Mariette, 1747); p. 12, no. 58, *Sammlung landschaftlicher Darstellung der schönsten Landsitze und Parks in England;* p. 12, no. 59, E. W. Glasewald, *Beschreibung des Gartens zu Machern: Mit besonderer Rücksicht auf die in demselben befindlichen Holzarten* (Berlin: Author, 1799); p. 15, no. 44, *Über den guten Geschmack bey ländlichen Kunst- und Gärten-Anlagen und bey Verbesserung wirklicher Landschaften: Durch Beispiele erläutert,* trans. from English (Leipzig: In der Kleefeldschen Buchhandlung, 1798); p. 16, no. 68, *Über die chinesischen Gärten: Eine Abhandlung* (1773); p. 17, no. 86, René-Louis, marquis de Girardin, *De la composition des paysages sur le terrain; ou, Des moyens d'embellir la nature autour des habitations champêtres* (Paris: Geneva: n.p., 1777; Mayer, 1795); p. 17, no. 91, Friedrich-August Krubsacius, *Wahrscheinlicher Entwurf, von des jüngern Plinius Landhaus und Garten* (Leipzig: B. C. Breitkopf & Sohn, 1763; Gilly had an edition published in Leipzig in 1768), and William Chambers, *Über die orientalische Gartenkunst* (Gotha: n.p., 1775; trans. of William Chambers, *A Dissertation on Oriental Gardening* [London: W. Griffin, 1772].); p. 19, no. 143, Stanislas Girardin, *Promenade; ou, Itinéraire des jardins d'Ermenonville* (Paris: n.p., 1788); p. 23, no. 1, Abbé Delille, *Les Jardins; ou, L'art d'embellir les paysages, poëme* (Paris: Impr. de F.-A. Didot l'aîné, 1782); p. 36, no. 29, *Gartenkalender,* year 1, ed. Christian Cai Laurenz Hirschfeld (Kiel: n.p., 1782).

219. Carl August Boettiger, *Reise nach Wörlitz, 1797* (1798), ed. from the ms., with commentary, by Erhard Hirsch (Wörlitz: Staatliche Schlösser und Gärten Wörlitz, Oranienbaum und Luisium, 1988), 63ff.

220. Gilly (see note 192): 110 [144].

221. Gilly (see note 192): 111 [144].

222. Gilly (see note 190): 116 [155].

223. Gilly (see note 190): 116, 119 [155, 158].

224. Gilly (see note 190): 121 [161].

225. Gilly (see note 190): 122 [162]: *"In der entfernteren stillen Gegend eines Gartens macht diese ganz natürliche Anlage mit ihrer mahlerischen Umgebung einen überraschenden und gefälligen Anblick, und eine solche Hütte ist mehr werth, als alles modische Drechselwerk von Tempeln und bunten Häuserchen."*

226. Friedrich Gilly, "Einige Gedanken über die Notwendigkeit die verschiedenen Theile der Baukunst in wissenschaftlicher und praktischer Hinsicht zu vereinen," *Sammlung nützlicher Aufsätze und Nachrichten, die Baukunst betreffend* 3, no. 2 (1799): 3–12 [165].

227. *Sammlung nützlicher Aufsätze und Nachrichten, die Baukunst betreffend* 1, no. 1 (1797): "Vorrede," vi.

228. Eytelwein (see note 21). This connection is also pointed out by Hanno-Walter Kruft, *Geschichte der Architekturtheorie* (Munich: C. H. Beck, 1985), 33, in his brief mention of the Gilly essays.

229. Christian Ludwig Stieglitz, *Encyclopädie der bürgerlichen Baukunst* (Leipzig: C. Fritsch, 1792–1798), not listed in the catalog of Gilly's library, which does, however, contain the following by the same author: p. 13, no. 5, idem, *Geschichte der Baukunst der Alten* (Leipzig: Dyksche Buchhandlung, 1792); p. 23, no. 241, idem, *Die Baukunst der Alten: Ein Handbuch für Freunde der Kunst* (Leipzig: Breitkopf & Härtel, 1796).

230. Gilly (see note 226): 5 [166].

231. Gilly (see note 226): 5 [165].

232. Gilly (see note 226): 4 [165–66].

233. Gilly (see note 226): 4 [165].

234. Gilly (see note 226): 4 [166].

235. Gilly (see note 226): 5 [166].

236. Gilly (see note 226): 5 [166].

237. Gilly (see note 226): 6 [167]: "Bald sehen wir ihn sein kunstmäßiges Talent auf dem Gebiet des Geschmacks üben. . . . Bald wird dieser Zweck strenger, der seinen Plan bestimmt, und alle Rücksichten verbinden zur Regel, die mit jener Kunst behandelt werden soll. Bald ist es der Zweck allein, das nothwendige Bedürfnis, wodurch als erstes Gesetz, die Art der Form des Werks bestimmt wird."

238. Gilly (see note 226): 6 [167].

239. Gilly (see note 226): 5, 6 [167].

240. Gilly (see note 226): 5 [166].

241. Gilly (see note 226): 8 [169].

242. Gilly (see note 226): 4 [165].

243. Gilly (see note 226): 7 [168].

244. Gilly (see note 226): 7 [169].

245. Gilly (see note 226): 8f. [169].

246. Gilly (see note 226): 8 [169]: "Mit der verbreiteten Gelehrsamkeit wurde auch die Baukunst größtentheils gelehrt behandelt. Es kam die Zeit der Lehrbücher. Die Mathematik nahm sich ihrer vorzüglich an, und selbst das Geschmacksproblem sollte durch sie . . . gelöst werden."

247. See also the criticism of Wolff in the preface to the first issue of *Sammlung nützlicher Aufsätze und Nachrichten, die Baukunst betreffend* 1, no. 1 (1797): iv. Sturm's works were listed in the catalog of Gilly's library, p. 8, nos. 109, 118; p. 9, no. 124; and p. 11, no. 37. On Wolff and Sturm, see also Ulrich Schütte, *Ordnung und Verzierung: Untersuchungen zur deutschsprachigen Architekturtheorie des 18. Jahrhunderts* (Braunschweig: F. Vieweg, 1986), esp. 18ff.

248. Wackenroder (see note 4), 7, in his chapter on Raphael.

249. Gilly (see note 226): 8 [169].

250. Johann Wolfgang Goethe, "Über Lehranstalten zu Gunsten der bildenden Künste," *Propyläen* 2, no. 2 (1799): 4–25, 141–71; 14: "Die Natur hat zwischen jedem Zeitalter gleichsam eherne Mauern errichtet, die kein Mensch überspringt."

251. Gilly (see note 226): 8 [169]: "Wie auch ihr Zustand überhaupt, ihre Verbindung mit der Wissenschaft beschaffen gewesen seyn mag, so war es natürlich, daß sie [die Baukunst] sich damals eigentlich und mehr wie je den Künsten anschloß. Aber eine in ihrer Art einzige Vereinigung von Kenntnissen und Talenten kann übrigens nur allein zu jener Vollkommenheit der damaligen Werke geführt haben" (emphasis in original).

252. Gilly (see note 226): 9 [170]: "Lange hatte man ihr zugestanden, eine wirkliche Gefährtin der schönen Künste zu sein; doch behielt sie damals wenig Vertheidiger dieses Rechts, selbst kaum ihres Kunst-Namens. Einige

gestanden ihr eine halbe Stimme unter den Künsten zu, doch andere strichen sie ganz von dieser Liste und verwiesen sie an ihre notwendige Dürftigkeit und Dienstbarkeit. So wurde sie als bloße Mechanik selbst betrachtet, bald unter diese, bald unter jene Herrschaft gegeben—zu dienen und zu nützen."

253. Friedrich Schiller, *Über die ästhetische Erziehung des Menschen* (1795), Letter 2, in idem, *Werke in drei Bänden*, ed. Herbert G. Göpfert (Munich: Carl Hanser, 1966), 2: 446–47: *". . . von der Notwendigkeit der Geister, nicht von der Notdurft der Materie . . . Der Nutzen ist das große Ideal der Zeit, dem alle Kräfte fronen und alle Talente huldigen sollen"* (emphasis in original).

254. Gilly (see note 226): 9 [170].

255. Schelle (see note 173), 282, alleges that Heydenreich himself intended to write a treatise on the art of the promenade.

256. Karl Heinrich Heydenreich, *System der Ästhetik* (Leipzig: G. J. Göschen, 1790); reprinted, with an epilogue by Volker Deubel, in *Texte zum literarischen Leben um 1800*, ed. Ernst Weber (Hildesheim: Gerstenberg, 1978). On his life and work, see *Allgemeine deutsche Biographie* (Leipzig: Duncker & Humblot, 1880), 12: 355–56, from which we learn that Heydenreich was savagely attacked by Goethe and Schiller. In 1799 Heydenreich resigned from his professorial appointment, and he died in 1801, at the age of thirty-seven, "in consequence of excessive consumption of spirituous liquors, and notably of large quantities of brandy" (ibid.: 355). Schelle, the author of *Spatziergänge; oder, Die Kunst spatzieren zu gehen* (see note 173), published a posthumous tribute to Heydenreich: *Karl Heinrich Heydenreich: Charakteristik als Mensch und Schriftsteller* (Leipzig: Martini, 1802).

257. Heydenreich, *System der Ästhetik*, reprint 1978 (see note 256), xxvii.

258. Heydenreich, *System der Ästhetik*, reprint 1978 (see note 256), 150.

259. Karl Heinrich Heydenreich, "Neuer Begriff der Baukunst als schoenen Kunst," *Deutsche Monatsschrift* (October 1798): 160–64.

260. Ibid.: 162: *"Soll es ein Werk schöner Architektur seyn, so müssen wir, so wie wir es in seiner Lage (die auch mit zu seiner Erfindung gehört,) sehn, ländliche Ruhe, sanfte Stille und Einfalt athmen, diese Gefühle müssen uns aus der Form entgegen kommen, wir müssen, hingerissen vom Anblicke, Dichter werden, und in diesem Zeitpunkte mit Bildern eines patriarchalischen Friedens, und idyllischer Unschuld ein schwärmerisches Spiel treiben."*

261. Heydenreich (see note 259): 162–63: *"Wenn es dem Künstler gelingt, seinem Gebäude solche Formen zu geben, daß der Gedanke des physischen Zweckes ganz verschwindet und der Betrachter sogleich durch den Anblick zu dem höhern Zweck erhoben, und zu einem freyern Spiele unter Bildern, die mit ihm zusammenhängen, begeistert wird, dann ist sein Werk ein Werk der schönen Architektur. Es versteht sich von selbst, daß es außerdem allen Gesetzen eines zweckmäßigen und verhältnißmäßigen Gebäudes Genüge leisten muß. . . . Man kann jedes Werk der schönen Architektur ansehn, als eine dichterische Darstellung des höhern Zweckes des Gebäudes in schönern architektonischen Formen, bey deren Empfindung alle blos physische Rücksichten gänzlich verschwinden.*

Einen höhern und edlern Standpunkt wird wohl schwerlich auch der enthusiastischste Freund der schönen Architektur für sie bestimmen. Sie erscheint, als wahre schöne Kunst. Ihre Werke sind nur durch Genie möglich, und der erfindende Architekt befindet sich mit dem erfindenden Dichter und Bildner in ziemlich gleicher Stimmung. Sein Plan wird nicht etwa vom physischen Zwecke herbeygezwungen, sondern er wird durch die dichterische Vorstellung des höhern Zweckes des Werkes erzeugt" (emphasis in original).

262. Schinkel (see note 28), 197f.

263. Gilly (see note 226): 10 [171].

264. Gilly (see note 226): 10 [171].

265. "Das älteste Systemprogramm des deutschen Idealismus, 1795/96," in Christoph Jamme and Helmut Schneider, eds., *Mythologie der Vernunft: Hegels "ältestes Systemprogramm des deutschen Idealismus"* (Frankfurt: Suhrkamp, 1984), 13: "*Polytheismus d[e]r Einbildungskraft u[nd] der Kunst, dis ists, was wir bedürfen!*" This is the surviving fragment of a draft for a programmatic philosophical statement, probably written down by Hegel. Possibly the most important German philosophical text of the 1790s, it has come to the notice of scholars only recently; for text and discussion, see Jamme and Schneider, as above. The text appeared in English translation in H.S. Harris, *Hegel's Development: Toward the Sunlight, 1770–1801* (Oxford: Clarendon, 1972), 510–12. That translation was not used here.

266. "Das älteste Systemprogramm" (see note 265), 11.

267. Johann Wolfgang Goethe, "Baukunst" (1795), in idem, *Werke* (see note 119), 47: 72: "*Puristen . . . , die auch in der Baukunst gern alles zu Prosa machen möchten.*"

268. Johann Wolfgang Goethe, "Baukunst" (1795), in idem, *Werke* (see note 119), 47: 328: "*Es ist eigentlich der poetische Theil, die Fiktion, wodurch ein Gebäude wirklich ein Kunstwerk wird.*" (The quote is not from the final version of "Baukunst," but rather from a preliminary draft dated 29 October 1795.)

269. "Das älteste Systemprogramm" (see note 265), 12–13: "*Der Philosoph muß eben so viel ästhetische Kraft besizen, als der Dichter. Die Menschen ohne ästhetischen Sinn sind unsre BuchstabenPhilosophen. Die Philosophie des Geistes ist eine ästhetische Philosophie. Man kan in nichts geistreich seyn, selbst über Geschichte kan man nicht geistreich raisonnieren—ohne ästhetischen Sinn. Hier soll offenbar werden, woran es eigentlich den Menschen fehlt, die keine Ideen verstehen,—und treuherzig genug gestehen, daß ihnen alles dunkel ist, sobald es über Tabellen und Register hinaus geht.*"

270. "Das älteste Systemprogramm" (see note 265), 12: "*Ich bin nun überzeugt, daß der höchste Akt der Vernunft, der, indem sie alle Ideen umfast, ein ästhetischer Akt ist, und daß* Wahrheit und Güte, nur in der Schönheit *verschwistert sind*" (emphasis in original).

271. Heydenreich, 1978 (see note 256), "Einleitung," xxi–xxii.

272. See the following titles in Gilly's book collection by Karl Philipp Moritz: p. 23, no. 9, *Mythologischer Almanach für Damen*, ed. Karl Philipp Moritz (Berlin: J. F. Unger, 1792); p. 15, no. 46, *Vorbegriffe zu einer Theorie der Ornamente* (Berlin: K. Matzdorff, 1793; facsimile reprint, Nördlingen: Dr. Alfons Uhl, 1986); p. 15, no. 49, *Über die bildende Nachahmung des Schönen* (Braunschweig: Schul-Buchhandlung, 1788); p. 17, no. 80, *Anthousa; oder, Roms Alterthümer: Ein Buch für die Menschheit* (Berlin: Friedrich Maurer, 1791); p. 19, nos. 138–40, *Reisen eines Deutschen in Italien in den Jahren 1786 bis 1788,*

3 vols. (Berlin: Friedrich Maurer, 1792–1793); p. 22, no. 201, *Götterlehre; oder, Mythologische Dichtungen der Alten* (Berlin: J. F. Unger, 1791); p. 33, no. 43, Johann Gottfried Bremer, *Die symbolische Weisheit der Ägypter aus den verborgensten Denkmälern des Alterthums*, ed. Karl Philipp Moritz (Berlin: K. Matzdorff, 1793); p. 35, no. 128, Karl Philipp Moritz, *Vom Unterschiede des Accusativ's und Dativ's. In Briefen* (Berlin, 1781; Berlin, 1792).

273. P. 5, nos. 64–65, Johann Joachim Winckelmann, *Alte Denkmäler der Kunst*, 2 vols., trans. from Italian by Friedrich Leopold Brunn (Berlin: n.p., 1791–1792); p. 10, no. 21, idem, *Sendschreiben von den Herkulanischen Entdeckungen* (Dresden: G. C. Walther, 1762); p. 10, no. 22, idem, *Anmerkungen über die Baukunst der Alten* (Leipzig: J. Gottfried Dyck, 1762); p. 10, no. 23, idem, *Abhandlung von der Fähigkeit der Empfindung des Schönen in der Kunst, und dem Unterrichte in derselben* (Dresden: In der Waltherischen Buchhandlung, 1763; Dresden, 1771); p. 11, no. 31, idem, *Gedanken über die Nachahmung der griechischen Werke in der Mahlerey und Bildhauerkunst* (Dresden: G. C. Walther, 1756); p. 12, nos. 66–68, idem, *Histoire de l'art de l'antiquité*, 3 vols., trans. from German by M. Huber (Leipzig: Author and J. G. I. Breitkopf, 1781); p. 21, nos. 193–94, idem, *Lettres familières de M. Winckelmann*, 2 vols., trans. from German by Hendrik Jansen (Amsterdam: Couturier fils, 1781).

274. Karl Philipp Moritz, "Die Signatur des Schönen: In wie fern Kunstwerke beschrieben werden können," *Monats-Schrift der Akademie der Künste und mechanischen Wissenschaften zu Berlin* 1, no. 3 (1789): 3ff.

275. On this see Hanno-Walter Kruft, "Introduction," in Karl Philipp Moritz, *Vorbegriffe zu einer Theorie der Ornamente* (1793; facsimile reprint, Nördlingen: Dr. Alfons Uhl, 1986), 7. On Moritz's life and influence, see also Karl Philipp Moritz, *Schriften zur Ästhetik und Poetik*, ed. Hans Joachim Schrimpf (Tübingen: M. Niemeyer, 1962).

276. Levezow (see note 11), 226.

277. First published in *Deutsche Monatsschrift* 5 (1785): 225–36; reprinted in Carl [Karl] Philipp Moritz, *Die große Loge; oder, Der Freimaurer mit Waage und Senkblei* (Berlin: E. Felisch, 1793).

278. Moritz, *Reisen eines Deutschen in Italien* (see note 272). Also reprinted in part in Moritz, *Vorbegriffe* (see note 275). (Both titles appear in the catalog of Gilly's books.)

279. Moritz, *Vorbegriffe* (see note 275), 4: "*Der Mensch will in einem Gebäude nicht nur mit Wohlgefallen wohnen—er will es auch mit Wohlgefallen ansehen—und es arbeiten für die Nahrung des Auges fast eben so viele Hände als für die Ernährung des Körpers.*"

280. On this, see esp. Christoph Jamme and Gerhard Kurz, eds., *Idealismus und Aufklärung: Kontinuität und Kritik der Aufklärung in Philosophie und Poesie um 1800*, Deutscher Idealismus, vol. 14 (Stuttgart: Klett-Cotta, 1988).

281. Friedrich Hölderlin, *Hyperion* 2 (Berlin, 1799); cited from idem, *Sämtliche Werke und Briefe*, ed. Günther Mieth (Munich: Carl Hanser, 1970), 1: 607: "*Immerhin hat das den Staat zur Hölle gemacht, daß ihn der Mensch zu seinem Himmel machen wollte.*" Ibid., 1: 661: "*Aber aus bloßem Verstand ist nie Verständiges, aus bloßer Vernunft nie Vernünftiges gekommen.*"

282. "Das älteste Systemprogramm" (see note 265), 13: "*Wir müßen eine neue Mythologie haben,*

diese Mythologie aber muß im Dienste der Ideen stehen, sie mus eine Mythologie der Vernunft werden" (emphasis in original).

283. "Das älteste Systemprogramm" (see note 265), 13: *"Sie wird am Ende wieder, was sie am Anfang war—Lehrerin der Menschheit"* (emphasis in original).

284. Friedrich Schiller, *Über die ästhetische Erziehung des Menschen* (see note 253), 2: 447: *". . . durch das ästhetische den Weg nehmen muß, weil es die Schönheit ist, durch welche man zu der Freiheit wandert."*

285. "Das älteste Systemprogramm" (see note 265), 13f.: *"So müssen endlich aufgeklärte und Unaufgeklärte sich die Hand reichen, die Mythologie muß philosophisch werden, und das Volk vernünftig, und die Philosophie muß mythologisch werden, um die Philosophen sinnlich zu machen. Dann herrscht ewige Einheit unter uns. . . . Dann erst erwartet uns gleiche Ausbildung aller Kräfte, des Einzelnen sowohl als aller Individuen. Keine Kraft wird mehr unterdrükt werden, dann herrscht allgemeine Freiheit und Gleichheit der Geister!"* (emphasis in original).

286. Gilly (see note 226): 10 [171]: *"Denn es muß überall dahin kommen, daß der Baumeister den Gelehrten, der Gelehrte den Baumeister schätzen lerne, daß der Baumeister unter sich mit ihren besonderen Kenntnissen, mit eigenthümlichen Anlagen sich vereinigen, sich achten und daß kein eitler Stolz unter ihnen den sogenannten Baukünstler auszeichne. Wechselseitig muß alles sich die Hände bieten und einander nützlich seyn, je entfernter und vielseitiger das Ziel des ganzen Strebens ist"* (emphasis in original).

287. Gilly (see note 190): 119 [158].

288. Gilly (see note 226): 11 [171].

289. Gilly (see note 226): 10f. [171–72].

290. Goethe, "Über Lehranstalten" (see note 250); the passages cited by Gilly are on pp. 10, 13, and 17: *"Wenn sie [die Kunst] aber beherrscht und gemeistert wird, wenn sie sich nach der Zeit richten soll, dann wird sie abnehmen und vergehen. . . .* Sollen die Künste steigen und blühen; so muß eine allgemeine Liebhaberey herrschen, die sich zum Großen neigt. . . . *Vergebens hofft man, daß Zierlichkeit, Geschmack, Zweckmäßigkeit sich durch alle Gewerbe wohlthätig verbreite! denn dieses kann nur alsdann geschehen, wenn der Kunstsinn allgemein ist, und die schöne Form überall gefordert wird"* (emphasis in original).

291. Gilly (see note 226): 12 [172].

292. GStA Merseburg (see note 12), Rep. 76 alt IV, Kuratorium der Bauakademie, Nr. 25.

293. Letter from Gilly to Minister Freiherr von Schrötter, 17 May 1799, in Staatsbibliothek zu Berlin—Preußischer Kulturbesitz, Sammlung Darmstaedter D 1798 (1): Gilly, Friedrich. Quoted from Internationale Bauausstellung Berlin 1987 (see note 11), 243: *"Die Perspektive und die dazu erforderliche Lehre der Optik werde ich, nach Vorausgeschickter Übersicht, der älteren Methoden, nach Lambertischem Systeme, mit Zuziehung der neusten Schriften von Mönich, Hindenburg, Breisig u.s.f. vortragen; worüber ich, bey dem bereits öfters ertheiltem Unterrichte im eigentlich praktischen und ausübenden dieser Wißenschaft, so wie über die gesamte Theorie und Ausübung der Zeichenkunst, als [auch?] über Licht, Schatten, Farbengebung, Komposition, geschmackvolle Behandlung der Zeichnungen pp. eigene Hefte aufgesetzt habe und zum Grunde zu legen denke, wovon ich demnächst die nähere Übersicht untertänigst einreichen werde. den Unterricht im architektonischen Zeichnen selbst, werde ich nach jenen Vorlesungen anordnen und die Schüler durch gute Muster, sowohl in der Richtigkeit, Sauberkeit und im Geschmake zu bilden, demnächst aber durch Aufgaben, zu eigener Ausarbeitung*

und eigenen Entwürfe zu üben suchen" [emphasis in original] (After first giving a prior outline of the older methods, I shall present *Perspective*, and the theory of Optics which is necessary for it, according to the Lambert system, with diagrams from the most recent works of Mönnich, Hindenburg, Breysig, and others. In delivering a number of previous courses of instruction in the practice and exercise of this science, in the general theory and practice of draftsmanship as well as in light, shade, color, composition, and the tasteful presentation of drawings, I have compiled albums of my own, on which I intend to base myself, and of which I shall shortly have the honor to submit a more detailed conspectus. I shall organize the instruction in *architectural draftsmanship* in accordance with those lectures and shall seek to train the students in accuracy, neatness, and good taste by providing good models; and, initially through assigned tasks, to prepare them to elaborate and then to initiate designs for themselves).

The catalog of Gilly's library lists the following titles by the writers mentioned: p. 14, no. 16, Johann Heinrich Lambert, *Grundregeln der Perspektiv*, ed. C. F. Hindenburg (Leipzig: n.p., 1799); p. 14, no. 13, idem, *Die freye Perspektive; oder, Anweisung, jeden perspektivischen Aufriss von freyen Stücken und ohne Grundriss zu verfertigen* (Zurich: Heidegger, 1759; 2nd ed., Zurich: Orell, Gessner, Füesslin, 1774); p. 14, no. 14, Johann Heinrich Lambert, *Kurzgefaßte Regeln zu perspectivischen Zeichnungen, vermittelst eines zu deren Ausübung so wie auch zu geometrischen Zeichnungen eingerichteten Proportionalzirkels* (Augsburg: n.p., 1772); p. 14, no. 19, Bernhard Friedrich Mönnich, *Versuch die mathematischen Regeln der Perspektive für den Künstler ohne Theorie anwendbar zu machen*, 4 vols. (Berlin: G. A. Lange, 1784–1801)—Gilly owned one volume, published in 1794; p. 14, nos. 20–24, five more copies, unbound; p. 14, no. 25, Johann Adam Breysig, *Versuch einer Erläuterung der Reliefs-Perspektive* (Magdeburg: G. Ch. Keil, 1798); p. 14, no. 26, idem, *Skizzen, Gedanken, Entwürfe, Umrisse, die bildende[n] Künste betreffend* (Magdeburg: G. Ch. Keil, 1799). Additionally, the following treatises on perspective are listed in the catalog of Gilly's books: p. 21, no. 175, Thomas Bonnor, *Illustration of all the Engraved Subjects Which Compose the Number of the Copper-Plate Perspective Itinerary* (London: Author, 1798–); p. 14, no. 17, Abel Bürja, *Der mathematische Maler; oder, Gründliche Anweisung zur Perspektive nach verschiedenen Methoden, nebst einem Anhange über die theatralische Perspektive und der Beschreibung eines neuen perspektivischen Instruments* (Berlin: C. G. Schöne, 1795); p. 7, no. 94, Courtonne, *Traité de la perspective pratique, avec des remarques sur l'architecture, suivies de quelques édifices considerables mis en perspective & de l'invention de l'auteur* (Paris: Vincent, 1725); p. 14, no. 27, Carl Gottlieb Horstig, *Briefe über die mahlerische Perspektive* (Leipzig: n.p., 1797); p. 7, no. 93, *Die Perspektive des P. Pozzo* [perhaps: Andrea Pozzo, *Perspectivae pictorum et architectorum*, bilingual German and Latin ed. (Rome, 1693; Augsburg?: Johann Fridrich Probst, 1706–1719)]; p. 11, no. 43, Jean Dubreuil, *Perspectiva practica; oder, Vollständige Anleitung zu der Perspektiv-Reißkunst*, trans. Johann Christoph Rembold (Augsburg: J. Wolff, 1710).

294. Leon Battista Alberti, *De re aedificatoria*, book 9, chapter 9. Among Gilly's books, p. 9, no. 6, is an edition of Alberti: *I dieici libri di architettura di Leon Watt. Alberti*, trans. [into Italian] Cosimo Bartoli (Florence: L. Torrentino, 1550; 1784).

295. Levezow (see note 11), 235.

296. Letter from Gilly to Minister Freiherr von Schrötter, 17 May 1799 (see note 293), quoted from Internationale Bauausstellung Berlin 1987 (see note 11), 243–44: "*Ob ich gleich eigene Zeichnungen und Vorschriften aus meiner Samlung so viel als möglich vorlegen werde; so dürfte dies doch kaum für die obere Klasse, in einem jährig fortwährendem Unterrichte hinreichen, und selbst der Vorrath von Originalien aus der bisherigen architektonischen Klaße, würde nach gehöriger Auswahl für die sämtlichen Zeichen-Schüler wohl zu gering seyn. Hierzu würden den die nötigen und doppelt vorhandenen Kupferwerke aus den Königl. Bibliothecken wohl abgetreten und einige neuere sehr nötige Werke angeschafft werden könen, deren Verzeichniß ich mit Ew. Excellenzien gnädiger Bewilligung sogleich anfertigen werde*" (Although, as far as possible, I shall present drawings of my own and examples from my own collection, this is unlikely to suffice for the senior class in a course lasting for several years; and even the stock of originals from the previous architecture class would be inadequate, if a proper selection were made, to cater for all the students of drawing. To this end, it is expected that it will be possible to secure the engraved works present in duplicate in the royal libraries and to acquire a number of highly necessary recent works, a list of which, with Your Excellency's gracious permission, I shall draw up without delay).

297. Letter from Gilly, 17 September 1799, GStA Merseburg (see note 12), Gen. Directorium, Bau-Akademie Deput. Tit. VI, Nr. 8, Acta wegen des Unterrichts in der Optik und Perspective: Professor Gilly, Simon: 1799–1809, fol. 2f.: "*Seinem hochlöblichen Direktoris der Kgl. Bau-Akademie überreiche ich ganz gehorsamst in den Beylagen den Plan welchen ich vorläufig zu den diesjährigen Vorlesungen über Optik und Perspektive, als Grundlage meiner allgemeinen theoretisch-artistischen Anweisung zur Zeichenkunst, welche ich mit diesen Vorlesungen zu verbinden gedenke, entworfen habe. Bey der Menge und Vielfaltigkeit der dabey vorkommenden und für die Praxis unentbehrlichen Materien, ist es mir nicht wohl möglich gewesen, die einzelnen Abschnitte dieses Entwurfes weitläufiger auszuführen; ich denke dies aber sowohl für die Folge zu thun*" (I herewith respectfully submit to His Honor, the director of the Royal Bauakademie, the provisional plan that I have drawn up for this year's lectures on optics and perspective as the foundation of my general theoretical and artistic instruction in draftsmanship, which I intend to link with these lectures. Because of the quantity and variety of the materials that are indispensable for teaching, I have been unable to set out the individual sections of this outline at greater length; however, I intend to do so for what follows). See also Appendix 1.

298. Friedrich Gilly, "Vorlesungen über Optik und Perspektive als Grundlage einer theoretisch artistischen Anweisung zur Zeichenkunst besonders für Architekten," in GStA Merseburg, Gen. Directorium (see note 297), fol. 4, 5.

299. Friedrich Gilly, "Vorlesungen über Optik und Perspektive als Grundlage einer theoretisch artistischen Anweisung zur Zeichenkunst besonders für Architekten," in GStA Merseburg, Gen. Directorium (see note 297).

300. Kruft (see note 228), 154.

301. Claude Perrault, *Les dix livres d'architecture de Vitruve* (Paris: Jean-Baptiste Coignard, 1673).

302. [Julien-David] Le Roy, *Les ruines des plus beaux monuments de la Grèce* (Paris: H. L. Guérin & L. F. Delatour, 1758).

303. Thomas Major, *The Ruins of Paestum, Otherwise Posidonia in Magna Graecia. Les ruines de Paestum, ou de Posidonie dans la Grande Grèce,* bilingual English and French ed. (London: Author, 1768).

304. Antonio Labacco, *Libro appartenente all'architettura nel qual si figurano alcune notabili antiquità di Roma* (Rome: In Casa Nostra, 1552).

305. Jean Barbault, *Les plus beaux monumens de la Rome ancienne* (Rome: Bouchard & Gravier, 1761); idem, *Denkmäler des alten Roms,* ed. Georg Christoph Kilian (Augsburg, 1767).

306. All titles mentioned are in the catalog of Gilly's library. Others include: p. 4, no. 19, Robert Wood, *Les ruines de Balbec, autrement dite Héliopolis dans la Coelosyrie* (London: n.p., 1757); p. 4, no. 18, idem, *Les ruines de Palmyre, autrement dite Tedmor au désert* (London: A. Millard, 1753); p. 4, nos. 20–24, Saint-Non (see note 188).

307. See Appendix 1, "List of a Selection of the Duplicates Present in the Royal Library of This City," 175–79.

308. Kunstbibliothek Berlin, Staatliche Museen Preußischer Kulturbesitz, HdZ 7718, 7719.

309. See Gilly's remarks on the subject in "Bagatelle" (note 192): 110 [143].

310. Goethe (see note 250), 169.

311. Goethe (see note 250), 169: *"Derjenige, der das Glück hat dieses zu bewirken, einen reinern Geschmack einzuführen, ist ein Wohlthäter seiner Zeit."*

Friedrich

GILLY

Essays on Architecture

1796–1799

On the Views of Marienburg, Castle of the Teutonic Order in West Prussia, Drawn in the Year 1794 by Mr. Gilly, Supervisor at the Royal Building Administration

To the uninitiated, this collection of ten different views of Marienburg Castle and certain of its details may at first sight appear to be merely the exercises of a novice, deserving of no admiration whatever. Yet, once one has discovered the right vantage point and the proper distance, this chaos of apparently aimless lines suddenly yields a most remarkable order and consummate beauty; everything falls into place and acquires both shape and vitality. This is especially true of the interior view of the chapter house, in which, all at once, there unfolds to view a stupendous and awe-inspiring vault resting on a single, slender granite pillar— certainly one of the boldest and most daring architectural feats ever accomplished. Seen in this way and from this distance, the work attests to its author's true artistic genius and masterly hand—all the more so, since these views did not offer themselves to immediate copying: it was Supervisor Gilly's own penetrating and burning force of imagination that combined the scattered ruins into a grand whole, which, having once impressed itself on his sensibility, had then to pass from the mind through the arm and thence to the brush. To enable the reader to judge all this, I shall allow the artist to speak for himself.

—Kosmann

T he castle of Marienburg in West Prussia presents a variety of interest. Architecturally remarkable for its colossal and audacious construction and for its truly grand simplicity of style, the castle is also a monument of great antiquarian and patriotic significance.

Prussia was still a trackless wilderness when Albert of Prague,[1] following the course of the river Vistula, discovered the first humble dwellings of Danzig. It was here that he began his work of conversion, only to be slain by the heathen Prussians. Bruno of Querfurt[2] and other missionaries who followed him in preaching salvation were put to flight. In vain did Bolesław of Poland,[3] inflamed with sacred zeal and allied with the lowland knights, march against the heathen; in vain did his successors pursue their crusades until, at last, powerful assistance was at hand. The Prussians, who had fought with the fury of desperation for their beliefs, their freedom, and their lives, were expelled and enslaved by the aid of several neighboring powers, notably the knights of the Teutonic Order.[4]

These had just moved their seat to Venice, and, in anticipation of secure conquests, they were glad to join the fray. Their success soon brought them considerable land-holdings by treaty, and their grand master, Herrmann von Salza,[5] installed Herrmann Balke[6] as provincial master with a large garrison. The little territory of Culm and Marienburg was taken in 1233, and further conquests followed. To overawe the often rebellious populace, fortified castles were built, the first of which was Vogelsang.[7]

The heights along the Nogat River, near the town of Marienburg, offered a propitious site for fortifications. There, in the center of a smiling and fertile river plain, the knights installed themselves in a safe and pleasant stronghold that dominated the plain as far as Elbing in one direction and the uplands in the other; and everywhere forts and castles were erected to form a protective chain around the precious lowlands. Located near the Montau triangle, where the Nogat and the Vistula separate, the site ensured the knights mastery of those rivers, of shipping, and of trade—most particularly of the trade from Danzig, whose grain barges were often intercepted.

An old fortress erected at Montau in 1244 by the Pomeranian duke Swentopolk was razed,[8] the materials were carted to Marienburg, and by 1276 (or 1280–1281, according to Hartknoch's *Chronik von Preußen*),[9] under the aegis of the grand master who completed the conquest of Prussia, Hartmann von Heldrungen,[10] Provincial Master Konrad von Thierberg[11] had erected a spacious residence for the provincial masters, together with conventual buildings.

This, the Old Castle, surrounded by breastworks and a deep moat, which presumably was once fed by the river, stands on the riverbank, adjacent to the town, on the crown of a gently sloping hill some sixty to seventy feet in height; it forms a colossal rectangle enclosing an inner court. Later, Provincial Master Meneko von Querfurt[12] built embankments along the Nogat to protect the town and valley, and from that time onward the agriculture of the region began to flourish.

Prussia offered increasingly attractive and important prospects to the now highly unsettled Teutonic Order. Siegfried von Feuchtwangen,[13] who was elected [grand master] in 1304, left stewards in charge of the minor possessions of the order and transferred the seat of the grand master to Marienburg. The castle expanded across the lower slopes of the hill; and, when the grand master took up residence, the so-called New or Middle Castle was constructed on a truly lavish scale. Soon after this, the Lower Castle was built; within an enclosure fortified with towers and walls, this incorporated ample storehouses, stables, and arsenals, as well as a large paddock, enclosed within the walls, that seems to have served as a secure pasture for the horses. The undertaking was continued without interruption by subsequent grand masters, and most notably by Dietrich von Oldenburg,[14] who, among other things, built beside the Old Castle the church of Saint Mary of the Teutonic Order (about 1355) and the funerary vault of the grand masters, as well as a cemetery reserved for the brethren.

Under this new regime, the agriculture of the Prussian provinces was improved; the knights applied to good effect the knowledge they had gained on their extensive travels. Cultivation and improvement increased the fertility of the soil; canals were dug; the rivers were made navigable; colonists—mostly Germans—were brought into the wastelands; and skilled artisans were recruited. It is not improbable that these foreign craftsmen included a number from Venice, where the knights had resided for a considerable time. Architecture flourished at that period in northern Italy, and the look of the knights' buildings suggests that considerable skill was lavished on their construction.

Several of the grand masters, among them Winrich von Kniprode,[15] were fine connoisseurs and patrons of the arts and sciences. Under the grand master and his successor, Konrad Zöllner von Rotenstein,[16] there was a vigorous dissemination of the learning of the day. Existing academies and schools received special care, and new ones were founded. And so it is with the greatest interest that we visit a place so closely bound up with the history of our country, from which learning and strong rule spread throughout these provinces, and which may be considered a cornerstone of the hereditary right of the House of Brandenburg to hold sway throughout Prussia.*

---

* In 1511, the knights, whose position had become precarious, elected Margrave Albert of Brandenburg to be their grand master. In Worms he made the acquaintance of Dr. Luther, who profoundly influenced him and many of the knights. The Peace of Krakau was signed, and Albert left the order, became duke of East Prussia under Polish suzerainty, converted to Lutheranism along with his entire country, married, and endowed the University of Königsberg as his own memorial. The knights dispersed, their chapter moved to Mergentheim, and the fury of the emperor and pope was unavailing.

Traversing the low plain to the banks of the Nogat, the traveler is astonished to come upon these towering walls and their granite columns. The picturesque ruins, the soaring vaults in the interior, and the spacious passages and halls
present a variety of surprising and impressive scenes, especially as the effects of
light are often extremely fine. The site challenges the draftsman to capture it and
the architect to linger and to survey the structure from within. One is aware, above
all, of the need for haste in recording the existence of these remains when one sees
how much has been destroyed by neglect or by thoughtless clearance and how
easily monuments of this kind can be obliterated without a trace.[17]

In addition to a plan of the whole, the drawings I made of these buildings
on my travels in the year 1794 include a series of views of the most interesting parts
of the castle, together with a survey of all the individual parts, connections, and dimensions, which will serve as an elucidation for the architect.

The first of these views [fig. i] illustrates the exterior of the Old Castle with
its entrance, the oldest section of the building; the second [fig. ii] depicts one of the
Old Castle gates of brick construction variously combined with glazed tiles in a
manner that exemplifies the masonry of almost all of the exterior walls.

The third plate shows the plan and sections of the Old Castle. The courtyard, which contains a deep well constructed in ashlar, is surrounded by a rank of
heavy, squat pillars of a type also found in the interior of the building; in the courtyard, these serve to support the open galleries of the upper floors. The remaining
fragments of these shafts and the old entry gate, still with its doorkeeper's grating,
are represented in the adjacent drawing. As for the restoration, the architect is
struck by the marked similarity between the cloisters and the style of several
Venetian buildings, particularly Saint Mark's Palace. Shafts, dressings, stairways,
and ornaments consist of massive ashlar blocks, and the walls are adorned with
various forms, including leaves and vines, in terra-cotta work of excellent style
and workmanship.

The interior vaults, which rise successively from the base of the hill to its
crown, are extraordinarily massive; indeed, it was once said in praise of this building that it stands as deeply embedded in the earth as it rises above it. The finest of
all castles—or so the saying went—were those of Marienburg, Buda, and Milan;
and the old chronicles are full of their praise.*[18]

---

*   During the period of Polish rule, as a result of negligence, the older section of the
castle burned down; much of what remained was destroyed when the building was
converted into a barracks and the old walls covered with fancy wooden decoration.

In the structure known as the New Castle, we entered a high, vaulted cloister, which is represented in the fourth plate [fig. iii]. One side of the cloister rests on red porphyry columns, and it is picturesquely illuminated by the subdued light that falls only from this one side. A tall, heavy doorway of ashlar [fig. iv], with columns eight feet apart, spanned by an architrave of three stones forming a flat arch, connects one side of the cloister to the chapter house, which is represented in the fifth plate [fig. v]. In the center of this stands a tall, monolithic granite pillar, on which converges the entire span of a room some sixty feet square. Following the Battle of Tannenberg,[19] the Poles are said to have aimed a cannon at this very column from outside, hoping to bring the ceiling down and bury the knights assembled in the chapter house. So say the chronicles; and the ball, which luckily missed its mark, is still shown embedded in the wall with an illegible inscription. The chapter house had precious stained-glass windows, which long survived. All the window frames throughout the castle were made of iron, and the existing mullions or muntins are composed of ashlar, very skillfully jointed.

Stone benches extended around the walls, and beside the stone counter one can still see the opening that afforded access from outside, permitting the servants to attend without entering the chapter house itself. The paintings on the walls, which local antiquarians described to me on the strength of their last surviving remnants, are now obscured by whitewash; and wooden partitions (added when this remarkable room was made into rooms for the spinning of wool)[20] now unfortunately obscure the effect of the whole—which, once one has labored to find its fortunately still unobscured parts in separate rooms, the imagination must now supply.

The two plates that follow represent the exterior of that section of the building in which the chapter house is located [fig. vi].[21] Viewed from below, it soars to an imposing height. A deep, carved cornice, preserved only in part, surmounts the plain brick wall, which encompasses the building in a series of massive wall piers separated by windows. With truly admirable boldness, the architect cuts these piers short at the level of the chapter house floor and supports the entire upper burden of each, as far as the roof, upon two granite columns barely a foot in thickness and each composed of several blocks. This construction repays the closest examination. Hardly has one gazed one's fill on the astonishing sight of this aerial rank of columns, suspended high above one's head, when one is led on to admire the magnificent vaults of the former knights' refectory [fig. vii]. This lies in the same section of the castle, and its vaults are supported, in a similar manner to those in the chapter house, by three tall monolithic pillars. The room measures ninety-six feet in length and forty-five feet in width. The vaulting seems to shoot aloft like a rocket from each pier and converges at the crown in alternating points. The arches are adorned only by single ribs. There is little ornamentation anywhere, and none of it is truly bad; the effect of the whole, as in every part of the castle, is one of grandeur and exhilaration.

I shall pass over such minor details as the various ingenious vaultings of the living chambers and cells; the manner of construction; the remarkable heating and other domestic facilities enjoyed by those who formerly dwelt there;* and the expanse of subterranean vaults, which provides a thousand picturesque views.

The castle church [fig. viii] affords an especially picturesque effect. Its end wall stands directly on the edge of a moat lined with masonry, from whose depths it rises sheer to the roof. This expanse of wall is punctuated by a large niche, ornamented with golden stars, which encloses a colossal image of the Virgin in high relief. Hartknoch gives the height of the figure as eight ells and the length of the Christ child in her arms as six ells, which is no exaggeration.[22] The entire image is executed in a kind of mosaic made of burnt bricks of medium size, its surface colored and overlaid with a transparent, glassy substance. In all likelihood, this work originated in Venice, where the most renowned glasswork of the age was produced, and it was no doubt prized by the knights.

The figure, executed in the style of the period, is somewhat rigid, particolored, and excessively ornate. And yet the whole makes a dignified impression by force of its sheer size, which is reinforced by the massive, ruinous, overgrown masonry. The Virgin Mary still protects her church, which is now the property of the nearby Jesuit community. Beneath the Madonna is a small window that provides illumination for the Crypt of Saint Anne, where the funerary vault of the grand masters now lies inaccessible. Visible in the [church] floor are several tombstones, the most noteworthy of which is a slab eleven feet in length and six feet in width, which reputedly covers the entrance to the crypt. The church itself now contains nothing of note, unless it be the treasures of its present owners. Among its points of interest in former times was the seat of the grand master, which could still be seen a few years ago. Placed opposite the altar, it resembled an armchair and was designed to be rotated. Such was the progress, even at that early date, of ingenuity in the pursuit of comfort.

---

* It is noteworthy, for instance, that several of the rooms, including the great chapter house, were heated from below. The heat was conducted upward through pipes— traces of which are still visible—from the lower stories and under the floor. Apart from a few fireplaces, these rooms apparently had no other heating arrangements.

The illustrations mentioned are supplemented by a depiction of the mill-race that the knights conducted to Marienburg from a great distance along a wide embankment across the plain [fig. ix]. The embankment is pierced by a massive tunnel that still provides drainage for the low-lying land. Together with several associated works, this is evidence of the care that the knights took for the good of the land, in this respect as in others.

Another plate shows the remarkable vaulted arcade of the old castle at Marienwerder [fig. x],[23] whose arches measure about eighty feet to the crown, and which, with the old castle, forms a colossal foreground for the delightful vista over the plain.

Source Note: Friedrich Gilly, "Über die vom Herrn Oberhof-Bauamts-Kondukteur Gilly im Jahr 1794 aufgenommenen Ansichten des Schlosses der deutschen Ritter zu Marienburg in West-preußen," in J. W. A. Kosmann and Th. Heinsius, eds., *Denkwürdigkeiten und Tagesgeschichte der Mark Brandenburg* 1 (June 1796): 667–76.

Addendum to the Essay on Marienburg
by Mr. Gilly, Supervisor
at the Royal Building Administration

Toward the close of the essay, mention is made of the special chair for the grand master installed in the church, and the statement was made that this was designed to be rotated. These words follow: "Such was the progress, even at that early date, of ingenuity in the pursuit of comfort." An explanation of the matter, which should have come between these two sentences, was omitted. Now, a revolving chair is not anything particularly remarkable in itself so long as its design does not serve, as here it does, a specific—and, in the present case, a truly extraordinary—purpose. The grand master was able to seat himself in this chair in his own parlor, which adjoined the church; then he had himself turned round on this suspended framework in order to appear, quite effortlessly, among the knights gathered in worship and later return in the same manner.

This is a remarkable refinement for its period: hence the need for this explanation. On the one hand, it sheds light on the luxurious circumstances in which those dignitaries lived; on the other, it provides a striking contrast to the otherwise generally rough and crude domestic arrangements and customs of the age, as described, for example, in Mr. Meiners's *Historische Vergleichung des Mittelalters mit dem jetzigen Jahrhundert, etc.;*[24] and I trust that the interpolation supplied here will not be unwelcome to attentive readers and antiquarians in particular. Other occasional lapses on the part of the compositor are of a kind that the reader will easily have been able to correct for himself.

Source Note: Friedrich Gilly, "Zusatz zu dem Aufsatz des Herrn Oberhof-Bauamts-Kondukteurs Gilly über Marienburg; im 6ten Stück der Denkw. S. 667," in J. W. A. Kosmann and Th. Heinsius, eds., *Denkwürdigkeiten und Tagesgeschichte der Mark Brandenburg* 2 (August 1796): 892.

Editor's Notes

1.   Bishop Adalbert of Prague (or Albert, as Gilly refers to him) was known as the "Apostle of the Prussians." He became a martyr when on 23 April 997 he was axed to death by a heathen priest while trying to convert the native Slav population of Prussia to Christianity.

2.   Bruno of Querfurt, also known as Boniface (circa 974–1009), was a Benedictine monk and missionary. Along with eighteen companions he was massacred by the Prussians while trying to convert them.

3.   After he had conquered Pomerania and Kraków, Bolesław I, "the Brave" (966/967–1025), was crowned the first king of Poland by Emperor Otto III in the year 1000. He obtained an independent archdiocese for the Polish church, burnt the heathen temples, and made the Prussians pay tribute to Poland and embrace Christianity. The Prussians, however, rejected Christianity as soon as Bolesław departed, a scene that was replayed under three of his successors, who were also named Bolesław. The Prussians were not fully brought to embrace Christianity until the thirteenth century.

4.   The Teutonic Order of Knights was a German military-religious order founded (1190–1191) during the siege of Acre in the Third Crusade. Its members were Germans of noble birth, who took monastic vows of poverty, chastity, and obedience. For a hundred years, until 1291, the order was headquartered at Acre. In 1226, at the request of the Polish duke Conrad of Masovia, the Teutonic Knights moved into Prussia to help Conrad in his crusade to christianize the heathen Prussians. During the 1270s the order founded the castle of Marienburg (Malbork), which became the seat of its government and grand master in 1309. The order was given vast privileges by the Holy Roman Emperor and was granted extensive lands from its conquests, thus acquiring great wealth. It subdued the Prussians and founded numerous towns and fortresses. Continuous warfare with the Poles, who laid claim to the lands the order ruled, led to the defeat of the Teutonic Knights at Tannenberg (Stebark) in 1410 and ultimately to the second Treaty of Thorn (Toruń), 1466, in which the knights were forced to cede West Prussia and Pomerania to Poland. In 1457 their capital was moved from Marienburg to Königsberg (Kaliningrad), whence the grand masters of the order ruled as vassals of Poland. In 1525 Grand Master Albert of Brandenburg-Ansbach accepted the Reformation, effectively putting an end to the order. Its remaining possessions in Catholic Germany were secularized by Napoleon in 1809. The order retreated to Austria, where it still exists; it has been a lay order, the Deutschherrenorder, since 1960.

5.   As grand master from 1210 to 20 March 1239 Herrmann von Salza developed the Teutonic Order from a humble group of perhaps ten knights to a power that was to rule and influence German history for centuries.

6.   Hermann Balke (Balco) was the first provincial master of the Teutonic Order of Knights in Prussia. He arrived on the Vistula in 1230 to start subjugating the Prussians, and he died in Germany on 5 March 1239.

7. Vogelsang was built shortly after 1233.

8. Montau, about five miles west of Marienburg, was built in 1244 by Duke Swentopolk of Pomerania.

9. Christoph Hartknoch (1644–1687) published his Prussian history in Latin in 1679; it was based on the work of Petrus of Dusburg, who chronicled the history of the Teutonic Order from 1226 to 1326. A German version of Hartknoch's work appeared later: *Alt- und Neues Preußen*, 2 vols. (Frankfurt: In Verlegung M. Hallervorden, Buchhandlern in Königsberg, 1684).

10. Hartmann von Heldrungen was grand master of the Teutonic Order from 1274 to 19 August 1283.

11. Two brothers who were both called Konrad von Thierberg were provincial masters of the Teutonic Order. The elder brother held the post from 1273 to 1279, while the younger had the office from 1283 to 1287 and again at a later time.

12. Meneko (Meinhard) von Querfurt was provincial master of the Teutonic Order of Knights from 1288 to 1299.

13. Siegfried von Feuchtwangen was the first grand master of the Teutonic Order to reside at Marienburg, from 1309 to 1311. Under him, the Middle Castle was added to the Old Castle.

14. Dietrich von Oldenburg, or Altenburg, was grand master of the Teutonic Order of Knights from 1335 to 6 October 1341. He is credited with the construction of the church of Saint Mary and the chapel of Saint Anne at Marienburg, enlarging and strengthening of the fortifications of the castle, and the first construction of a bridge across the Nogat River.

15. During Winrich von Kniprode's reign as grand master, from 1351 to 24 June 1382, the Teutonic Order reached the height of its glory.

16. Konrad Zöllner von Rotenstein succeeded Winrich von Kniprode (see note 15) as grand master from 1382 to 20 August 1390.

17. After 1457 Marienburg served as a garrison for various groups of Polish soldiers. During the seventeenth and early eighteenth centuries the castle was occupied by the Swedes on several occasions, and during the Seven Years' War Russian soldiers wintered at Marienburg. Finally, at the first partition of Poland, in 1772, the castle once again fell into Prussian hands. Part of the castle was then inhabited by Jesuits, while much of it was occupied by soldiers. The latter used the refectory, which for years had had no windows and had thus been exposed to the ravages of the elements, as a parade ground, in spite of repeated complaints by the commanders about the risk of the vaults collapsing. An army school and spinning and weaving workshops were installed in the chapter house and adjoining rooms; the large kitchen of the convent was used as a horse stable. The parapet facing the Nogat River was steadily broken apart so that its pieces might be used for construction elsewhere.

In 1794 Friedrich Gilly's father, David Gilly of the Royal Building Administration in Berlin, set forth an official plan to tear down the Old Castle and Middle Castle to make room for a large storage facility, and in order to develop his plans, he undertook an official trip to Marienburg. He was accompanied on the journey by his son, who availed himself of the occasion to make a series of drawings of the castle. These drawings (see pp. 118–27) were exhibited at the Akademie der bildenden Künste in Berlin in 1795. In 1796 Friedrich Gilly published the present text, which clearly argues for the preservation of the buildings rather than their destruction. The beauty of the buildings so impressed King Frederick William III that he put an end to plans to tear down the castle.

Over the years Marienburg has repeatedly suffered damage, through war, fire, and neglect. The latest assault on the castle occurred in January 1945 when forces of the German army set up defenses there against the advancing Soviet army. During several days of fighting the castle church was completely destroyed; the chapel of Saint Anne was directly hit and severely damaged; the main tower collapsed; and most of the castle suffered heavily. The Agency for the Preservation of Historical Monuments in Poland undertook a massive restoration effort after the war, which suffered a setback in 1959 when a major fire destroyed a large part of the roof of the Middle Castle. Today, however, the exterior of the castle appears much as it did in the Middle Ages.

18. For a more detailed history of Marienburg and its use and abuse, see Wilhelm Salewski, ed., *Schloß Marienburg in Preußen: Das Ansichtswerk von Friedrich Gilly und Friedrich Frick: In Lieferungen erschienen von 1799 bis 1803* (Düsseldorf: Galtgarben, 1965), "Introduction."

19. At the Battle of Tannenberg in 1410, the Teutonic Knights, led by Ulrich von Jungingen, grand master from 1407 to 15 July 1410, suffered a bloody defeat at the hands of the Poles under King Władysław II Jagiłło. After the battle, Władysław laid siege to Marienburg, which, however, withstood his every effort to conquer it, including his attempt, with the help of a traitor, to shoot down the single column in the chapter house while the knights were all assembled there.

20. The conversion of the chapter house into spinning and weaving workshops apparently took place after Marienburg was returned to Prussia in 1772.

21. It is no longer possible to identify more than one view by Gilly of the exterior of the chapter house.

22. In the publication of Marienburg from 1799 to 1803, Friedrich Frick gives the height of the statue of the Virgin as "sixteen to twenty feet." Scales on the tables in the publication are given in *rheinische Füsse*, or Rhenish feet, the same measurement that seems to have been used to give the scale of the rooms. It therefore seems reasonable to assume that Frick uses this same form of measurement in his estimation of the height of the Madonna image. Gilly usually used Rhenish feet in his architectural plans. A Rhenish foot is 1.0298 English feet, making Frick's estimated height of the image between 16.5 and 20.6 feet, or between 5 and 6.3 meters. There are two-and-a-half feet to the Rhenish ell, so Gilly's estimate of the height of the image coincides with the higher of Frick's estimates.

23. Marienwerder (Kwidzyn), twenty-three miles south of Marienburg, was another castle founded by the Teutonic Order, in 1233. Several grand masters of the order are buried in its cathedral. Gilly also visited that castle during the summer of 1794, and in 1795 he exhibited drawings

of a vaulted passage and a tower from Marienwerder, "drawn from nature," as no. 202 in the Akademie der bildenden Künste exhibition: *Beschreibung derjenigen Kunstwerke* (see note 17). The vaulted passage shown here as figure x was, however, published by Frick as being from Marienburg.

24. Christoph Meiners, *Historische Vergleichung der Sitten, und Verfassungen, der Gesetze, und Gewerbe, des Handels, und der Religion, der Wissenschaften, und Lehranstalten des Mittelalters mit denen unsers Jahrhunderts in Rücksicht auf die Vortheile, und Nachtheile der Aufklärung*, 3 vols. (Hannover: Helwingische Buchhandlung, 1793–1794).

·

Note on the Marienburg Illustrations

In September 1795 ten drawings that Friedrich Gilly had made during the summer of 1794 of the castles of Marienburg and Marienwerder were exhibited at the Akademie der bildenden Künste in Berlin (nos. 200–202 in the catalog). See *Beschreibung derjenigen Kunstwerke, welche von der Königlichen Akademie der bildenden Künste und mechanischen Wissenschaften in den Zimmern der Akademie über dem Königl. Marstalle auf der Neustadt den 26. September und folgende Tage Vormittags von 9 bis 1 Uhr und Nachmittags von 2 bis 5 Uhr öffentlich ausgestellt sind* (Berlin, 1795), 47, nos. 200–202. The catalog is reproduced in facsimile in Helmut Börsch-Supan, ed., *Die Kataloge der Berliner Akademie-Ausstellungen, 1786–1850*, vol. 1, Quellen und Schriften zur bildenden Kunst, no. 4, ed. Otto Lehmann-Brockhaus and Stephan Waetzoldt (Berlin: Bruno Hessling, 1971).

Later, the engraver Friedrich Frick collaborated with Gilly to reproduce the Marienburg drawings. The first published example of their work was the frontispiece in *Sammlung nützlicher Aufsätze und Nachrichten, die Baukunst betreffend* 1, no. 2 (1797), showing the exterior of the chapter house at Marienburg (see fig. 9, p. 28). After Gilly's death in 1800, Frick visited the castle at Marienburg, accompanied by the architect Martin Friedrich Rabe, Gilly's friend and a member of the Privatgesellschaft. Frick's stated intention was to correct the views and hence to represent the castle more accurately.

The castle was measured by Rabe, and in addition to a number of plans and several plates of architectural elements, Frick made a new drawing and etching of at least one of Gilly's views—the aquatint of the chapter house facade published in 1803 (see fig. vi, p. 123). The drawing includes the top story of the building, which was not part of the earlier, and more romantic, engraved version. The following etchings (figs. i–x) approximate, as accurately as can be determined, the images that Gilly recorded and exhibited in 1795.

—F. N.

i. Friedrich Gilly, *Entrance to the Oldest Part of the Castle* (*Portal des ältesten Theils des Schlosses*), 1794–1803, aquatint and etching by Friedrich Frick, 37.2×24 cm. From Friedrich Frick, *Schloß Marienburg in Preußen* (Berlin: n.p., 1803), pl. v. Staatliche Museen zu Berlin, Preußischer Kulturbesitz, Kunstbibliothek.

ii. Friedrich Gilly, *Entrance to the Middle Castle* (*Eingang zum mittleren Schlosse*), 1794–
1803, aquatint and etching by Friedrich Frick, 19.8 × 19 cm. From Friedrich Frick, *Schloß
Marienburg in Preußen* (Berlin: n.p., 1803), pl. xiv, no. 3. Staatliche Museen zu Berlin,
Preußischer Kulturbesitz, Kunstbibliothek.

iii. Friedrich Gilly, *Corridor in Front of the Chapter House* (*Korridor vor dem Kapitel-Saal*),
1794–1803, aquatint and etching by Friedrich Frick, 35.2×23.6 cm. From Friedrich Frick,
Schloß Marienburg in Preußen (Berlin: n.p., 1803), pl. ɪx. Staatliche Museen zu Berlin,
Preußischer Kulturbesitz, Kunstbibliothek.

iv. Friedrich Gilly, *Entrance to the Chapter House* (*Eingang zum Kapitel-Saal*), 1794–1803, aquatint and etching by Friedrich Frick, 52×43 cm. From Friedrich Frick, *Schloß Marienburg in Preußen* (Berlin: n.p., 1803), pl. x. Staatliche Museen zu Berlin, Preußischer Kulturbesitz, Kunstbibliothek.

Kapitel-Saal im vormaligen Zustande

v. Friedrich Gilly, *Chapter House in Its Former State* (*Kapitel-Saal im vormaligen Zustande*), 1794–1803, aquatint and etching by Friedrich Frick, 27.8×45.5 cm. From Friedrich Frick, *Schloß Marienburg in Preußen* (Berlin: n.p., 1803), pl. XI. Staatliche Museen zu Berlin, Preußischer Kulturbesitz, Kunstbibliothek.

vi. Friedrich Gilly, *Facade of the Chapter House (Fassade des Kapitel-Saals)*, 1794–1803, aquatint and etching by Friedrich Frick, 35.2 × 47.5 cm. From Friedrich Frick, *Schloß Marienburg in Preußen* (Berlin: n.p., 1803), pl. XII. Staatliche Museen zu Berlin, Preußischer Kulturbesitz, Kunstbibliothek.

Refectorium im gegenwärtigen Zustande.

vii. Friedrich Gilly, *Refectory in Its Current State* (*Refectorium im gegenwärtigen Zustande*), 1794–1803, aquatint and etching by Friedrich Frick, 35.7 × 48.5 cm. From Friedrich Frick, *Schloß Marienburg in Preußen* (Berlin: n.p., 1803), pl. xiii. Staatliche Museen zu Berlin, Preußischer Kulturbesitz, Kunstbibliothek.

Schloß Kirche

viii. Friedrich Gilly, *The Castle Church* (*Schloß-Kirche*), 1794–1803, aquatint and etching by
Friedrich Frick, 52 × 41 cm. From Friedrich Frick, *Schloß Marienburg in Preußen* (Berlin:
n.p., 1803), pl. VII. Staatliche Museen zu Berlin, Preußischer Kulturbesitz, Kunstbibliothek.

125

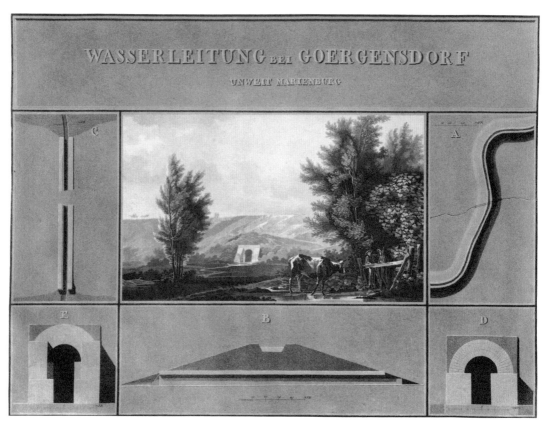

ix. Friedrich Gilly, *Aqueduct near Goergensdorf, not far from Marienburg* (*Wasserleitung bei Goergensdorf unweit Marienburg*), 1794–1803, aquatint and etching by Friedrich Frick, 37×50 cm. From Friedrich Frick, *Schloß Marienburg in Preußen* (Berlin: n.p., 1803), pl. XIX. Staatliche Museen zu Berlin, Preußischer Kulturbesitz, Kunstbibliothek.

x. Friedrich Gilly, *Exit from the Old Castle* (*Ausgang aus dem alten Schlosse*), 1794–1803,
aquatint and etching by Friedrich Frick, 20 × 32.5 cm. From Friedrich Frick, *Schloß
Marienburg in Preußen* (Berlin: n.p., 1803), pl. VIA. Staatliche Museen zu Berlin, Preußischer
Kulturbesitz, Kunstbibliothek.

i. Friedrich Gilly, sketch for memorial for Frederick II, 1797, watercolor, 59.6 × 135.2 cm. Staatliche Museen zu Berlin, Preußischer Kulturbesitz, Kupferstichkabinett und Sammlung der Zeichnungen, Gilly sz Nr. 5.

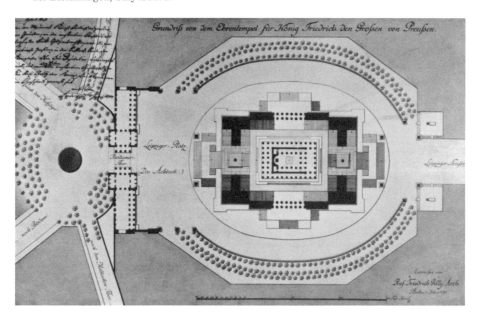

ii. Friedrich Gilly, memorial for Frederick II, plan, 1797, watercolor, 36 × 57 cm. Lost. From Alfred Rietdorf, *Gilly: Wiedergeburt der Architektur* (Berlin: Hans von Hugo, 1940), 58, fig. 44. Santa Monica, The Getty Center for the History of Art and the Humanities.

Note on the Friedrichsdenkmal
[*Version 1*]

Your Excellency will please find herewith the project devised by me for a
memorial to Frederick II, together with a brief description of the project.
As I have presented the drawings themselves to my father, Superintending
Architect Gilly, as a keepsake on the occasion of my impending absence, I
must most respectfully request Your Lordship to be so kind as to return
them to my father after use.[1]

T he plan rendered in this drawing [figs. i, ii] depicts the temple intended to
be built in the middle of the Octagon at the Potsdam Gate as a monument
for Frederick II. This temple rises on a rectangular podium, and vaulted
passages open up the view through the podium.[2] In its center a spacious vault is
built to contain a sarcophagus, above which, as envisaged by the designer, a diadem of stars would appear in the soffit of the vault. If Frederick's remains were indeed to rest in the bosom of his monument, the significance of this inner section
would be greatly enhanced.

In order to heighten the effect, the temple itself will be made of a material
lighter in color than the podium and roofed with bronze; it offers to the eye, in a
simple, ancient Doric form, no ornamentation other than two bas-reliefs of ungilt
bronze. One of them depicts Frederick armed with thunderbolts, smiting his ene-
mies, in a chariot drawn by winged horses, and with an eagle above him clutching
a victor's wreath. The second portrays Frederick enthroned, beneath the palm of
peace, before his assembled people; the eagle with the thunderbolts rests beside
him.

Two altars are erected on stepped bases in front of the pedimented ends
of the temple.

The altar at the front is consecrated to the Protector, who is represented
by a thunderbolt and a diadem entwined with laurel. The altar at the rear is consecrated to the Peaceful Ruler, symbolized on one side by the lyre and the caduceus,

on the other by the plowshare and the sickle entwined with oak and olive leaves. Inside the temple, facing the entrance, the statue stands in a niche, on a massive plinth. The light enters the temple from above. No side lighting—for a statue, above all—can ever match the effect of this form of light.

The entrance to the square from Leipziger Straße is marked by four obelisks, that from the gate by two obelisks. Around the monument is a street for carriages and pedestrians, transformed into a veritable promenade.

It is necessary for the gate to form a unity with the monument; to achieve a similar impression, it must therefore be built in a similar style. On it stands a quadriga, in which—following the example of antiquity—there is nothing but a palm of victory to which the reins are tied. The horses are not rendered at full gallop but at the moment of drawing to a halt.[3]

The arguments that have induced the author to choose the square at the Potsdam Gate are the following:

1. It is spacious enough for the monument to be seen in its entirety.
2. It contains no buildings of unusual size and height that might interfere with the effect of the monument, as would be the case, to some degree, in any of the other squares of the city.
3. Conversely, the monument on the square does not mar the appearance of any other principal building of the Royal Capital, as would be inevitable in any other square.
4. It possesses the particular distinction of being somewhat removed from the bustle of daily life and at the same time, by virtue of its location, among the most frequented of squares. It is quiet, spacious, and animated without being clamorous. The same thing can hardly be said of any other square.
5. The view that meets the eye on leaving the temple—the whole of Friedrichstadt at the visitor's feet[4]—is so grand and so singular that no other [location] affords its equal.
6. On no square of similar perfection does the artist have such freedom to create a grand ensemble. The size and the openness of the square, the proper embellishment of the surrounding houses, the gate, the open space in front of the gate, which—aptly enough—represents the entrance to the road to Potsdam; the proximity of the Tiergarten: how much this offers not only for the immediate creation of this monument, unique as its subject is, but also for the continuing and ever-growing glorification of that subject![5]

—Fr. Gilly, 21 April 1797

[*Version 2*]

In executing the idea of a memorial to Frederick, a *temple with the statue of the late king*, it has been the designer's primary concern to find a setting well suited to the perfect execution of the work itself. It is his belief that no better place is to be found within the city walls than the Octagon at the Potsdam Gate. This marks the termination of one of the longest and finest streets in the city;[6] and, to the stranger who enters through the principal gate from one of the most-traveled and most convenient military roads between the two royal residences,[7] it conveys the most stately and favorable impression of the beauty of the capital. In other respects, also, this location unites all the indispensable advantages that would be found in no other place:

It is not out of the way but is much frequented by citizens and travelers alike.

It forms a part of the finest section of the city and lies within that district that owes its present elegance to the late king himself.

It is of such a size as to offer the necessary space for the projected work.

Were the work to be put into execution, the square—through an appropriate embellishment of the surrounding residential buildings and through the planting of trees that offer pleasant walks—would both attract more people to the monument and, because of its proximity to the Tiergarten, offer a more pleasant and convenient access to that park.

While the square is much frequented in itself, and the embellishments suggested above would render it even more so, it is nevertheless remote from the bustle of affairs, which would infallibly have introduced scenes of profanity and scandal and desecrated the atmosphere of this shrine.

On this square, the memorial would be seen at its best, in its true grandeur, for none of the existing buildings stands out by virtue of size or height in such a way as to weaken the extraordinary effect that the memorial is called upon to create. This would be only too likely in any of the other squares in the city, to the great detriment of the work.

This location, with the intimate connection between the gate and the highway to Potsdam, cannot fail to evoke in the beholder the thought of Potsdam, the second home of the late king and the place from which Frederick's hand lavished so many blessings upon Prussia.

It might be objected that if so large a building, in a colossal style, were to present itself to the stranger immediately on his entry to the city, this would set his imagination working on too vast a scale; should the other buildings fail to match the impression thus created, they would appear slight and mean. But if those buildings are built on a scale appropriate to their own purposes, no stranger of any taste and judgment will allow such a thought to enter his mind; on the contrary, the initial impression created by the memorial will be all the more securely maintained. To place the memorial in the center of the city, surrounded by a host of buildings, would render that impression weaker and more short-lived. Again, those buildings themselves, if seen alongside the memorial or even in its vicinity, would sacrifice something of their own intrinsic effect.

The *memorial* itself stands in the center of the elongated octagon of the square. The temple rises on a rectangular podium, dark in color, which incorporates the steps up to the temple. Vaulted passages afford a clear view through the podium from the gate to the end of the street. Within it is a second vault, which might possibly be used to house a sarcophagus, thus enhancing the value of the memorial still further. Above the sarcophagus, which is placed so that it cannot be touched,[8] the diadem of stars is to be seen in the flat of the cavetto vault. The temple itself, roofed in bronze, is built of a lighter material, to enhance its resplendent effect when seen against the sky. It is an elongated rectangle, in the Doric order, and like the ancient Greek temples it is devoid of any frivolous ornament; only a few elements of the columns and some of the architectural ornaments of the entablature are picked out in gilt bronze. In the pediments of the temple are two bas-reliefs in ungilt bronze:

(a) Armed with thunderbolts, Frederick strikes down his foes from a chariot drawn by winged horses: above him hovers the eagle with the victor's laurels;
(b) Frederick appears enthroned, with the palm of peace, before his assembled people; the eagle at his side holds the thunderbolts.

The open colonnades of the porticoes lead to the interior of the temple, where the statue stands on a large plinth in a niche, facing the entrance. Light enters the temple from above; this is the most beautiful of all forms of lighting, especially for a statue, which is never adequately lit in the open air or from the side, especially when there are several lateral openings or, worse, windows. Emerging from the temple, the visitor commands a view from the top of the steps across that large expanse of the royal capital city that is Frederick's own creation. A prospect unique of its kind!

Below, on the square, around the memorial, runs the road for carriages and equestrians. Slightly raised and adjoining the residential buildings is the tree-lined walk—or rather the promenade—for pedestrians. The entry to the square from Leipziger Straße is adorned by four obelisks, and on the side toward the Potsdam Gate by two. At the corners of Leipziger Straße are two couchant bronze lions that serve as fountains.

The gate, together with the portions of city wall on either side and the environs as a whole, must appear in a style that agrees closely with the effect of the ensemble. The gate has an arch wide enough for two carriages abreast; on either side, between the columns, is a walk for pedestrians. Beneath the covered gateway, both carriages and persons are scrutinized by guards and by officials as they pass in and out. The two lateral openings between the colonnades are large enough to accommodate a convenient mustering place for the guards and, on the other side, the business of the officials.

On top of the gate stands a quadriga without any representation of the victor himself or of a goddess of victory but with a simple victory banner to which, in accordance with the example of the ancients, the reins are tied; the horses are seen at the moment of taking their last step. The portion of land outside the city walls and closest to the gate as well as along the highway must be planned so that, at the very least, it offers no disagreeable effect that might mar the approach to the gate and to the square containing the memorial; indeed, it must be laid out in such a way as to enhance it.

To this end, the vicinity should be suitably planted with trees, the groundwater that accumulates there should be drawn off into a large reservoir,[9] a number of small and unprepossessing houses that now stand along the near part of the highway should be cleared away, and a number of avenues should be laid out to connect the entire new composition with the nearby Tiergarten.

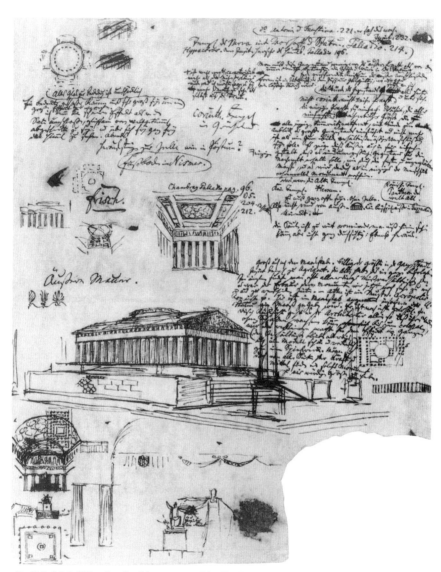

iii. Friedrich Gilly, sketch of the memorial for Frederick II, with annotations, 1796–1797, 25.2 × 20.2 cm. Lost. From Alste Oncken, *Friedrich Gilly, 1772–1800* (Berlin: Deutscher Verein für Kunstwissenschaft, 1935), pl. 27. Santa Monica, The Getty Center for the History of Art and the Humanities.

[*Notes on a Sheet of Sketches for the Friedrichsdenkmal, fig. iii*]

*Temple of Nerva fronted by statue, Palladio, 214; ditto Antoninus and Faustina, 221;
still there when he saw it. Jupiter, 232.*

Hypaethros to Jupiter, Ruler of the Heavens. Palladio, 196.[10]

*This object must be seen less in terms of outward strength than of inward
values. Grandeur and dignity count for more in the statue and lend it more character
than the king's features would ever do; in my opinion, this must take precedence even
over a faithful likeness.*

*To the beholder, all superfluous enrichment of external form is indifferent,
if not positively vexatious.*

*Not Corinthian, not rich splendor. The dignity of the subject in itself takes
precedence over all other considerations. May the only splendor be that of simple
beauty, the* simplest possible; *a reverential grandeur, remote from all sensual lures,
leading up to the aspect of the awesome object itself and remaining no more than a
frame appropriate to the picture. In all its simplicity, the external aspect must show
that it is built to preserve a single, unforgettable object for posterity, holding it fast,
as if by the force of its unshakable proportions; and so it will appear as a unique memorial, one that deserves to attract the reverence of all mankind.*

*Any covered, enclosed space must be very large if it is to make a grand ef-
fect. All glass for covering is contrary to decorum. I know of no more beautiful effect
than that of being enclosed on all sides—cut off, as it were, from the tumult of the
world—and seeing the sky over one's head, free, entirely free. At evening.*

Climb up to the cella, *as at Paestum? Floor at Nîmes.*

What were the old temples. Not a temple. Heroum.[11] *It must be completely
open. With no* cella. *So, not round externally. No example except at Pozzuoli. Roman
temples. Pantheon the Universe. Rectangular.*

Chambray, Palladio, pp. 96, 105, 204. Coffering, 212.[12]

*The columns not too far apart: It must be possible to look inside—but not
to see through. The same goes for looking out from within.*

Also grand in scale. May well be the largest in the whole city. Jupiter temple at Agrigentum. The ancients followed this in general. In the individual case, however, we often find false proportions, for the architects whose monuments we now see were too numerous and belong to too many different periods.

Athens is a model. Acropolis. Not so Rome. Here a scale is assumed, insofar as a size is assigned to the A. [?] statue. This size is not colossal. In this respect architecture is unique in that its works [?] can grow to colossal size with no detriment. Only reduction turns the overall effect into a toy (though the proportions would remain beautiful and excellent, even in a model). From every side, may strength and means be found to endow such a monument with a worthy grandeur.

Source Notes

VERSION 1: Friedrich Gilly's letter is in the Geheimes Staatsarchiv Preußischer Kulturbesitz, Abteilung Merseburg, Rep. 76 alt III, Kuratorium der Akademie der bildenden Künste und mechanischen Wissenschaften, Nr. 382, fol. 18ff.

VERSION 2: This translation was made from the copy in Alfred Rietdorf, *Gilly: Wiedergeburt der Architektur* (Berlin: Hans von Hugo, 1940), 57–61. Rietdorf gives as his source a (now-lost) transcript by "Moser" of a holograph by Gilly (see Introduction, n. 154). Alste Oncken, *Friedrich Gilly, 1772–1800* (Berlin: Deutscher Verein für Kunstwissenschaft, 1935; reprint, Berlin: Mann, 1981), 43 n. 195, refers to the same transcript, which she ascribes to volume 1 of the now-lost sketchbooks of Gilly's works in the Technische Hochschule. She also cites an earlier publication of Gilly's text and gives the source as *Berliner Blätter* of 18 October 1797. This is actually a reference to a lecture given by Carl Gotthard Langhans to the Akademie der bildenden Künste on the king's birthday, 25 September 1797, in which Langhans describes the various proposals for the memorial to Frederick the Great that were on display at the Akademie: Carl Gotthard Langhans, "Nachricht von den Entwürfen zu dem auf Sr. Majestät Befehl zu errichtenden Monumente Friedrichs des Großen," *Berlinische Blätter* (Wednesday, 18 October 1797): 65–83, esp. 71–73.

NOTES ON A SHEET OF SKETCHES: Formerly Library, Technische Hochschule, Berlin, Gilly notebooks, vol. 2, p. 2, no. 8, recto, now lost. This translation was made from the copy in Alste Oncken, *Friedrich Gilly, 1772–1800* (Berlin: Deutscher Verein für Kunstwissenschaft, 1935; reprint, Berlin: Mann, 1981), pl. 27, cat. no. B 162, and pp. 45, 48.

Editor's Notes

1. Friedrich Gilly submitted the drawings of the ground plan and perspectival view of his proposal for the Friedrichsdenkmal (reproduced here as figs. i and ii) along with this letter dated 21 April 1797 and the explanatory text published here as Version 1.

2. The podium is more than a hundred meters long and more than sixty meters wide. The temple measures thirty-six meters by twenty-four meters.

3. The text to this point was printed, with minor variants, in the 1797 exhibition catalog of the Akademie der bildenden Künste: *Beschreibung derjenigen Kunstwerke welche von der Königlichen Akademie der bildenden Künste und mechanischen Wissenschaften in den Zimmern der Akademie in dem Königlichen Marstalle auf der Neustadt den 26. September und folgende Tage Vormittags von 9 bis 1 Uhr und Nachmittags von 2 bis 3 Uhr öffentlich ausgestellt sind* (Berlin, 1797), no. 313, 64–66. The catalog text ends at this point, except for the following words: "The monument is represented on two sheets: (a) plan and section; (b) perspectival drawing." The catalog is reproduced in facsimile in Helmut Börsch-Supan, ed., *Die Kataloge der Berliner Akademie-Ausstellungen, 1786–1850*, vol 1, Quellen und Schriften zur bildenden Kunst, no. 4, ed. Otto Lehmann-Brockhaus and Stephan Waetzoldt (Berlin: Bruno Hessling, 1971).

4. The Friedrichstadt was the quarter of Berlin immediately inside the Potsdam Gate. It was laid out in 1688 under Frederick I and further developed under Frederick II, following a master plan by the Dutch-trained civil engineer and military architect Johann Arnold Nering. The new buildings were characterized by their lack of stylistic and decorative differentiation, and the Baroque layout followed a rigid block grid. See David Leatherbarrow, "Friedrichstadt—A Symbol of Toleration," *Architectural Design* 53, no. 11/12 (1983): 22–31.

Among the inhabitants of the Friedrichstadt were numbers of so-called Réfugiés, or French Huguenots, who like Gilly's family had escaped intolerance in France following the revocation of the Edict of Nantes (1685) and settled in Prussia, where the Edict of Potsdam (issued the same year, in response to the revocation of the Edict of Nantes) granted them liberty of conscience and religion.

5. Gilly's reference to the Tiergarten (Deer park) is an attempt to tie in his proposed memorial with this popular attraction and with the development of the Tiergartenviertel (Tiergarten district), a stylish new quarter of the city.

The Tiergarten was founded as a royal game preserve just west of Berlin's city wall by Elector Joachim I (1499–1535). The park was opened to the public by King Frederick William I (1713–1740), and shortly after the ascent of Frederick II to the throne in 1740, the fence around the Tiergarten was removed, making the park even more accessible. Located immediately outside the Brandenburg Gate (and just north of the Potsdam Gate), bordering the Spree River, the park became a favorite excursion goal of Berliners.

The development of the Tiergartenviertel—the area bordered by the Tiergarten on the north and the Landwehr Canal on the south, immediately outside the Potsdam Gate—into an elegant residential quarter began around 1790. At the same time the park was remodeled, and much of its former Baroque design was replaced with landscaping in the style of an English garden. It was here, directly across from the southern edge of the Tiergarten, at Tiergartenstraße 31, among the inns and coffeehouses that catered to visitors to the park and the cottages of gardeners who supplied fruits and vegetables to the city of Berlin, that Friedrich Gilly in 1799 designed a summer residence for Privy Councillor Mölter (see Introduction: p. 52 and fig. 20). Although a few villas had already been built in the area, 1799 was the year when the construction of villas began in earnest. In the years until Napoleon's entry into Berlin (27 October 1806), fourteen villas were built along Tiergartenstraße, forever changing the character of the district. On the development of the Tiergartenviertel, see Hartwig Schmidt, *Das Tiergartenviertel: Baugeschichte eines Berliner Villenviertels, 1790–1870*, Die Bauwerke und Kunstdenkmäler von Berlin, Beiheft 4 (Berlin: Mann, 1981).

6. Leipziger Straße runs straight east from the Potsdam Gate, then veers northeast to the Spree River.

7. The Potsdam road ran from the Potsdam Gate in Berlin to Potsdam, where Frederick II had built his summer palace, Sans Souci.

8. Gilly envisaged the sarcophagus placed on a platform and separated from the area where visitors would walk by a waterless "moat." See Jutta von Simson, *Das Berliner Denkmal für Friedrich den Großen* (Berlin: Propyläen, 1976), figs. 36b, 37c.

9. Drainage of low-lying, swampy areas was part of the renovation of the Tiergarten undertaken during the 1790s, so Gilly's proposal would merely extend the drainage efforts further south.

10. Gilly's references are to the French translation of Andrea Palladio's sixteenth-century text on architecture: Roland Fréart, sieur de Chambray, trans., *Les quatre livres de l'architecture d'André Palladio* (Paris: Edme Martin, 1650). This edition of Palladio is listed in the inventory of books Gilly owned (see Appendix 2, p. 5, no. 53). The last reference, to a hypaethral temple to Jupiter, alludes to a chapter on the propriety of various forms of temples for different deities. According to Palladio, *"à Iupiter, comme maistre de l'air & du ciel, ils dresserent des temples ouverts au milieu, avec des portiques tout à l'entour"* (for Jupiter, as lord of the air and the sky, they [the Romans] constructed temples that were open in the center, with porticoes all around).

11. Latin *heroum*, from Greek *heroion*, "the shrine of a hero."

12. Fréart de Chambray (see note 10). These references are all to various drawings by Palladio that Gilly used as inspiration and models for his memorial.

A Description of the Villa of Bagatelle, near Paris

The whole aspect of the building that I here describe in detail is among the most beautiful of its kind and incontestably one of the finest works of recent French architecture. In both distribution and style, it may serve as an excellent model; one, moreover, that is executed with such neatness and care as to mark the highest degree of perfection in every respect: a testimony to the skill of the artists employed that is rendered yet more admirable by the well-nigh incredible rapidity with which the project was planned and executed.

The illustration given on plate v [fig. i] is very much constricted by the small space, and allowance should be made for this as well as for the minor shortcomings of the engraving in which the drawing has been reproduced. I trust, however, that this plate and the following brief essay will be not unwelcome to connoisseurs of architecture, little detailed information having as yet been provided on this work, although its name is well known and the reputation of its beauty has been carried abroad in the accounts of a number of travelers. The only comparatively precise depictions that I have seen are those published in Paris as tinted engravings by Mr. Vancléemputte, the architect;[1] but in these, although the whole is represented quite clearly, the outside of the building, in particular, fails to appear to its full advantage.

The celerity with which this project was set in hand and completed and the method employed entitle it to be considered something of an architectural miracle. Here, just outside Paris, close to the lovely woodland of the Bois de Boulogne, and not far removed from the Seine, the comte d'Artois, brother of King Louis xvi, owned a small property that was used only occasionally as a hunting lodge.[2] The queen in particular had grown attached to this charming place and had often expressed the wish to have a comfortable residence there. This wish prompted the prince to set in hand the layout of the garden and the villa. He called it Bagatelle, probably more in reference to the character of the undertaking than to its scale.[3] No sooner was the idea conceived than the decision was taken. Within a matter of days,

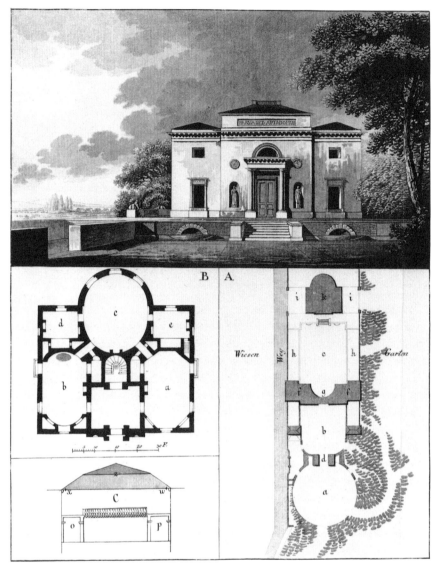

i. Friedrich Gilly, *The Chateau of Bagatelle by Bellanger, near Paris* (*Das Schlösschen Bagatelle von Bellanger, bei Paris*), 1799, aquatint and etching by Ostermeier, 22.6 × 17.8 cm. From *Sammlung nützlicher Aufsätze und Nachrichten, die Baukunst betreffend* 3, no. 3 (1799), pl. v. Santa Monica, The Getty Center for the History of Art and the Humanities.

the able Bélanger, then principal architect to the prince, had completed the plan of the whole, and construction began without delay.[4] Were it not that eyewitnesses are still living, one would scarcely think it possible to erect the building or indeed to lay out the larger part of the garden in no more than six weeks.[*5] Short though the time was, the prince's wishes were fulfilled to the letter. As the enterprise was kept entirely secret from the queen, she was astonished on her return by the magical spectacle of this almost inconceivable creation.

From the outset, Mr. Bélanger took charge of all the workmen and all the artists involved; all hands were at work simultaneously.

While the foundations were still being laid, all the ashlar walls were completed almost to the point of laying the stones. Soon work was proceeding on the base and the cornice concurrently; day and night, by torchlight, the site was overrun with workmen. As the foundation stone was laid, an active start was made with the smallest details of the interior decoration—marble floors, columns and chimneypieces, plasterwork, bronzes, mirrors, crystal chandeliers, and so on; the wainscoting of the rooms was being made in distant workshops; and the painters were already at work on decorations for walls that had yet to be built. Every effort had been set in motion, and—most necessary of all, without doubt—no expense had been spared to keep industry and skill employed. And so the work was completed that now stands foursquare and bears throughout the stamp of patient and ingenious art. The work reveals no trace of the miraculous speed of its making, which will be passed down in anecdote and one day, perhaps, lost in legend.

Nowhere are signs of haste visible; solidity of material is everywhere combined with solidity of workmanship, down to the last detail; and careful selection, directed by taste, prevails throughout. Such an undertaking calls to mind a striking image of all those concerned in devoting such exceptional exertions to a common activity: each thinking of his own task as a whole in itself, completing it, and contributing it to the grand design, without ever grasping the interconnection of all the parts. That was visible, perfect in every detail, only to the ordering imagination of its deviser. Some may take the view—unseasonably enough, in many instances, although I choose to say no more on this matter here—that such a work is an object of idle and willful extravagance; but in itself it remains a fine and

---

* Professor Huth (in *Magazin für die bildenden Künste* 1, no. 2: 253) has also given a description of this, adding that the former Paris Opera building was completed within seventy-five days. Other examples of such rapid construction exist, although they remain extremely rare.

gratifying monument to artistic effort: all the more gratifying, indeed, because in the midst of ruins it still remains intact in all its beauty.[6]

The Neuilly road, which, commencing at the Tuileries, leads by way of the delightful Champs-Elysées, through the *barrière* and thence to the allée de Bagatelle (which still from time to time is brilliantly lit, as it always was in former times), offers a splendid and much-frequented walk to the place. In barely half a league, one arrives at Bagatelle, which, bordered by the lush, low-lying meadows of the nearby Seine on the one side and by the Bois de Boulogne (now largely felled) on the other, lies between the half-demolished Château de Madrid[7] and the ruins of the once so splendid abbey of Longchamp.[8]

This route brings one first to the gatehouse; built in the English manner, in a picturesque style, this stands at the entrance to the park, backed by a semicircle of trees. To the right, the park opens out and extends to the château—if this modest structure can be referred to by such an exalted name. The garden is laid out in the modern manner, which the French, too, have adopted under the name of the English style, in order to free themselves of the monotonously scrupulous regularity of their older style of garden design. To explain how far this transformation has succeeded and what they may have gained or lost thereby would lead us too far afield. The grandeur of many of the older French gardens, coupled as it is with a certain character of richness and antiquity—above all when the arrangement incorporates architectural elements—indisputably lends an imposing aspect to the proportions and to the overall impression that nothing could adequately replace. Without wishing to put myself forward as a defender of these trimmed and imprisoned gardens (an issue that has been debated at unnecessary length, both pro and con), I cannot deny having received in many such parks a very strong impression— as have others—of sublimity; nor can I deny that I have in vain sought such an effect in many of the more recent gardens laid out as settings for truly excellent buildings, not to mention those petty, misapplied, so-called English enclosures. There is, without doubt, such a thing as an artistic treatment of ordered plans; and it is an exaggeration to say of them, flatly: "Symmetry is surely born of indolence and vanity."*[9]

Even in such an arrangement, there is a way of preserving nature in all her grandeur and delightful freedom. It is enough to recall Marly, Saint-Cloud, and Chantilly;**[10] the truly majestic impression of whose wonderful parks cannot sim-

---

*   Girardin, *De la composition des paysages*, etc. 8 (Geneva, 1777), 4.

**   Delille, *Les Jardins*, Chant i.

ply be dismissed, scornfully, as "majestic tedium."*[11]

Whatever the abuses to which this may have led, the art of gardening in France has by now perhaps lost more than it has gained by taking a different path. Felicitous though some of the eminently successful parks in the picturesque style may appear (such as Rincy and Ermenonville),**[12] the taste for that style has generally fallen far short of the ideal. It has kept pace with that country's current taste in the art of the landscape; and, in moving toward picturesque freedom and the seeming absence of constraint, it has been marked more by pettiness than by grandeur. It is doubtless true that, with the progress of taste, the French artists of today can and will turn this particular aspect of style in an entirely different direction; but for the present, the term "picturesque"—referring to this treatment of landscape—has been as much misused as misunderstood, for all the frequent warnings of the critics. What Mr. Girardin says in this connection is quite true:

> *The majestic tedium with symmetry has led abruptly from one extreme to the other. If symmetry has too long abused a mistaken conception of order and imprisoned everything, irregularity has soon enough abused disorder by bewildering the eye with a mass of vagueness and confusion.*†[13]

A tendency to affectation and artifice, which seems characteristic of that nation in several respects, seems to have contributed to this development, and gardens in France have very largely been transformed into diminutive, artificial models of gardens. The same tendency is now all too often seen in Germany, where it is common to do no more than imitate the shop-bought books that contain only the gleanings of English garden design. Even so, the Germans are perhaps more than anyone capable of grasping the strong sense of the picturesque in Nature that is innate in the English and of infusing it into their own art. Only an earnest and disinterested study of grand effects‡[14] can lead to the perfection that compensates,

---

*   Ibid., 5 (Mr. Girardin is the owner and designer of the park at Ermenonville).

**   The latter, in particular, has become widely known through the illustrated description, [Stanislas Girardin,] *Promenade; ou, Itinéraire des jardins d'Ermenonville* (Paris: n.p., 1788).

†   Girardin, *De la composition des paysages*, etc., op. cit.

‡   It is a true pleasure to hear what a young English author has to say of this study of grand effects in a work recently translated under the title *Über den guten Geschmack bei ländlichen Kunst- und Garten-Anlagen* (Leipzig, 1798).

and more than compensates, for all that has been lost by the abandonment of rule.

In describing a modern French garden that conforms to the style now fashionable, one is reduced to speaking of artificial mounds of earth, known as hills; of groves; of temples and cottages of all descriptions; of little bridges; and of accumulated frivolities that are often childish and wearisome in the extreme. Rarely does one find a quiet place to sit. Everywhere, Nature is merely bedizened; the brooks, pretentiously set in masonry and yet still made to meander, call to mind the lovely verses of Delille:

> ... *Where once a girdle of green*
> *enfolded the river,*
> *the waters now complain of their stony prison;*
> *and costly marble mocks the grass.*[15]

Such is the impression derived from the gardens of Mousseau—inviting though they admittedly are—and from the Folie de Chartres,[16] near Paris, or from the otherwise so charming Petit Trianon.[17] Even the gardens of Bagatelle, especially in the detail of their adornments, cannot be entirely absolved of this playfully trivial style, which strikes one as being so much in contrast with the rest: an impression that is mitigated, if not erased, by the beauty of Nature alone—by the woods, so delightful in themselves, and by the glorious groups of tall trees that, in contrast to the open, distant views, enclose the building proper.

From the dwelling of the Swiss porter a principal drive leads to the left, through orchards and kitchen gardens screened by ornamental planting, to the villa itself, whose various outbuildings are incorporated with the dwelling proper into an ensemble. This ensemble, the ground plan of which (A) is here illustrated on plate v [see fig. i], is bordered on the side nearest the Seine by the road from Longchamp to Neuilly; the other side is enclosed by the garden. The drive terminates here, emerging from the woods into a circular outer court (a), where guards are posted in the entry pavilion (d). The forecourt, or *basse-cour* (b), is enclosed by walls.[18] Stables and domestic offices are located in the side courts and outbuildings, and these abut a larger building (f), which contains the kitchens and the lodgings of stewards and domestics. With great neatness of design throughout, the exemplary plan combines order and comfort with a style whose simplicity is entirely fitted to the purpose of the whole. The upper servants' building divides this whole section from the house itself.

A semicircular entry (g) leads to the spacious great court, *la cour royale* (c),[19] in front of the main elevation of the château, as illustrated here. The lateral sections of this court (h) are bounded by parapet walls of the same height as the terrace of the building; they are used as walks. These low enclosing walls serve to very good effect as divisions of the whole, providing the necessary link between the architecture and the surrounding planting, which overhangs them in picturesque masses.

Broad stone steps, at either side of which water runs from a pipe into a large basin, lead up to the terrace, on which stands the principal structure (k). Its door, between two statuary niches, is flanked by detached columns that harmonize very pleasingly with the articulation of the whole. The exterior, every detail of which is executed with great care and precision, has the natural color of the ashlar blocks of which the building is composed. Its pale yellow hue, mellowed by weathering, lends the building, in common with the majority of those in Paris, an extremely pleasing appearance. Windows and doors are made of unpainted brown wood, which makes the muntins less visible from a distance and lends luster to the glass. The panels of the door are fitted with grilles of mat bronze and, with the fanlight above, give light to the vestibule.

Passing between two columns, which are matched by two others at the foot of the stairs, one enters the vaulted vestibule, whose plain ashlar walls are adorned with bas-reliefs in stucco and with four flanking pedestals of porphyry. On the right is the salon (a), on whose long side a door opens onto the garden. Its walls, which form an elongated octagon, are covered in simply but charmingly decorated paneling, as is the ceiling; and the furnishings, more elegant than splendid in style, harmonize admirably with the ensemble. On the left, opposite this salon, lies the dining room (b), overlooking the Seine. A door leads onto the terrace, whose balustrade, extending between a pair of plinths, affords a superb prospect. Directly opposite, across the river, lie the heights of Calvaire and a fertile range of hills planted with vineyards and orchards. Visible to the left are Longchamp and a number of villages. The meadows are strewn with flocks; and at some distance, among the trees, can be seen a tower-shaped structure, built to house a steam engine that pumps water to the gardens and buildings of Bagatelle. To the right, and higher up the Seine, is Neuilly; beyond a picturesque island (the Ile des Peupliers) can be seen the great bridge of Neuilly, the masterpiece of the celebrated Perronet.[20]

No more pleasant location could have been chosen for the dining room, and the extreme simplicity of its decoration does much to sustain the pleasure. White paneling touched with finely gilded ornament in the simplest of styles—a pattern that is found almost everywhere in the newer rooms of the royal palaces and is usually a mark of the greatest luxury—adorns the walls of the dining room; the chimneypieces of white marble and the other furnishings are in the same style.

The ceiling is equally plain; the floor is of marble. The ends of the room are rounded, and at one end stands a fountain and pool of lovely design.

The grand salon (c) connects with this room. It is oval in shape and projects into the garden, which at this point is laid out in regular parterres, which provide a transition to the wild woodland. The salon has a domed ceiling, decorated in a tasteful arabesque style, as are the walls, whose panels alternately bear paintings and mirrors. Adjacent to this room on the left [d] is a small, highly inviting cabinet, whose paneling is adorned with picturesque architectural views created by the genius of Robert.[21] A similar cabinet (e), embellished with paintings by Callet[22] and furnished with extraordinary elegance as a bathroom,[23] lies on the other side of the salon and is connected with the upper living rooms and bedrooms by a small stair. The corners and niches of this cabinet, like those above, are ingeniously arranged to provide the greatest convenience.

The stairway, designed with the utmost ingenuity, is perfectly suited for daily use, in keeping with the scale of the upper rooms. The stairs ascend in two curved flights separated by a rectangular landing. At the foot of the stairs and precisely at the center of its curvature, a beautifully worked female figure holding a crystal lamp stands on a pedestal.[24] The steps of polished brown oak are fashioned with the greatest imaginable care, and, having no face string, are ingeniously joined together in the manner of those solid, cantilevered stairs whose steps support themselves against each other. This method of construction, very commonly used in France and England and already imitated in Germany (at Dessau, for example), has many advantages with regard to space and presents an uncommonly light and pleasing appearance. One baluster stands on each step. These balusters are made of metal, steel-gray, with gilded rings and ornaments; the handrail is of mahogany. The light-yellow ashlar walls of the stairwell are adorned with plaster panels bearing colored paintings after the antique.

The head of the stairs (see the section, C) leads to a corridor (o, p) that provides access to the upper rooms, and above is the balustered ascent to the roof and to a few servants' rooms. This section of the building is illuminated from above by a glass roof (z). The light as it enters is pleasantly softened and distributed by a white linen sheet stretched horizontally below (x, w). This device is in use throughout France; in England the panes of skylights are frequently painted on the inside with a thin coat of white paint to achieve the same effect as well as to render less visible the fine wire mesh that is stretched above the panes to protect them from hailstones and other damage.

On the upper floor, one first enters a small antechamber that connects with the apartments located here. The bedchamber has been furnished to resemble a tent. Its walls are covered with white- and blue-striped silk hangings, draped tentlike from upright lances that stand around the room. The alcove, with matching decorations, contains a bed in the shape of a long couch or seat; and this, together with the ornamental weapons hung around the walls, produces a very picturesque effect. The remaining rooms are plainly but elegantly decorated with painted panels, outstanding among which are the arabesque paintings of one cabinet; with exceptional taste in design and invention, these represent Cupid and Psyche in various modern guises. This taste, applied with sensitive discrimination throughout and coupled with an equal perfection of workmanship, delights the eye at every turn and adds the utmost charm to the character of the building, as expressed by the owner in the inscription above the entrance: "PARVA SED APTA DOMUS."[25]

With this project, Mr. Bélanger firmly established the reputation that he now so properly enjoys.* He is one of the few artists to have given an entirely new direction to French architecture, one that in due course will undoubtedly raise it to the heights of perfection, exalting it far above the prevailing frivolity of the age, which artists in that country have long resisted with such valiant perseverance.**[26] Their bold endeavors have been attended with much success; and yet abroad, even in Germany, they have been misunderstood or else too little known.

Apart from the scattered comments of German observers, we have heard little on this subject beyond the narrative of one recent traveler, who treated French architecture and architects at some length.†[27] However, we have no such correct and tasteful selection of the best recent works of French architecture as Mr. Vogel set out to provide in the work cited; and the compendia now extant, like such valuable earlier works as the remarkably full presentations of entries submitted to competitions held at the erstwhile Paris Academy of Architecture,‡ are little known abroad.

---

* As yet, very few good illustrations of Mr. Bélanger's works are available, except for those included in *Musée de la nouvelle architecture française*, edited by the architect Mr. Vogel and published by Firmin-Didot, Paris.

** In this regard, see the remarkable preface, written in the true language of art, to a volume recently edited by one of the leading architects in Paris, *Palais, maisons de Rome* (fol., 1798–1799), and the announcement for it in the *Magazin encyclopédique*, etc.

† An essay by Mr. Wolzogen in the *Journal des Luxus*, 1798.

‡ These have been published in a folio volume of outline etchings with wash, and are being continued by Mr. Vancléemputte; I should be glad, on request, to provide more information to lovers of art.

The royal villa of Bagatelle, formerly a tranquil retreat from the clamorous diversions of the court, was incidentally open to anyone in possession of an easily obtained ticket of admission.[28] Now the property of the nation, it has been leased to a restaurateur for public banqueting. Given over to the round of fleeting pleasures, it has become a favorite resort of fashionable Parisian society.*[29]

---

* See the descriptions in the journal *London und Paris*.

Source Note: Friedrich Gilly, "Beschreibung des Landhauses Bagatelle bey Paris," *Sammlung nützlicher Aufsätze und Nachrichten, die Baukunst betreffend: Für angehende Baumeister und Freunde der Architektur* 3, no. 3 (1799): 106–15.

Editor's Notes

1.   As government architect in the year IV (1796), Pierre-Louis Van-Cléemputte, a student of the royal architect Jacques-Ange Gabriel, was in charge of public festivals in Paris, and he worked on the construction of prisons in the city as well. Also known as an engraver, he published, among other things, engravings of the prize projects submitted to the Académie d'architecture from 1779 to 1789.

2.   On 1 November 1775 the comte d'Artois (later King Charles X, r. 1824–1830) acquired the property of Bagatelle, which then consisted of some acres of land in the Bois de Boulogne and a small dilapidated château built in 1720 by the maréchal d'Estrées. In 1777 the comte d'Artois had the tottering château demolished and built the present Château de Bagatelle.

After the comte d'Artois fled France in late July 1789, Bagatelle became property of the state. In 1793 the Convention ordered that the contents of the château be sold. The grounds were opened to the public, and the château was used for dinner parties by rich Parisians. Napoleon acquired Bagatelle in 1806, but in 1815 it was returned to the comte d'Artois, who gave it to his son. After that the château had a series of different owners, one of whom altered it in the 1870s by adding an attic story and a balcony. The building for servants, at the far end of the main courtyard, was torn down, and a new building, in the style of the Grand Trianon at Versailles, was built along the east side of the courtyard. In 1905 Bagatelle was sold to the city of Paris, and today its public park, a showcase for flowers, is frequently used for concerts.

3.   The name "Bagatelle" was not invented by the comte d'Artois: it was recorded in 1721 for the previous château on the site.

4.   François-Joseph Bélanger became principal architect to the comte d'Artois in the spring of 1777. On 21 September 1777 Bélanger started drawing up the plans for Bagatelle; construction started forty-eight hours later and was completed on 26 November 1777.

5.   Gilly's reference in his footnote is to the temporary Opéra on the boulevard Saint-Martin, built from August to October 1781 by Samson-Nicolas Lenoir "le Romain." See Allan Braham, *Architecture of the French Enlightenment* (London: Thames & Hudson, 1980), 239.—Trans.

6.   When Gilly was in Paris in 1798, some of the scars left upon the city by the French Revolution must still have been visible. Although Gilly's description of ruins everywhere would seem exaggerated, some damage was inflicted in the heat of passion during the Revolution and more was occasioned by decree during the Reign of Terror.

Gilly's remarks in his next paragraph also allude to changes in the city that had occurred since the construction of Bagatelle.

7.   François I started the construction of the Château de Madrid in 1528. It was located in the Bois de Boulogne, immediately northeast of the site where Bagatelle was later built. The château remained a royal possession, but after the middle of the seventeenth century no king stayed there, and as a result it was not properly maintained.

By the 1770s its decay had progressed to the point where it was feared that it would collapse, potentially causing a disaster. Despite this, Louis XVI could not make up his mind to rectify the situation. The château was finally sold by the National Assembly on 27 March 1792 to an entrepreneur, Nicolas-Jean Le Roy, who promptly started demolishing it. When simply tearing down the structure proved to be difficult, the remnants were set on fire. The spectacular fire, which onlookers likened to the eruption of a volcano, did not, however, succeed in destroying the château. Forced to spend a great deal of money to continue the demolition, Le Roy went bankrupt and had to sell the land and burnt ruins in October 1795. That was the condition in which Gilly must have seen the place in 1798. An alleged former caretaker of Château de Madrid built a restaurant on the site in the early nineteenth century. See Monique Chatenet, *Le Château de Madrid au Bois de Boulogne* (Paris: Picard, 1987).

8.   The Blessed Isabel of France (1225–1270), sister of Louis IX, known as Saint Louis, founded the convent of the Order of Saint Clare at Longchamp in the 1250s on a site that is today inside the Bois de Boulogne, just southwest of Bagatelle. The abbey was closed during the French Revolution, and the buildings were destroyed. In 1857 the walls were pulled down except for one tower.

9.   René-Louis, marquis de Girardin, *De la composition des paysages sur le terrain; ou, Des moyens d'embellir la nature autour des habitations champêtres* (Geneva: n.p., 1777; 4th rev. ed., Paris: Debray, 1805), ch. 1: 30: *"La symétrie est née sans doute de la paresse et de la vanité."*

10.   The reference in Gilly's footnote is to l'abbé Delille, *Les Jardins; ou, L'art d'embellir les paysages, poëme* (Paris: Impr. de F.-A. Didot l'aîné, 1782; rev. ed., London: Ph. Le Boussonnier, 1801), chant I, pp. 21, 4.

The Château de Marly was built by King Louis XIV between 1679 and 1686 as a retreat near Versailles, west of Paris. Its extensively graded park, designed by Jules Hardouin-Mansart, was laid out in the formal French style with statues, large water basins, cascading waterfalls, and geometric plantings, all arranged symmetrically. An engineering marvel known as the *machine de Marly* (machine of Marly) brought water from the Seine to Marly for the many hydraulic arrangements in the park, including a grand cascade.

Originally constructed in the sixteenth and seventeenth centuries as a country house for the bishops of Paris, the Château de Saint-Cloud was located southwest of Paris. It was purchased in 1658 by Philippe d'Orléans, brother of Louis XIV. He undertook a renovation of the park with the help of the royal landscape architect André Lenôtre, who laid it out in formal, symmetrical style, with flower beds, large cascades of water, water basins with spouting jets, and statues. Expropriated during the French Revolution, the château survived until 1870 when German soldiers occupied it during their siege of Paris and burnt it down. The park, however, still exists.

Lenôtre likewise designed the park of the Château de Chantilly north of Paris. In 1666 Louis II, known as the Great Condé, retired to Chantilly after a long military career and entrusted the remodeling of the park of the ancient château to Lenôtre, who laid it out with long views tracing geometric and symmetric designs of flower beds, vast esplanades, groves embellished with grottos and statues, and large basins with spouting water requiring complicated hydraulic machinery.

11. *"Ennui majestueux."*

12. The present château of Ermenonville, northeast of Paris, was built in the second half of the eighteenth century. Its park, laid out in 1763 for René-Louis, marquis de Girardin, was the first and one of the most famous Anglo-Chinese gardens in France. Its pleasing disorder included lakes, waterfalls, hills, and groves.

Among the buildings in the park was a Temple of Philosophy and the tomb of Jean-Jacques Rousseau, who died at the estate in 1778 and was buried there on an island in a lake; his remains, however, were transferred to the Pantheon in Paris during the Revolution.

13. Girardin (see note 9), ch. 1: 31, "[*Le majestueux*] *ennui de la symétrie a fait tout d'un coup sauter d'une extrémité à l'autre. Si la symétrie a trop long-temps abusé de l'ordre mal entendu pour tout enfermer, l'irrégularité a bientôt abusé du désordre pour égarer la vue dans le vague et la confusion.*"

14. The complete reference for the source in Gilly's footnote is *Ueber den guten Geschmack bei ländlichen Kunst- und Gärten-Anlagen und bei Verbesserung wirklicher Landschaften: Durch Beispiele erläutert* (Leipzig: In der von Kleefeldschen Buchhandlung, 1798). Translation of Uvedale Price, *An Essay on the Picturesque, as Compared with the Sublime and the Beautiful; and, on the Use of Studying Pictures, for the Purpose of Improving Real Landscape* (London: J. Robson, 1794).

15. L'abbé Delille, *Les Jardins; ou, L'art d'embellir les paysages, poëme* (Paris: Impr. de F.-A. Didot l'aîné, 1782; rev. ed., London: Ph. Le Boussonnier, 1801), Chant III, p. 75:

> . . . *Au lieu de la verdure*
>
> *Qui renferme le fleuve dans sa molle ceinture,*
>
> *L'eau dans des quais de pierre accuse sa prison:*
>
> *Le marbre fastueux outrage le gazon.*

16. Gilly's spelling—Mousseau—corresponds to the French Mouceau, more commonly called Monceau. In 1778 Louis-Philippe-Joseph d'Orléans, duc de Chartres (known as Philippe Egalité), bought a large piece of land at Monceau, outside the *barrière* at Roule immediately north of Paris, and had an Anglo-Chinese garden installed there to the designs of the painter Louis de Carmontelle.

Among the features of the park were a Dutch windmill, a Tartar tent, a minaret, ruins of a temple of Mars, and a naumachia—a lake that served as a setting for a replica of a Roman naval battle. In the park the duc de Chartres built one of the most extravagant of all the châteaux in the environs of Paris. Completely remodeled in 1861, and reduced to less than half its original size, Monceau is today a public park.

17. The Petit Trianon was built by Jacques-Ange Gabriel for Louis XV in 1762–1768 near Versailles. The château was a favorite of Marie-Antoinette's, who had its garden renovated after 1777 in the Anglo-Chinese style, with a temple to Amor, a hamlet, a mill at the edge of a pond, a dairy and a farm, a lake, an artificial mountain, and a theater.

18. Gilly mistakenly uses the word *basse-cour* (poultry yard or stable court). His German *Vorhof* actually corresponds to the French *avant-cour* (forecourt), which is the word Bélanger used to designate this space.

19. Bélanger called the main courtyard *la cour d'honneur*.

20. The French civil engineer Jean-Rodolphe Perronet was famous for his stone-arch bridges. The Pont de Neuilly, built in 1774, is one of the best examples.

21. Hubert Robert, a French painter known for his landscapes and his portrayals of romantic Roman ruins, created six panels for this cabinet, illustrating *les plaisirs champêtres* (rustic pleasures). The panels are now in the Metropolitan Museum of Art in New York, and copies have been installed in Bagatelle.

22. Antoine-François Callet was a history and portrait painter. Although the subjects of Callet's six paintings for this room are not known, they may have been portraits of members of the royal family, destroyed during the Revolution. See Barbara Scott, "Bagatelle: Folie of the Comte d'Artois," *Apollo* 95 (June 1972): 476–85.

23. Gilly calls this room a bathroom (*Bade-Zimmer*), but on Bélanger's plan of Bagatelle, it is called a *boudoir*, or lady's dressing room, bedroom, or private sitting room.

24. Oddly, Gilly omits to mention that the "pedestal" on which the statue stands is an oval charcoal burner.

25. "A small but convenient house." The description is an abbreviation of the words written on the entrance of the house in Ferrara built by the Italian poet Ludovico Ariosto (1474–1533).

26. The complete references for the sources in Gilly's footnote are Charles Percier and Pierre-François-Léonard Fontaine, *Palais, maisons, et autres édifices modernes, dessinés à Rome* (Paris, 1798; reprint, Hildesheim: Georg Olms, 1980) and *Magasin encyclopédique; ou, Journal des sciences, des lettres et des arts*.

27. The complete reference for the source in Gilly's footnote is Wilhelm von Wolzogen, "Über die Barrieren von Paris," *Journal des Luxus und der Moden* 13 (February 1798): 76–82.

28. Bagatelle was an instant success; everyone wanted to visit the château. Such was the demand that the comte d'Artois opened his estate to the public on Thursdays, Sundays, and holidays. See Béatrice de Andia et al., eds., *De Bagatelle à Monceau, 1778–1978: Les folies du XVIIIᵉ siècle à Paris*, exh. cat. (Paris: Musée Carnavalet, 1978), 10.

29. The description to which Gilly refers in his note is in "Öffentliche Vergnügungsplätze," *London und Paris* 1, no. 1 (1798): 51: *"An festlich heitern Tagen ist er [der Bois de Boulogne] der Vereinigungsplatz von einer Menge Fußgänger, und ausserdem ist er täglich der äusserste Zielpunkt unserer Elegants und Elegantes. Gewöhnlich geht's denn da nach Bagatelle, für dessen Eingang 15 Sous bezahlt werden, wenn man sich nicht mit 48 Livres den freyen Eingang fürs ganze Jahr erkauft hat; und nach etlichen tours de promenade und etwa einem Sorbet oder Glace rollt man wieder nach Hause. Der Garten von Bagatelle, so wie das Innere des Schlosses, das noch ganz unversehrt ist, sind wirklich ganz allerliebst eingerichtet, und man darf sich nicht wundern, daß unsere schöne Welt so sehr daran Wohlgefallen findet"* (On special days when the weather is good, it [the Bois de Boulogne] is the rendezvous for crowds of pedestrians, and in addition it is daily the ultimate

destination for our gentlemen and ladies of fashion. The goal is usually Bagatelle, where one pays 15 sous to get in, unless one has bought free admission for the entire year for 48 livres; and after quite a few *tours de promenade* and perhaps a sherbet or ice cream, one heads for home again. The garden of Bagatelle and the interior of the château are really most charmingly arranged, and it is no wonder that the sophisticated people take such pleasure in it).

A Description of Rincy, a Country Seat near Paris

From the countryside, learn the art of adorning the countryside.[1]

—Delille

Rincy, a country seat located not far from Paris,[2] offers a composition that is a splendid pendant to Bagatelle.*[3] These two princely domains, among so many, share a simplicity and charm that invite us to make a comparison of the varied scenes that they offer to the eye. In both, the splendor of château and grounds, which commonly prevails in the rich estates associated with elevated rank, has been cunningly avoided. No exaggerated pomp strikes the eye, and nowhere does a sense of effort subdue the spontaneous charm that attracts and delights every beholder. For all their princely grandeur, these estates reveal themselves as places of repose in the true sense of the word; and a spirit of privacy, far removed from the needless splendor of the court, is much in evidence everywhere. It is a sheer delight to linger in these haunts of pleasure; undistracted by gratuitous artifice, we survey well-considered arrangements that might serve as patterns for any similar undertaking elsewhere—patterns that are rightly held to be among the best of their kind.

For all their similarities, the two compositions nonetheless differ in character, and this makes it all the more interesting to view them side by side, as pendants, affording a revealing comparison of the considerations on which their various arrangements were based.

Bagatelle presents the picture of a delectable country villa, adorned with decoration of the most refined sort, which unites Art with Nature in the happiest conceivable manner. Set in a delightful countryside and surrounded by inviting gardens and groves, it is pervaded by a solemn stillness that heightens the native

---

* See the previous issue of this journal.

charms of the site; it is a haven of repose and of the associated, nobler pleasures; and this effectively determines the character of the whole.

The original purpose of Rincy, by contrast, was to further the active business of country life. This prime consideration has continued to inform its recent arrangement; and that purpose, all the requirements of which have been met with special care, has been incorporated in the plan of beautifying the whole.

Richly appointed, the residence is surrounded by informal plantings that appear to be more the work of Nature than of Art. Here the art of garden design appears innocent of all ornament: its simple forms are everywhere linked with rustic concerns. Woods and fields are incorporated in the park, and a picturesque relation unites them into a whole. This park presents us with a free and manifold variety combined with the most careful cultivation. In the park and in its environs, the fields are animated by the work of cultivation; the pastures abound with flocks; the woods and the game preserves are protected; in the yards and outbuildings, all is industry: a rich image of variety and beauty, in which labor and utility are everywhere allied with pleasure and grace.

Such is the character of the beautiful country estate of Rincy, in whose center rises the princely dwelling, which—for all the opulence of its appointments—is neither ostentatious nor unduly dazzling in exterior appearance, tending rather to elevate the effect of the surrounding landscape.

The extent of the estate is considerable. Its agreeable, partly hilly location; the proximity of the great Forest of Bondy,[4] wherein lie the abbey of Livry,[5] the villages of Livry, Clichy, and others; the hunting for which this forest was famous; and many another amenity of the region, which is dotted with villages and hamlets—all served to enhance the attractions of the place. Most important of all, no doubt, its proximity to Paris doubled the enjoyment. Rincy has always had wealthy owners, for one of whom, the marquis de Livry, it was elevated to the rank of a marquessate (in the year 1700). By that time this château, set in the loveliest part of the region, had been fitted out as a hunting lodge and was frequented by the king and his retinue; encompassed as it was by gardens and parks, it was widely admired as an establishment of the most notable kind.

The true improvement of the place, however, began only when it came into the possession of the ducs d'Orléans. With dispatch and with a more refined taste they set out to eliminate superfluous display, to expunge the artificiality of the previous arrangements, and to reveal the truly rural character of the delightful landscape, employing only the simplest means of art. This was principally the work of the last owner of Rincy.[6] The execution conformed perfectly to that well-considered system of improvement that can and should be an inspiration for many a similar property: for both in the overall plan and in its separate parts the two prime difficulties of such improvements—well-considered demolition and careful reconstruction—were wonderfully calculated and resolved.

Additionally, the undertaking enjoyed all the advantages of a delightful and beautiful situation; a picturesque and diverse terrain of hills, valleys, and plains presented itself to the eye; and every advantage was present for the embellishment of garden and landscape alike. To animate the simple and informal rural views with all kinds of agricultural activity while constantly improving cultivation was a happy achievement, both for the yield of the estate and for the many delightful features that quite naturally resulted. The location was favorable to all kinds of animal husbandry, and the fertility of the soil encouraged and rewarded cultivation, from the simplest crop to the most artificial garden and fruit planting.

All this could not but encourage the owner to look upon the care of the estate and its embellishment as a labor of love. He may therefore be excused if in places he has overstepped the bounds of economy and employed many a superfluous adornment. It must be remembered that this was an opulent landed proprietor, who set apart this one portion of his otherwise adequately profitable possessions for purposes of pleasure, and who devoted considerable effort to its development. He even planted exotic varieties beside domestic ones, as in a hothouse and nursery for plants of various climes, and he provided the visitor with the most varied view of rural activities and customs.

The exemplary agriculture and landscape gardening of the English school supplied the prime model for these arrangements, even down to the smallest detail. A number of workmen and animal keepers were brought here to work in the various parts of the estate, and they formed a remarkable little colony of their own. Some of the tasks, especially horse breeding, were entrusted to Englishmen; the care of the herds, dairies, and the like was in Dutch or Swiss hands, depending on the department; sheep were raised with meticulous care in the Spanish style; and the variety of selected herds and flocks, spread out across the landscape, together with the most varied menageries in the dairy farms, was truly astonishing to look upon.

All of the necessary installations—the stables and outbuildings—were suitably designed and, for purposes of comparison, erected side by side with those typical of the region. The dwellings of the foreign communities were likewise characteristic in their form, and these little farmsteads were devised as varied and picturesque features of the landscape.

What a magnificent task for the artist whose job it was to arrange these manifold groups and structures, to beautify them, and to transform them into a single parkland scene. In this, as in other things, he succeeded to perfection; and there could be no greater praise than that accorded to his work by Delille,*[7] who wrote that the Graces, by electing and adorning their favorite places, had traced the plan of Rincy with their own fair hands. This would also seem to be the place where the poet discovered the ideal that is so delightfully depicted in his accounts of country life and of its simple pleasures. Here, all embodies that judicious combination of utility with beauty that he proclaims:

> *Nor seek there an idle ornament.*
> *Disguise pleasure in the garb of utility.*
> *The farm, its master's treasure and joy,*
> *will first claim its rustic ornament.*
> *Let not the proud castle disdain the farm,*
> *to which it owes its wealth, and whose simple charms*
> *excel its luxury . . .***[8]

Thus, in this delightful landscape the great house was encompassed by rural farmsteads, whose skillful disposition bore the stamp of prosperity and decent neatness that is characteristic of this fortunate region.

While all the pleasures that wealth can purchase were united inside the great house for the owner's delectation, in the surrounding park arrangements had been made for every kind of enjoyment and comfort.

Such was Rincy.

Now, by contrast, the place is deserted and silent. Only a handful of visitors and lovers of the rural life still make their pilgrimage to it. The whole still stands, as to its principal features; order still reigns in the production of its farms; and even those parts of the estate that were intended as mere embellishments have somehow been maintained. Their survival will depend on the efforts of the present purchaser and his successors. It is to be hoped that they will be able to prevent the decay that has hitherto been kept in check by the devotion of faithful servants. Judicious precautions have protected the estate from destruction, from whatever quarter; and perhaps the respect commanded by its beauty will in itself continue to inspire some care for its maintenance.

An old overseer, a native of England, was still performing his office at

---

*   Delille, *Les Jardins,* Chant i.

**   Ibid., Chant iv.

Rincy. Held here by his love of the place, whose former transformation he had witnessed and to which he himself had transplanted much from his native country, he shows particular interest in foreign visitors, offering his services as a guide with unforced goodwill.

The road from Paris to Rincy is no more than two leagues in length and leads through the two charming villages of Pantin and Bondy. Near the latter, one leaves the paved highway for the lovely avenue de Rincy. Bordered by six rows of poplars, it is about five hundred rods in length,[9] as the crow flies. The central avenue includes the roadway, which is cambered and graveled in the manner of English country roads; a hedge of thorn and beech, five feet high, protects the tree trunks and ditches from damage. The two outermost rows of poplars, planted close together, form a well-beaten and shaded path for pedestrians on either side, so that the road is actually a triple one. As a special amenity in wet weather, there is a line of large paving stones in the center of the footpath; although here, too, a camber and ditches are carefully arranged so that rainwater is carried off.

The entrance to these wonderful avenues is adorned by two small pavilions where the road overseers formerly lived, and it is closed off by light wrought-iron gates. At the far end, one comes to the barred gate of Rincy itself and, adjacent to it, the gatekeeper's lodge. On entering, one finds oneself on a wide green partly enclosed by rural buildings of various kinds and partly bordered with planted trees, the intervals of which afford glimpses of the surrounding country. Encompassed by these views, the visitor hesitates whether to stop here or to follow the path that leads on. But his attention is soon captured by a small group of farm buildings that lies immediately to the right of the entrance gates. This is a dairy built adjacent to the park on a stream that also supplies water for the animals. Its buildings extend around three sides of a rectangular yard, the fourth and nearest side of which is closed off by a wall pierced with grilles and doors. The exterior of these structures has an unassuming solidity that is pleasing; the walls are plastered smooth and framed with raised tiles. The stalls inside are laid out entirely in the Dutch manner. It is a great pleasure to see the order and cleanliness that reign throughout, especially in the milk rooms, kitchens, and other aspects of the enterprise, where careful provision has been made for even the smallest appliances; any ornament is applied with a purpose and without compromising its utility.

After the impression made by these appointments, not even the most rigorous agriculturalist will complain upon being led into a room that, serving principally for the storage of milk, is perhaps one of the most elegant of its kind [fig. i]. Its interior plan is represented in the appended engraving. The room is about thirty-six feet long and approximately eighteen feet wide.[10] The high walls are

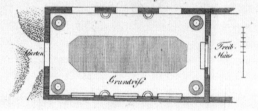

i. Friedrich Gilly, *Dairy at Rincy* (*Die Milch-Kammer zu Rincy*), 1799, aquatint and engraving by [Anton] Wachsmann, 11.8×21.7 cm (interior view). From *Sammlung nützlicher Aufsätze und Nachrichten, die Baukunst betreffend* 3, no. 2 (1799), frontispiece. Santa Monica, The Getty Center for the History of Art and the Humanities.

divided into panels without decoration and finished in light yellow, marbled plaster. The ceiling is very plainly framed by a simple cornice; the floor is paved with marble flagstones. In the center of the room stands a long table made of white marble slabs of remarkable size.* Its supports are straightforward in design and, together with the exquisite tabletop, form a splendid base for the milk vessels arrayed on the gleaming marble surface. The varied shapes of these vessels and bowls, in blue and white glass or in porcelain decorated with delicate paintings (the transparent rims of the former being adorned with cut decoration of various kinds), are a most pleasing and diverting sight. One loses oneself in contemplation of their lovely forms without a thought for the costliness of their material or workmanship; one enjoys the simplicity that makes them so pleasing and that serves to adorn and ennoble even the most commonplace implements, vessels, and other objects. Examples of this kind rekindle the fervent desire, which is still so seldom fulfilled, to encourage at every opportunity this application of pure and pleasing forms—which can be accomplished without great expense and indeed frequently obviates it.

In the four corners of the room are stands of the same pleasing design supporting circular slabs on which milk bowls stand. In the centers of these slabs rise wide basins, in which fresh water constantly bubbles up, led up through the base. All of these features lend so agreeable and delightful an overall appearance that one lingers in the room and returns to it with pleasure. What more inviting scene could be imagined than to come upon so tranquil and refreshing a place on a walk through a beautiful park? In winter it is most comfortably warmed by an orangery that abuts the short side of the room: the pipes of the heating system are attached to an iron plate in the partition and continue under the floor. This greenhouse contributes much to the pleasing atmosphere of the place; in summer, the orange trees set outside at intervals add charm to the open vistas that are enjoyed from within.

Three arched, glass doors are let into the long wall, and there is a door of the same kind in the end wall. Opposite these doors are niches of similar design, fitted with upholstered seats; and against the wall piers stand graceful female figures bearing lamps for illumination.[11]

One is finally tempted to forsake this lovely room only in order better to enjoy the magnificent landscape, and one is carried away by new delights. One enjoys a view of a large part of the park, which is surrounded by meadows and crossed here and there by watercourses. The green valley with its bushes, paths, and

---

* These lovely tables are now said to have been taken to the Museum in Paris.

Schweitzer Meierey

ii. Friedrich Gilly, *Swiss cottage at Rincy* (*Schweitzer Meierey*), 1799, engraving by Ant.[on]
Wachsmann, 9.4 × 15.5 cm. From *Sammlung nützlicher Aufsätze und Nachrichten, die
Baukunst betreffend* 3, no. 2 (1799), title vignette. Santa Monica, The Getty Center for the
History of Art and the Humanities.

bridges offers an unconstrained and smiling landscape, in which one longs to lose
oneself. Once more the scene is entirely rural.

Not far distant lies a lush meadow, which has been fenced in for a small
herd of Swiss cows. Erected there is an unpretentious structure that contains the
necessary stalls and the herdsman's dwelling. Built entirely from timber frame and
wattle and daub, it is roofed with clapboard and shingles, and its interior is equally
unassuming but neat. The title vignette [fig. ii] gives a view of this little building, a
pretty imitation of rural Swiss architecture.

Located in a distant, quiet corner of the park, this entirely natural construction, in its picturesque setting, presents a surprising and pleasing prospect. A
chalet of this kind is indeed worth more than all the modish overelaboration of temples and gaudy pavilions.

To be continued.[12]

Source Note: Friedrich Gilly, "Beschreibung des Landhauses Rincy unweit Paris," *Sammlung nützlicher
Aufsätze und Nachrichten, die Baukunst betreffend: Für angehende Baumeister und Freunde der Architektur* 3, no.
2 (1799): 116–24.

1. Abbé Delille, *Les Jardins; ou, L'art d'embellir les paysages, poëme* (Paris: Impr. de F.-A. Didot l'aîné, 1782; rev. ed., London: Ph. Le Boussonnier, 1801), Chant I, p. 4, l. 4: *"Des champs apprenez l'art de parer les champs."*

2. Rincy, or Le Raincy, originally sixteen kilometers east of Paris (measured from Notre-Dame Cathedral), is now in the eastern suburbs of Paris. The château was built in the early 1640s by Jacques Bordier, *intendant de finances* to the king. The architect was Louis Le Vau, and the garden was designed by André Lenôtre.

In 1769 Louis-Philippe d'Orléans acquired Rincy. Between 1769 and 1783 he replaced Lenôtre's park with one of the first English parks in France "to free itself from the sad regularity of classical gardens" (see Caisse nationale des monuments historiques et des sites, *Jardins en France, 1760–1820*, exh. cat. [Paris: Caisse nationale, 1978], 9, 11). The changes to the park included construction of a hamlet with a cow byre, a sheepfold, and a timber-framed hermitage. His son Louis-Philippe-Joseph, the future Philippe Egalité, inherited the château upon his father's death and proceeded with the help of the Scottish gardener Thomas Blaikie to install a *jardin anglais*. Blaikie describes his work at Rincy in his diary for 1786: "The begining of the year the Duc d'Orleans died and the Duc de Chartres became Duc D'Orleans and proprietaire of Rainsy & as his highness wanted to Make changes in the Park he desired Me to go and examine the Park and Make him a Plan of the Same; the 15 fev 1786 went to Rainsy to examine the ground. . . . All this requires a great deal of work; the Dukes father has been trying to make some part of it into an English garden but without taste or judgement" (Thomas Blaikie, *Diary of a Scotch Gardener* [London: George Routledge & Sons, 1931], 195).

At the time of the Revolution, Rincy was included in a decree that ordered the royal estates to be preserved and maintained as property of the republic in order to serve the needs of agriculture and the arts. The château was sold shortly after to a descendant of the second owners, and after the empire it was returned to Louis-Philippe, son of Philippe Egalité, and later king (r. 1830–1848). The château was torn down in 1852 when the possessions of the House of Orléans were confiscated. Four years later the land was carved up and sold off in twenty-three lots. See Patrick Bracco and Elisabeth Lebovici, "Les vestiges du parc du Raincy," *Monuments historiques: Ile-de-France* 129 (October–November 1983): 47–52.

3. Gilly is referring in his note to his essay on Bagatelle, published here on pages 139–53.

4. The Forest of Bondy (*la forêt de Bondy*) is a remnant of the extensive forest that formerly covered the region east of Paris, from the Bois de Vincennes in the north to the Forest of Fontainebleau in the south.

5. The abbey of Livry had its origin in a chapel built in 1186 near Livry, the town that today has merged with Le Raincy to form the township of Livry-Raincy. The abbey, which produced a number of scholars and historians, was destroyed during the Revolution and the land sold off as national property.

6. The last owner of Rincy before the Revolution and before the time of Gilly's writing was Louis-Philippe-Joseph, duc d'Orléans, who was executed during the Revolution (see note 2).

7. For the complete reference for the source Gilly cites in his note, see Delille (note 1).

8. Delille (see note 1), Chant IV, p. 94, ll. 3–9:

N'y cherchez pas non plus un oisif ornement.
Et sous l'utilité déguisez l'agrément.
   La ferme, le trésor, le plaisir de son maître,
Réclamera d'abord sa parure champêtre.
Que l'orgueilleux château ne la dédaigne pas;
Il lui doit sa richesse; et ses simples appas
L'emportent sur son luxe . . .

9. Five hundred rods (*Ruthen*) equal 2,059.5 yards, or 1,883 meters.

10. Here Gilly uses the Rhenish foot as his measurement. The room measured approximately 37 feet by 18.5 feet, or 11.3 meters by 5.6 meters.

11. The fashion of constructing dairies in the parks of palaces for the amusement of the nobility originated in French royal circles in the late eighteenth century. The dairy at Rincy served as a model for Gilly when, after his return to Berlin in 1799, he designed a dairy near the summer palace of Bellevue in the Tiergarten outside the capital. It was built for the amusement of Princess Louise, wife of Prince Ferdinand, the youngest brother of Frederick II.

12. Gilly had apparently intended to publish more about Rincy, but his untimely death prevented that. This text was the last one published during his lifetime.

Some Thoughts
on the Necessity of Endeavoring to Unify
the Various Departments of Architecture
in Both Theory and Practice

I n a journal whose purpose it has been, and will remain, to publish the more important results of inquiry and experience in the entire realm of architecture—as well as the latest and most interesting historical and literary accounts of developments, works, and elaborations in the theory and practice of this art, the scope of whose influence has expanded so much of late—in such a journal it may not seem entirely out of place to advance a few thoughts on the necessity of attempting to unify all aspects of the various departments of architecture, in both theory and practice, for their mutual benefit and in order to further their general influence. So vast is the range of the several arts and sciences, and so numerous are the fields of action that they encompass, that practitioners, mindful of their own limitations, must for their own sakes restrict themselves to one or another aspect of their chosen subject; they may nevertheless, on occasion, profitably adopt a more elevated vantage point and survey the whole, of which their own work is a part, and which endows that work with its characteristic form and purpose.

Although the present survey can embrace only a few general features, it may nevertheless for the moment serve a purpose that is certainly not without importance to the art itself and to its theoretical understanding.

Any comparative view of *the entire realm of construction* must begin by considering the association, or rather the combination, of the various branches of the discipline and the great differences that arise in their application and in their treatment. No term has been more variously and loosely applied than "construction" [*Bauen*]. Usage and chance associations as well as varying national interpretations have expanded it ever further; in consequence, it would be difficult to name any other discipline that entails the study and practice of more subjects. In many cases it is merely a tenuous and contingent connection or the initial application of certain common principles that has caused such highly disparate subjects to be associated as if they were closely akin. When they are viewed severally, their traditional association with an entity to which we refer by the generic name of "science of construction" [*Baukunde*] frequently comes to seem surprising. For this reason, any comparative and evaluative account of construction in its widest sense is inevitably diverse and heterogeneous and requires the application of quite distinct criteria to each separate field of inquiry. It therefore seems best to consider this extensive topic and the combination or association of the various disciplines that embrace its disparate parts with a view to the *advantages* inherent in the traditional union between them, their shared or reciprocal effects, and the initial *coincidence* of their general principles, rather than to any *direct or intrinsic relevance*. How else could river engineering and hydraulics as such be reconciled with mechanical engineering in all its forms; or with elements of mining and the various associated trades; or with the making of roads, which also goes by the name of construction? And how are all these to be reconciled with the art of erecting monumental edifices, or cities, or houses?

Such are the considerations that lead us to reflect on the relations between these subjects, all of which—many and diverse as they are—carry great importance for the state, for civil society as a whole, and for the welfare of every individual.

The *art of architecture itself,* in its own *proper domain,* is also characterized by an extraordinary multiplicity not only in the individual topics with which it deals but also in its associated purposes, wants, and inquiries. Its study, like its practice, involves a great variety of interconnected topics; its essential concerns therefore demand to be considered from distinct points of view.

These concerns nevertheless connect to form a *whole* once they are seen in terms of the points of contact that arise in practice between them; and this *connected view becomes necessary* because *the purposes and wants themselves necessarily form connections*. If architecture were once viewed in terms of these connections, which are essential both for its practice and for its study, then its logical sequence and pattern would emerge. A description of this kind would amount to *an outline of the entire education of an architect;* and such a work, which would unarguably be of the greatest importance and interest, may perhaps in time be expected from the pen of some knowledgeable writer.

Along with this necessary association between its diverse concerns and purposes, the expansion of architecture has continued apace. With the constant progress of science and art in invention, in application, and in general use, the scope of architectural inquiry—both specific and general—and of architectural practice has continued to grow. This expansion, the product of much thoughtful effort both in science and art, has brought with it a daily increase in the mass of essential knowledge that any architect—however rich he may be in experience—is required to master.

To follow the youthful architect through so various and so interesting a course of instruction must inevitably enhance our respect for his calling. Now we see him exercising his artistic talent in the realm of taste and pursuing art amid the lovely and copious models supplied by antiquity; he learns to design and shape his creations freely, as objects of pure gratification and noble purpose. Now, as the purpose that determines his plan grows more rigorous, all the requirements inherent to that purpose unite to present a rule, to which his art must be applied. Now it is purpose alone, the dictate of necessity, that becomes the prime law of his work and determines its nature and its form; here he must judiciously observe the most minute considerations of function and of needs of all kinds—those of domestic labor, or of the practice of a craft, or the demands and arrangements of agricultural economy—and must make them his constant study. On that great stage that is architecture, with all its forms of arrangement, objects of the most varied nature will present themselves to his view. From the smallest dwelling to the largest, he will be expected to observe a thousand variations and alterations in every regard. Nor will he encounter domestic and private requirements alone: public installations, the planning of cities, streets, and squares; traffic in general; trade; manufacture; workshops; and countless public needs will demand equal attention. Rural economy, husbandry, and the bonds of trade and traffic in the shape of canals, bridges, and roads will constantly, and at times imperatively, extend the scope of his inquiry. Everywhere the architect will find occasion for active employment of his powers, and for each of these manifold concerns, he will be expected to discover the fittest, the best, and the most convenient solution.

Now he must begin to combine good and convenient construction with lasting solidity; and this is learned through study and experience of a quite different kind. To ground a building securely, to join its parts durably together—in a word, to erect it—he must place his reliance in laws as well as in mechanical accessories and contrivances. In this, the scientist will come to his aid, bringing to him the manifold results of investigations in the pure sciences; the study of mathematics, in particular, will prove a sure guide. In addition, science will teach him to understand and verify the nature and durability of building materials and of the substances that join them and to observe the manifold practical consequences of their use.

In pursuit of experience, the young architect now makes his way to the construction site itself, where he must begin to learn through practice. Here he must apply the knowledge he has gained and witness the application of his rules. He must concern himself with all manner of technical factors, methods, and expedients; each and every trade will demand his continual attention: for one day he will assume the important position of general overseer of all these tradesmen and will constantly have to confer with them. Here, at last, the difficulty of practice and the often arduous nature of the work will be brought home to him. He will have to learn to observe binding instructions: time, space, and means will be laid down for him; and, as for economy, he must select the best possible means from those that are also the most economical.

To survey the elementary principles of the subject is to become aware of the connection—so necessary in practice and yet by no means constant in its nature—that unites these manifold demands. This leads to a clear understanding of the separate steps involved and of the manner in which they are linked by the requirements of the matter at hand. A course comprising the artistic, the theoretical, the practical, and the purely technical, united in the plan and purpose of the whole, is thus seen to be indispensable to the study of architecture; and whatever view is taken of the whole or of its parts, nothing in the sequence must be omitted.

The more these requirements, *viewed in conjunction,* are seen *necessarily to be bound up with* the attainment of the purpose and the completeness of the execution, the more justly they should (or might) all be demanded of any individual architect. Whether this is *feasible* in any literal sense and with perfect consistency is a question that would require a more detailed examination of the study of architecture and its attendant difficulties. Close consideration will readily show how difficult it is to fulfill so many and such varied requirements to an equal degree; and we shall soon come to honor the man who in his own sphere of activity, however limited, achieves an eminent degree of perfection by devoting himself to specific concerns.

Yet, while the man of exceptional talent may be permitted, for this very reason, to concentrate on the development of his special powers, the general considerations mentioned suggest that the aspiring architect would be well advised to place no *limitations* of any kind on the totality of his training or studies. In his chosen profession he must learn to judge all the demands that confront him, to assess them in all their implications, and to keep the whole in view at every point. Anyone who believes that a *limited and exclusive course of study can supply the want* of all the rest, or who even regards the rest as *dispensable,* will certainly *err* in the former case or become *one-sided* in the latter case. A man may be great and preeminent in one respect, but this does not make him so in all. At times, he may be in no position to judge what is required, let alone to supply it; and sound judgment, at least in those parts of his profession most closely related to his own, is the least that can be expected of any architect. There is a degree of one-sidedness that frequently proves pernicious for the individual and for society; and this must stand as a warning, especially to those youthful novices who are inclined to be overhasty in their judgments.

At this juncture a few remarks would seem to be in order concerning the changes in the *status of architecture itself, especially of late:* the way in which it has been regarded and treated has necessarily affected its status, leading to differences on matters of substance and opinion, both in general and in particular, that have often been mutually damaging. A glance at this issue is therefore very much in the general interest.

The status of architecture in antiquity—quite apart from the many difficulties attendant on any attempt to describe it—is too remote for comparison with the present situation. Whatever may have been its status or its connection with the sciences, it was then, more than at any other time, that architecture naturally enjoyed a close alliance with the *arts.* Yet only an unequaled combination of knowledge and talent could have produced the perfection of the works of that age.

As architecture declined, it sank to the level of mere craftsmanship, a state from which it then had to be rescued. At length, the country that is the cradle of all the arts fortunately produced architects of force and vigor, to whom we owe a rebirth of architecture in its capacity as an art. In that connection, however, the teaching and dissemination of architecture thenceforward took a noteworthy course. With the spread of learning, architecture came to be treated as a largely scholarly pursuit. The age of the manuals now dawned. Mathematics, in particular, took architecture in hand and even presumed—if only in an appendix—to solve the problem of taste. This did not, of course, put an end to the existence of craftsmanship; and for the first time architects emerged who were master builders in the true sense and who were capable of combining the two.

It cannot be denied that, as a result of these developments, first one aspect of the subject and then another suffered and was suppressed; that a pernicious *one-sidedness,* not to say *division,* prevailed within a combined art and science that always has to function *in unison* and as an *entity.* As a result, the practice of architecture came to be governed by the character and methods of each individual nation, or by mere force of opinion, or even by fashion; and so it remains to this day, divided into national variants that seldom work to its advantage.

The want of that precious balance that leads to a higher and shared perfection has undoubtedly been due, first and foremost, to this one-sidedness; to this individual caprice; and, worst of all, to this division. This has been so in a number of otherwise excellent schools of architecture; and what reader will not recall, in this connection, the futile feuds and controversies between the academic architects and their various adversaries in France and England, with all the dire consequences that ensued?

Along with the schools of art, there arose critiques of art and theoretical formulas; and these, whatever their intrinsic value, served to exacerbate the prevailing feuds. In the course of imposing a general classification, criticism was compelled to include architecture; but the systems that emerged were naturally as controversial as they were diverse. Architecture had long since been admitted as a true companion of the fine arts; but few now came forward to defend this right or even its right to the name of art. Some conceded it half a vote in the congress of the arts, but others struck it entirely from the list, citing its ignominious subservience to necessity and utility. And so architecture came to be considered merely a mechanical pursuit, and it was subordinated first to one superior authority and then to another: its task was to serve and be useful.

So harsh a verdict has compelled more recent critics to review the case and to pass a more temperate judgment; and one philosopher, by advancing an *entirely new conception*, has shown that—on certain conditions—architecture can still be recalled from exile and restored to its ancient rights.* In the schools and among the architects themselves, the old, one-sided categorization of architecture was not without its practical effect. One-sidedness frequently brought division and disaster in its train; for many it was an incitement to division—and even, be it said, to mutual contempt.

At a time when art and science are everywhere so closely allied, a general community of interest must necessarily prevail, the more so as their interdependence increases; and all who are conscious and desirous of the general good must surely strive toward this end. And so, first of all, there must surely be no more talk of division, utterly opposed as it is to all secure achievement, to the true and reciprocal advantages of education, and to progress.

Those advantages can be secured for architecture only when every individual—while advancing his own abilities and his own talent, wherever these may lie—simultaneously seeks to improve himself in other directions: the more so, the closer they lie to his own concerns. He will add to his store of always profitable knowledge by following others in studies more or less closely related to his own. At the very least, we may surely expect that he will not be a total stranger to all that lies outside his own field, and that he will welcome the interest of others in that field; and no one, I trust, will seek to assert that such an enhanced breadth of concern would threaten the talents or the interests of anyone.

---

* [Karl Heinrich Heydenreich,] "Neuer Begriff der Baukunst als schönen Kunst," *Deutsche Monatsschrift* (October 1798): 160–64.

In this way alone can the preeminent abilities and particular studies of one individual bear fruit for others, exert an influence on them, and elicit from them a respect that must become mutual. For everywhere the architect must learn to *value* the scientist, and the scientist to value the architect; architects, each with particular talents and native gifts, must *work together in mutual respect;* and no vain pride must mark out the supposed "artist" [*Baukünstler*] among them. Each must extend a hand to all in the interest of mutual aid—all the more so as the goal to which all aspire grows ever more distant and more manifold.

Only from such an association and from such reciprocal influence can we expect any general advance toward perfection, especially as things are at present; and for this the ground cannot be laid too soon. Above all, if a school duly combines all the important and related parts of so extensive a discipline, it can have the most beneficial effects and spread the true advantages of learning. And thus the great institution recently established in London for the dissemination and application of scientific principles in industry and allied matters and based on these principles of mutually beneficial association will undoubtedly prove a powerful influence and, in countless ways, a model of its kind.*[1]

The influence of this important association between disciplines will gradually expand, and by virtue of this alone it will attract the *universal interest* that architecture requires, perhaps more than anything else, for its practical advancement and dissemination. There is every reason to expect that, by such means, the public will come to appreciate an art that is as useful as it is pleasurable; an art that is the natural ally of order, tranquillity, and the blessings of civilization; an art that involves human activity of every kind in its pursuit of mutual advantage; an art that—wherever it flourishes—is itself a *sign of a cultivated society.* As such, it will enjoy the most attentive public support; and a gratifying example is set by any state that gives its practical patronage to architecture as an important agent of the common good. This is also a particular instance of the attention that must be devoted to the pursuit of the *whole:* and on this a great deal will indeed depend. For whatever means may exist for the instruction of individuals and whatever their learning and culture, the daily practice, the advancement, and in a sense the fate of every science, and still more that of the needful, practical arts and even crafts, all ultimately depend on the *interest* and the *response*—and thus on the *level of education—of the public* at large and on its *receptivity* to excellence, grandeur, and

---

* Information concerning this institution, whose founder was the distinguished count Rumford, may be found in *Der Neue Deutsche Merkur,* July 1799, etc.

beauty. It is well to urge the importance of this more general interest, this practical appreciation of culture. The judicious words of a universally revered author concerning the appreciation of the arts in general find a useful application here:

> *If art be controlled and subdued, if it be made to conform to the dictates of its age, it will wither and perish. . . . If the arts are to flourish and advance, there must be a* universal and active love of art, *with a predisposition toward greatness. . . . It is vain to expect that* elegance, taste, and fitness for purpose *will spread their influence through every craft; for this can never happen until a* feeling for art has become general, *and until those qualities are in* demand.[2]

Nothing, therefore, could be more desirable, more supportive, or productive of happier consequences than this widespread interest in an art so manifold and important and the union that springs from the numerous considerations outlined above.

The maintenance and furtherance of this universal interest are thus the twofold duty of everyone who calls himself a supporter and lover of the arts. Interest will grow at every step as the aims of architecture become interconnected and unified, and as its influence extends further, even to the remotest associations. When science and art unite at a common central point, when they work in concert, and when they place equal reliance on the lessons of experience, then they will progress more swiftly toward their goal; and each stands to gain by the mutual extension of their powers to encompass even the remotest social purposes. The more extensive and various the specialized studies in every field of human knowledge and skill, the richer their common yield of experience and example; and the wider their application, the more complete will be the appreciation manifested by individuals and hence by society at large.

It may be hoped that the same public appreciation will be enjoyed by an undertaking that devotes itself—as does the present compilation—to all the important topics and inquiries in the realm of architecture; an undertaking that will be pursued with all possible diligence and with an ever-growing concern for the principles of breadth of view, mutual association, and social utility; and one that will, preeminently, be enriched by the support of the ablest men.

Source Note: Friedrich Gilly, "Einige Gedanken über die Notwendigkeit, die verschiedenen Theile der Baukunst, in wissenschaftlicher und praktischer Hinsicht, möglichst zu vereinen," *Sammlung nützlicher Aufsätze und Nachrichten, die Baukunst betreffend: Für angehende Baumeister und Freunde der Architektur* 3, no. 2 (1799): 3–12.

Editor's Notes

1. In 1799 the British-American physicist and philanthropist Benjamin Thompson Count Rumford was instrumental in the organization of the "Royal Institution of Great Britain for diffusing the knowledge and facilitating the general Introduction of useful mechanical Inventions and Improvements," which received its charter of incorporation from George III in 1800. The report about the new institution that Gilly refers to in his note appeared in *Der neue Teutsche Merkur*, 7. Stück (July 1799): 263–5, where it is described in glowing terms: " . . . *[es] verspricht schon jetzt in seiner ersten Kindheit soviel, daß man ohne alle Übertreibung ihm einen außerordentlichen, die ganze kultivirte Erde umfassenden Wirkungskreis baldigst versprechen darf*" ([it] promises already in its earliest infancy so much that we may without any exaggeration expect it very quickly to achieve an extraordinary sphere of activity comprising the entire educated world).

2. "*Wenn die Kunst beherrscht und gemeistert wird, wenn sie sich nach der Zeit richten soll, dann wird Sie abnehmen und vergehen. . . . Sollen Künste blühen und steigen, so muß eine allgemeine Liebhaberey herrschen, die sich zum Großen neigt. . . . Vergebens hofft man auch, daß Zierlichkeit, Geschmack und Zweckmäßigkeit, sich durch alle Gewerbe wohlthätig verbreiten! denn dieses kann nur alsdann geschehen, wenn der Kunstsinn allgemein ist, und jene Eigenschaften gefordert werden.*" Gilly has slightly changed both the wording and the emphasis of the quotation, which is drawn from three separate passages in Johann Wolfgang Goethe, "Über Lehranstalten zu Gunsten der bildenden Künste," *Propyläen* 2, no. 2 (1799): 10, 13, 17.

Some Thoughts

173

Appendix 1
List of a Selection of Duplicates Present in the Royal Library of This City

No. 1

Highly important for instruction in architecture and in draftsmanship.

1. Edifices antiques de Rome. p. Degodetz. 1682.—fol. [folio]
    [Desgodets, Antoine. *Les edifices antiques de Rome.* Paris: Jean-Baptiste
    Coignard, 1682.]
2. Fragmenta vestigii veteris Romae. fol. [folio]
    [Bellori, Giovanni Pietro. *Fragmenta vestigii veteris Romae.* Rome: J.
    Corvi, 1673.]
3. L'architect. de Vitruve p. Perrault. fol. [folio]
    [Perrault, Claude. *Les dix livres d'architecture de Vitruve.* Paris: Jean-
    Baptiste Coignard, 1673.]
4. Libro d'archit. d'Antonio Labacco. fol. minor. form. [small-size folio]
    [Labacco, Antonio. *Libro d'Antonio Labacco appartenente a l'architettura
    nel qual si figurano alcune notabili antiquità di Roma.* Rome: In Casa nos-
    tra, 1552.]
5. Les Ruines de Balbek. fol. [folio]
    [Wood, Robert. *Les ruines de Balbec, autrement dite Héliopolis dans la Coe-
    losyrie.* London: n.p., 1757.]
6. Les Ruines de Palmyre. fol. [folio]
    [Wood, Robert. *Les ruines de Palmyre, autrement dite Tedmor au désert.*
    London: A. Millard, 1753.]
7. Les Ruines des monumens de la Grece. p. le Roi. fol. 1ste Ausgabe. [folio 1st
    edition]
    [Le Roy, Julien-David. *Les ruines des plus beaux monuments de la Grèce.*
    Paris: H. L. Guérin & L. F. Delatour, 1758.]
8. Voyage pittoresque de Naples et Sicile.—ein Band einzeln. [1 detached volume]
    [Saint-Non, Jean Claude Richard de. *Voyage pittoresque; ou, Description*

des royaumes de Naples et de Sicile. 4 vols. Paris: Imprimerie de Clousier, 1781–1786.]

9. Les Ruines de Paestum p. Major. fol. [folio]

   [Major, Thomas. *Les ruines de Paestum, ou de Posidonie dans la Grande Grèce.* London: Author, 1768.]

10. Monumens de Rome ancienne. p. Barbault. fol. [folio]

   [Barbault, Jean. *Les plus beaux monumens de la Rome ancienne; ou, Recueil des plus beaux morceaux de l'antiquité romaine qui existent encore.* Rome: Bouchard & Gravier, 1761.]

11. Opere d'architettura du Piranesi. 4 fol. Bände. [4 folio volumes]

   [Piranesi, Giambattista. *Opere varie di architettura, prospettive, grotteschi, antichità sul gusto degli antichi romani.* Rome: Author, 1750.]

No. 2

Extraordinarily useful for instruction in figure and freehand drawing; nevertheless, as these are very costly works (some of them, at least), they are to be requested from the library only by way of a loan, and on the supposition that they are not to be sold elsewhere.

1. Raccolta d'antiche Statue. fol. [folio]

   [Cavaceppi, Bartolomeo. *Raccolta d'antiche statue, busti, bassirilievi ed altre sculture.* 3 vols. Rome: P. Manno, 1768–1772.]

2. Statues antiques p. Perrier. Kl. fol. [small folio]

   [Perrier, François. *Segmenta nobilium signorum et statuarii. . . .* Rome: n.p., 1638; Paris: Chez la veufue de deffunct Perier, 1638.]

3. Maffei Raccolta di statue antiche—1. fol. [folio]

   [Maffei, Paolo Alessandro. *Raccolta di statue antiche e moderne.* Rome: Stamperia alla pace, 1704.]

4. Galleria Giustiniana. 2 Th. fol. imperil. [2 imperial folio volumes (a paper size)]

   [*Galleria Giustiniana del marchese Vincenzo Giustiniani.* 2 vols. Rome: n.p., 1631.]

5. Delle antiche statue greche e Romane. 2 Th. fol. [2 folio volumes]

   [Zanetti, Antonio Maria. *Delle antiche statue Greche e Romane che nell'antisala della Libreria di San Marco.* 2 vols. Venice: Eccellentissimo Senato, 1740–1743.]

6. Admiranda Romanorum d. Bellori. quer fol. [oblong folio]

   [Bartoli, Pietro Santi. *Admiranda romanarum antiquitatum. . . .* Rome: J.J. de Rubeis, 1693?]

7. Lucernae fictiles v. Gori. fol. [folio]

> [Perhaps: Academia Pisaurensis. *Lucernae fictiles Musei Passerii*. Pisa: Aedius Gavellius, 1739.]

8. Sandrart Deutsche Akademie d. B. K.—7 Bände fol. [7 folio volumes]

> [Sandrart, Joachim von. *Teutsche Akademie der Bau-, Bildhauer- und Maler-Kunst*. 8 vols. Nuremberg: J. A. Endter, 1768–1775.]

9. Zwei einzelne Bände von der Voyage pitt. de la Suisse.—[2 single volumes of the Voyage pitt. de la Suisse (reading of "Suisse" uncertain)]

> [Perhaps: Zurlauben, Béat Fidèle Antoine Jean Dominque, Baron de. *Tableaux de la Suisse; ou, Voyage pittoresque fait dans les treize cantons. . . .* 4 vols. Paris: Impr. de Clousier, 1780–1786.]

(Perhaps from these also, according to the stock of books available for teaching purposes, a number of works could be loaned to us, which the instructor would have to specify each time.)

No. 3

Works that, for the Akademie, would not be indispensable acquisitions, or urgently required for specific teaching purposes, but might be purchased on readily acceptable terms, at *very low prices,* to become the foundation of a future library solely dedicated to the use of the Akademie.

1. Colonna Traiana di Petr. S. Bartolo. qfol. [oblong folio]

> [Bartoli, Pietro Santi. *Colonna Traiana eretta dal Senato, e popolo romano all'imperatore Traiano Augusto nel suo foro in Roma*. Rome: Giovanni Giacomo de Rossi (1673).]

2. Architettura di Scamozzi. 4°. [quarto]

> [Scamozzi, Vincenzo. *L'idea della architettura universale*. Venice: Author, 1615.]

3. Fontane di Roma da Falda.

> [Falda, Giovanni Battista. *Le fontane di Roma nelle piazze e luoghi publici della città*. Rome: Giovanni Giacomo de Rossi, 1675–1691?]

4. Bandinius de Obelisco Caesaris Augusti.

> [Bandini, Angelo Mario. *Dell'obelisco Cesare Augusto*. Rome: Nella stamperia di Pallade, 1750.]

5. Columna Antonini d. Bellori qfol. [oblong folio]

> [Bellori, Giovanni Pietro. *Columna Cochlis M. Aurelio Antonino Augusto*. Rome: n.p., 1704.]

6. Winckelmann, Über die Bauk. d. Alten. 4°. [quarto]

   [Winckelmann, Johann Joachim. *Anmerkungen über die Baukunst der Alten*. Leipzig: Johann Gottfried Dyck, 1762.]

7. Torino architettura civile. fol. [folio]

   [Guarini, Guarino. *Architettura civile*. Turin: G. Mairesse, 1737.]

8. Architektur von Dieterlein.

   [Dietterlin, Wendel. *Architectura von Außtheilung, Symmetria und Proportion der fünff Seulen, und aller darauss volgender Kunst Arbeit, von Fenstern, Caminen, Thürgerichten, Portalen, Bronnen und Epitaphien*. Nuremberg: Hubrecht & Balthasar Caymox, 1598.]

9. Del Palazzo de Cesari d. Bianchino. fol. [folio]

   [Bianchini, Francesco. *Del palazzo de' Cesari*. Verona: P. Berno, 1738.]

10. Representation de Venise.

11. Palazzi di Genova.

    [Rubens, Peter Paul. *Palazzi di Genova*. Antwerp: n.p., 1622.]

12. Beschreibung des Weißensteins beÿ Kassel. fol. alt. [folio (?)]

    [Perhaps: Apell, David Phillip von. *Kurze Beschreibung der Wilhelmshöhe beÿ Cassel*. 2nd ed. Kassel: n.p., 1797.]

13. Reliquiae antiquae urbis Romae ab Overbek. fol. [folio]

    [Overbeke, Bonaventur van. *Reliquiae antiquae urbis Romae*. Amsterdam: J. Crellius, 1708.]

14. Resolution des 4 principaux Problems de l'archit.

    [Blondel, François. *Resolution des quatre principaux problemes d'architecture*. Paris: De l'Imprimerie royale, 1673.]

15. L'Arco di Susa. fol. [folio]

    [Massazza, Paol' Antonio. *L'arco antico di Susa*. Turin: Stamperia Reale, 1750.]

16. Architettura di Ruggieri. 4 Thl. fol. [4 folio volumes]

    [Ruggieri, Ferdinando. *Scelta di architetture antiche e moderne della città di Firenze*. 4 vols. Florence: Giuseppe Bouchard, 1755.]

17. Anfiteatro Flavio d. Fontana. fol. [folio]

    [Fontana, Carlo. *L'anfiteatro Flavio*. The Hague: I. Vaillant, 1725.]

18. Roma sotteranea da Bosio.

    [Bosio, Antonio. *Roma sotteranea*. Rome: G. Facciotti, 1632.]

19. Statues antiques de Nismes.

    [Perhaps: Clérisseau, Charles-Louis. *Antiquités de la France*. Part 1, *Monumens de Nismes*. Paris: De l'imprimerie de Phillipe-Denys Pierres, 1778.]

20. Antiquités expliquées par Montfaucon. 5 Bände fol. [5 folio volumes]
    [Montfaucon, Bernard de. *L'antiquité expliquée, et représentée en figures.*
    Paris: F. Delaulne, 1719.]

21. Pitture ant. di Ercolano. 2er, 3er, 4er Theil. [volumes 2, 3, 4]
    [Real accademia ercolanese di archeologia. *Delle antichità di Ercolano.* 8
    vols. Naples: Regia stamperia, 1757–1792.]

From these, a special selection should be made of those that are the most useful.

—Fr. Gilly

12 September 1799

Source Note: "Verzeichnis einer Auswahl der auf der hiesigen Kgl. Bibliothek vorhandenen Doubletten." Geheimes Staatsarchiv Preußischer Kulturbesitz, Abteilung Merseburg, Gen. Directorium, Bau-Akademie Deput. Tit. VI, Nr. 8, Lektionen und Lehrer, Acta wegen des Unterrichts in der Optik und Perspective: Professor Gilly, Simon: 1799–1809, fol. 3, 3a.

Appendix 2
Friedrich Gilly's Book and Engraving Collection— Introduction and Facsimile List of Titles

The "List of the Choice Collection of Books and Engravings, Mostly on Architectural, Antiquarian, and Artistic Subjects, Left by the Late Professor and Royal Building Inspector Gilly," reproduced in facsimile on the following pages, is known to have survived in only one copy, which is in the Geheimes Staatsarchiv Preußischer Kulturbesitz, Abteilung Merseburg (Zivilkabinett, Rep. 96 A Tit. 12 M). The list is a unique document, which reaches far beyond biographical information: it mirrors the intellectual and artistic activities of a century of paradigmatic shifts in thinking and social reality, which opened up new perspectives and territories for the theories of art and architecture, their production and perception.

Gilly's books, collected during the last decade of the eighteenth century but spanning a much longer period of time, comprise a wide range of artistic interests, including poetry, cultural history, art history, aesthetic theory and philosophy, and the art of building in both its practical and theoretical aspects. For Gilly the range of these interests determined the conceptual framework within which his notion of architecture could be conceived.

Most of the significant authors of eighteenth-century theory can be found among those listed in Gilly's private book collection. In French architectural theory the discourse ranges from the famous *querelle des Anciens et des Modernes*, opposing sides of which are represented by François Blondel and Charles Perrault, to the important, and more recent, arguments advanced by prominent authors such as the abbé Marc-Antoine Laugier and Nicolas Le Camus de Mézières, by Charles-Etienne Briseux, Jean-François de Neufforge, Pierre Patte, Charles Percier and Pierre-François-Léonard Fontaine, Marie-Joseph Peyre, or Antoine-Chrysostome Quatremère de Quincy. English sensualism was represented by Edmund Burke's treatise on the sublime, as famous as it was seminal, and by the studies on taste published by Archibald Alison and William Hogarth. German idealistic philosophy and aesthetic theory were marked by names fundamental to the "theoretical" progress of the age, such as Immanuel Kant, Johann Gottlieb Fichte, and Johann Joachim Winckelmann, accompanied by a group of such important writers and theoreticians as Karl Philipp Moritz, Johann Georg Sulzer, Gotthold Ephraim Lessing, Johann Wolfgang Goethe, Friedrich Schiller, Wilhelm Wackenroder, Ludwig Tieck, and others.

In an architect's library of that time, the recent publications of classical antiquities with their more or less imaginary depictions of ancient Greek and Roman monuments were essential. Hence it is not surprising but nevertheless impressive to find in Gilly's library a string of such important names as Robert Adam, James Stuart and Nicholas Revett, Julien-David Le Roy, and Thomas Major, not to mention Giambattista Piranesi. Indispensable, of course, to the architect were canonical authors such as Palladio, of whom Gilly owned seven editions, and Vitruvius, listed in eleven different editions, the earliest by de Ponte dated 1521, the latest a German edition from the year 1796 by August Rode. Three different editions of Perrault's Vitruvius prove an intense interest in the modern interpretation of this classic. How much David Gilly contributed to the library in general and particularly to this set of editions, which is a remarkable collection for a twenty-eight-year-old architect, we do not know.

The printed inventory lists about seven hundred books and hundreds of engravings. It had been Friedrich Gilly's intention to build up an architecture library that would meet the needs and demands of young architects and to open it for use by fellow members of the Privatgesellschaft junger Architekten. Acquisitions of the latest French publications, which Gilly presumably purchased in Paris during his study tour, evidently were meant to serve that purpose. In view of his son's intentions, it was logical that David Gilly donated the collection to the library of the recently founded Bauakademie in 1801.

The printed inventory of the books and engravings collected by the late "Professor and Royal Building Inspector Gilly" was a private publication obviously compiled on the occasion of the joining of the two libraries in 1801. In 1884 the library of the Bauakademie became part of the Technische Hochschule in Berlin-Charlottenburg, whose entire library was lost at the end of World War II.

—F. N.

Verzeichniß

der

von dem verstorbenen Professor und Hof=Bau=Inspektor Gilly

hinterlassenen auserlesenen

Sammlung von Büchern und Kupferstichen,

meist architektonischen, antiquarischen und artistischen Inhaltes.

———————

Berlin, 1801.

184

In Folio.

<table>
<tr><td>Nro.</td><td></td></tr>
<tr><td>1 — 3</td><td>The antiquities of Athens, measured and delineated by James Stuart and Revett. London 1762, mit schönen Kupfern, 3 Bände.</td></tr>
<tr><td>4</td><td>Les ruines de Paestum ou de Posidonie dans la grande Grèce, par F. Major. London 1768, mit schönen Kupfern.</td></tr>
<tr><td>5 — 6</td><td>Jonian antiquities, published by Chandler, Revett and Pars. London 1769, mit schönen Kupfern, 2 Bände.</td></tr>
<tr><td>7</td><td>Description de l'école de chirurgie à Paris, par Goudoin. Paris 1780.</td></tr>
<tr><td>8</td><td>Les édifices antiques de Rome, dessinés & mesurés par M. Desgodetz. Paris 1799, Prachtausgabe, mit Kupfern.</td></tr>
<tr><td>9</td><td>Prix de l'académie d'architecture de Paris. Collection de divers plans en contours, Oeuvre très rare.</td></tr>
<tr><td>10</td><td>Ruins of the palace of the emperor Diocletian at Spalatro in Dalmatia by R. Adam, 1764, blos Kupfer.</td></tr>
<tr><td>11</td><td>Palais, Maisons, & autres édifices modernes, dessinés à Rome, publiés à Paris an VI, 15 Hefte, jedes Heft zu 6 Blatt.</td></tr>
<tr><td>12</td><td>Gallerie antique, ou collection des chef-d'oeuvres d'architecture, sculpture & peinture antiques. 6 livraisons, avec 74 planches.</td></tr>
<tr><td>13</td><td>Choix & costumes civils & militaires des peuples de l'antiquité, leurs instruments de musique, meubles, & décorations intérieurs de leurs maisons, d'après les monuments antiques 4 livraisons avec 24 planches, par Willemin. Paris an VI.</td></tr>
<tr><td>14</td><td>Arabesques antiques des bains de Livie de la ville Adrienne, avec les plafonds de la ville Madame, peint d'après les desseins de Raphael, & gsavés par de Ponce, à Paris, blos Kupfer.</td></tr>
<tr><td>15</td><td>Les ruines des plus beaux monuments de la Grèce, par M. le Roi, 1758, 2 Bände, Prachtausgabe, mit Kupfern.</td></tr>
<tr><td>15 — 16</td><td>Le loggie di Rafaele Sanctio d'Urbino nel Vaticano, lauter schöne Kupfer.</td></tr>
</table>

A 2

185

Nro.

18 Les ruines de Palmyre, autrement dite Tedmor au defert, à Londres 1753, Prachtausgabe, mit ſchönen Kupfern.

19 Les ruines de Balbec, autrement dite Heliopolis dans la Coeloſyrie, à Londres 1757, Prachtausgabe, mit ſchönen Kupfern.

20 — 24 Voyage pittoresque ou defcription des Royaumes de Naples & de Sicile, à Paris 1781 — 86, Prachtauſg., mit ſchönen Kupf., 2 Bände.

25 Voyage pittoresque de l'Iſtrie & de la Dalmatie, contenant la defcription hiſtorique des monuments, fites, productions, coſtumes, moeurs, & uſages des habitans, & enrichi d'eſtampes, pris ſur les lieux par Caſſas.

26 Voyage pittoresque de la Grèce par Choiſeul - Gouffier, à Paris 1782, Tom. I, Prachtausgabe, mit Kupfern.

27 — 30 Voyage pittoresque des Isles de Sicile, de Malte & de Lipari, par J. Houël, à Paris 1782 — 97, Prachtausgabe, mit ſchönen Kupfern, 4 Bände.

31 Fragments & ornements d'architecture deſſinées à Rome d'après l'antiques, par Moreau, architecte, blos Kupfer.

32 Antichità Romane de tempj della Republica e de' primi Imperatori, da G. B. Piraneſi, blos Kupfer.

33 Darſtellung römiſcher Ruinen, von G. B. Piraneſi, blos Kupfer.

34 Sammlung von antiken Caminen, herausgegeben von G. B. Piraneſi, blos Kupfer.

35 Della magnificenza d'architettura de' Romani, opera di G. B. Piraneſi, mit ſchönen Kupfern.

36 Vitruvio Pollione, de architectura libri dece, tradotti de latino da G. de Ponte 1521, Como, mit Holzſchnitten.

37 J dieci libri della architettura di M. Vitruvio, tradutti e commentati da Monſignor Barbaro. Vinegia 1556, mit Holzſchnitten.

38 M. Vitruvii Pollionis de architectura libri X. Amſterdam 1649, mit Holzſchnitten.

39 Les dix libres d'architecture de Vitruve, édition de M. Perrault, à Paris 1684, avec Eſtampes.

40 L'architettura di M. Vitruvio Pollione, colla traditione Italiana e commentata del Marq. B. Galliani. Napoli 1758, Prachtausgabe, mit Kupfern.

41 Commentaire ſur Vitruve, éclaircis par des figures, par W. Newton, architecte. Londres 1780.

186

Nro.	
42	Les plus beaux monuments de Rome ancienne qui exiſtent encore, deſſinés par Barbault. Rome 1761, mit Kupfern.
43	Della antichità di Ercolano, rappreſentando i bronzi ivi retrovati, mit ſchönen Kupfern.
44	Les Reſtes de l'ancienne Rome, meſurés, deſſinés & graves par B. d'Overbecke, à la Haye 1763, mit Kupfern.
45	Original deſigns in Architecture, conſiſting of Plans, Elevations and ſections for villas, manſions, townhoules &c. by J. Lewis. London 1780, Prachtausgabe.
46 — 47	Les Bâtimens & les deſſeins d'André Palladio, recueillis & illuſtrés par O. B. Scamozzi, 1 Theil Beſchreibung, 1 Theil Kupfer.
48 — 49	The four books of Architecture by A. Palladio, translated from the original Italian by Iſaac Ware. London, 2 Bände, mit Kupfern.
50	Les Bâtimens inedits d'André Palladio, mit Kupfern, Tome I, à Veniſe 1760.
51	Vorſtellung der vornehmſten Gebäude in und um Wien, blos Kupfer.
52	Architecture de Palladio, miſe au jour par J. Leoni, mit ſchönen Kupf.
53	Les quatres livres d'architecture d'André Palladio, mis en françois, à Paris 1650, mit Holzſchnitten.
54	Opere varie di architettura proſpettive, groteſchi, antichità, ſul guſto degli antichi Romani, inventate & inciſe da G. B. Piraneſi. Roma 1750, mit Kupfern.
55	Architecture de Philibert de Lorme, à Paris 1567, avec figures (livre très rare).
56	Nouvelles inventions pour bien baſtir & à petits fraix, par Philibert de l'Orme. Paris 1561 (livre très rare).
57	Manière de bien baſtir pour toutes ſortes de perſonnes, par P. Le Muet, architecte, à Paris 1647, mit Kupfern, (livre très rare).
58	Les oeuvres d'Architecture d'Antoine le Pautre, architecte, à Paris, lauter Kupfer.
59 — 62	Abbildung der Gemählde und Alterthümer aus Herkulanum, herausgegeben von Kilian, mit vielen Kupfern, 1781, 4 Bände.
63	L'Anfiteatro flavio, deſcritto e delineato dal Cavaliere C. Fontana, nell Haia 1725, mit Kupfern.
64 — 65	J. Winkelmann alte Denkmäler der Kunſt aus dem Italiäniſchen, von Fr. K. Brunn. Berlin 1791, 2 Bände, mit vielen Kupfern.

187

Nro.

66 — 67   Oeuvres d'Architecture de M. J. Peyre, ancien penfionaire de l'Académie à Rome, à Paris an IV, 2 Bände, Prachtausgabe.

68   Nuovi difegni dell' architetture e piante di palazzi di Roma de piu celebri architetti, defign. & intagl. da G. B. Falda, lauter Kupfer.

69   Defcription des travaux qui ont procedé, accompagné & fuivi la fonte en bronze d'un feul jet, de la Statue équeftre de Louis XV, à Paris 1768, mit Kupfern.

70   Antiquités de la France par Cleriffeau, architecte, première partie. Paris 1778, mit Kupfern.

71   Collection (fans titre) de 198 planches, contenants les deffeins de divers meubles, & ornements de portes, cheminés, & fenêtres.

72   Befchreibung aller Kirchen-Gebäude der Stadt Danzig, von Bertolt Ranifch, 1695, mit Kupfern.

73   Columna Cochlis, M. Aurelio Antonino dicata. Romae 1704, blos Kupf.

74   Etudes d'architecture de differents maitres Italiens, mifes au jour par Dumont, blos Kupfer.

75   Eglifes des Stations de Rome, & vues de Lyon, Grenoble &c., par Dumont, blos Kupfer.

76   Paralellè de plans des plus belles fales de fpectacle d'Italie & de France, avec des détails de machines theatrales, par Dumont. Paris, mit Kupfern.

77   Oeuvres d'architecture de M. J. Peyre, à Paris 1765, mit Kupfern und Plänen.

78   Mascarade à la Grecque, par Boffi. Parma 1771, blos Kupfer.

79   Architettura della Bafilica di St. Pietro in Vaticano. Roma 1684, mit Kupfern.

80   De la Gueppière architecture, blos Kupfer.

81   Del palazzo de' Cefari, opera poftuma di F. Bianchini. Verona 1738, Prachtausgabe, mit Kupfern.

82   Hotels & maifons de ville en France, blos Kupfer.

83   Sammlung italiänifcher Ruinen und Profpekte, blos Kupfer.

84   Stato prefente degli antichi monumenti Siciliani 1767, mit Kupfern.

85   Romanarum antiquitatum libri X, autore Bartolomaei. Bafel 1583, mit eingedruckten Holzfchnitten.

86   Antiquae urbis Romae fplendor. Romae 1612, mit Kupfern.

188

Nro.	
87	Infigniorum Romae templorum profpectus, curâ de Sandrat. Nürnberg, blos Kupfer.
88	Ruinen und Ueberbleibfel von Athen und andern Gegenden Griechenlands, herausgegeben von R. Sayer in London, aus dem Euglifchen. Augsburg 1782, mit Kupfern.
89	Denkmäler des alten Roms, nach Barbaults Zeichnungen, herausgegeben von Kilian. Augsburg 1767, faft lauter Kupfer.
90	A Series of Plans for Cottages or habitations of the labourer &c., by the late G. Wood, architecte. London 1792, lauter fchöne Kupfer.
91	F. Perrier Darftellung der übrig gebliebenen alten Statüen. Rom, 100 Blatt, ohne Text.
92	Daffelbe Buch nochmals.
93	Die Perspektive des P. Pozzo, mit vielen Kupfern.
94	Traité de la perspective pratique avec des remarques fur l'architecture, par Courtonnne, architecte. Paris 1725, mit vielen Kupfern.
95	Recueil élémentaire d'architecture, compofé par l'architecte de Neuforge, à Paris 1768.
96	Traité des manières de deffiner les ordres de l'architecture antique, par Boffe, à Paris, ganz in Kupfer geftochen.
97	Magazin der Alterthümer, von Ch. F. Prange. Halle 1783, mit Kupfern.
98	Abbildung der Marmorarten, herausgegeben von Wirfing. Nürnberg 1775, mit fchönen nach der Natur illuminirten Probetafeln.
99	Raccolta de Tempj e fepolcri difegnati dell antico da G. B. Montano. Roma 1638, blos Kupfer.
100	Befchreibung der Statüe zu Pferde Friedrichs V. von Dännemark in Coppenhagen, 1774, mit Kupfern.
101	Larven im Innern des Berliner Zeughaufes, nach Schlüters Modellen, von B. Rode, blos Kupfer.
102	Difegne del monte, preffo Caffel 1706, mit Kupfern.
103	Spectacles des vertus, des arts & des fciences repréfentés dans les palais des dieux, a Paris, mit Kupfern.
104	Six livres de divers trophées, contenant divers attributs &c., par J. C. de la Foffe, à Paris, blos Kupfer.
105	Plan, Aufriffe und Durchfchnitte der katholifchen Kirche zu Dresden, vom Architekten Gät. Chiar. Romano. Dresden 1740, blos Kupfer.

189

Nro.

106 Entwurf einer historischen Architektur, in Abbildung unterschiedener berühmter Gebäude des Alterthums und fremder Völker. gezeichnet von Fischer v. Erlachen, meist Kupfer.

107 Ansichten der vorzüglichsten Partien im Garten zu Machern, 1stes Heft.

108 Description des travaux exécutés pour le déplacement, transport & élévation des groupes de Couston, par Grobert, à Paris an IV, (geheftet).

109 L. Ch. Sturms getreue und gründliche Anweisung zu der Civil-Baukunst. Augsburg 1714, mit Kupfern.

110 Description de la grotte de Versailles, à Paris 1679, mit Kupfern.

111 Eigentliche Vorstellung der Kaiserlichen Bibliothek zu Wien, mit Kupfern, 1737.

112 Collection de châteaux & maisons de campagne en France, blos Kupf.

113 Nouvelle Iconologie historique, ou attributs hyeroglophyques de divers oqjets, par J. Ch. de la Fosse. Paris 1768, mit Kupfern.

114 Sale de Spectacle de Bordeaux, par M. Louis, à Paris 1782, mit Kupfern.

115 Prospectum aedium viarumque insigniorum Venetiarum, collectio. 1763, mit Kupfern.

116 Ordonances des cinq espèces de colonnes, selon la méthode des anciens, par M. Perrault. Paris 1683, mit Kupfern.

117 Mahlerische Skizzen von Deutschland, 1stes und 2tes Heft, von Günther und Schlenkert.

118 L. Ch. Sturms Regel des Ebenmaaßes, wie sie zuvörderst an dem Exempel des Tempels Salomons wahrzunehmen. Augsburg 1720, mit Kupfern.

119 Ausführliche Anleitung zur Civil-Baukunst von Weigel. Nürnberg, blos Kupfer.

120 Versuch über die Harmonie der Gebäude zu den Landschaften von J. C. Klinski. Dresden, mit Kupfern.

121 Theoretisch praktische Anweisung zu Schlosser-Arbeiten ꝛc. von Zipper. Augsburg 1795, mit Kupfern.

122 Freudenbezeugung der Stadt Danzig über die Wahl und Krönung Augusts II. von Polen, Gerike, mit Kupfern.

123 Bauanschlag, oder Anweisung zu deren Fertigung von J. F. Penther. Augsburg 1753, mit Kupfern.

124 L.

Nro.	
124	L. Ch. Sturms durch einen großen Theil von Deutschland und den Niederlanden gemachten architektonischen Reise-Anmerkungen. Augsburg 1719, mit Kupfern.
125	Gnomonik von J. Fr. Penther. Augsburg 1734, mit Kupfern.
126	Collection de façades & plans de divers maisons, blos Kupfer.
127	J. R. Fäsch, dito.
128	Ragguaglio delle solenne esequie di Frederico Augusto, Re di polonia, celebrate in Roma 1733, mit Kupfern.
129	Rede über das Verhältniß verschiedener der vornehmsten Städte in Europa, von Langhans, mit Kupfern, 1796.
130	Stetters Säulen-Ordnungen, blos Kupfer.
131	J. B. Taverniers orientalische Reisen. Genf 1681, mit Kupfern.
132	Traité de la construction des Théatres & des machines théatrales, par M. Rubo le fils, Maitre menusier. Paris 1777.

In Quarto.

1 — 2	Traité du beau Essentiel dans les beaux arts, avec les cinq ordres d'architecture, par C. E. Briseux, architecte, ganz, auch der Text, in Kupfer.
3	Cours d'architecture, qui comprend les ordres de Vignole avec des commentaires, par P. J. Mariette. Paris 1750, mit Kupfern.
4 — 5	Des M. Vitruvii Pollio Baukunst, aus dem Lateinischen, von A. Rode. Leipzig 1796, 2 Bände.
6	J dieici libri di architettura di Leon Watt. Alberti, tradotti in Ital. da Cos. Bartoli, 1784, mit Kupfern.
7	M. Vitruvii Pollionis de architectura libri X, Argentorati, 1550, mit Holzschnitten.
8	Idea d'un teatro, nello principali sue parti, opera d'Andrea Palladio. Vicenza 1762, mit Kupfern.
9	Principes de l'ordonnance & de la construction des bâtimens, avec des recherches sur le nouveau pont de Paris construit par Perronet, par Ch. F. Viel. Paris 1797.
10	Dissertation sur les dégradations survenues au piliers du dôme du panthéon françois, & sur les moyens d'y remedier, par E. M. Gauthey. Paris an VI.

B

11   Mémoire historique sur le dôme du panthéon françois, par J. Roudelet.

12   Mémoire sur l'application des principes de la Mécanique à la construction des voutes & des dômes, relatifs au panthéon françois, avec divers pièces concernant cet objet, par Gauthey, 1771.

13   Etudes d'architecture par P. Patte, architecte. Paris, lauter schöne Kupfer.

14   Recueil de principes élémentaires de peinture, sur l'expression des passions, ou Extrait des oeuvres de Ch. Lebrun, Winkelmann, Mengs, Wattelet &c. Paris an V.

15 — 16   Des Gr. Caylus Sammlung von Egyptischen, Hetrurischen, Griechischen und Römischen Alterthümern, aus dem Französischen. Nürnberg 1766, 1 Band Schrift, 1 Band Kupfer.

17   Recueil d'antiquités dans les Gaules, ouvrage qui peut servir de suite aux antiquités du comte de Caylus, par de Sauvagere. Paris 1770, mit Kupfern.

18   Regles des cinq ordres d'architecture de Vignole, par de la Gardette, architecte. Paris an V, mit Kupfern.

19 — 20   Des Gr. Caylus Abhandlungen zur Geschichte der Künste, aus dem Französischen übersetzt von Meusel, nebst einer Vorrede von Klotz, mit Kupfern. Altenburg 1768.

21   J. Winkelmanns Sendschreiben von den Herkulanischen Entdeckungen. Dresden 1762.

22   Anmerkungen über die Baukunst der Alten, entworfen von J. Winkelmann. Leipzig 1762.

23   J. Winkelmanns Abhandlung von der Fähigkeit der Empfindung des Schönen in der Kunst, und dem Unterrichte in derselben. Dresden 1771.

24   L'art de peindre, poëme avec des réflexions sur les différentes parties de la peinture, par Wattelet. Paris 1760.

25   Roma sotteranea, opera postuma di Ant. Bosio Romano. Romae 1650, mit Kupfern.

26   Ueber die Gemmenkunde, von J. Gurlitt. Magdeburg 1798.

27   Ueber Erfindung, Construktion und Vortheile der Bohlendächer, von D. Gilly. Berlin 1797, mit Kupfern, Velinpapier.

28   Zergliederung der Schönheit, die schwankenden Begriffe von dem Geschmack festzusetzen, von W. Hogarth, aus dem Englischen. Berlin 1754, mit Kupfern.

Nro.	
29	F. C. v. Cancrin praktische Anweisung wie Decken durch neue Spreng- und Hängwerke zu bauen; nebst Beschreibung und Abbildung eines Exercier-Hauses, mit Kupfern. Gießen 1796.
30	Diarium Italicum, five monumentorum veterum notitiae fingulares. Paris 1702, mit Kupfern.
31	Gedanken über die Nachahmung der griechischen Werke in der Mahlerey und Bildhauerkunst, von J. Winkelmann. Dresden 1756.
32	Die Gottesdienstlichen Alterthümer der Obotriten, aus dem Tempel zu Rhetra am Tollenzer See, von D. Wogen, mit vielen Kupfern. (ungeb.)
33 — 35	Briefe über Rom ꝛc., von Chr. Fr. Weinlig, mit Kupfern und den dazu gehörenden Prospekten, 3 Bände.
36	Pianta esteriore e spaccato del nouvo teatro di Reggio di Lombardia.
37	Ausführliche Anleitung zu der Civil-Baukunst nach Vignola und Mich. Angelo, von L. Chr. Sturm. Augsburg 1725, mit Kupfern.
38	Vues de Versailles, gravées sur les desseins au naturel, par G. Swidda.
39	Beschreibung des alten Athens, und dessen Schicksalen in der bürgerlichen Verfassung und den Wissenschaften, nebst Grund- und Aufrissen, 1794.
40	Méthode pour apprendre le dessein, par Ch. A. Joubert. Paris 1754, mit vielen Kupfern.
41	La théorie & la pratique du Jardinage. Paris 1747, mit Kupfern.
42	Zieglers Beantwortung der Preisfrage, über die Ursachen der Festigkeit alter Römischer und Gothischer Gebäude, und die Mittel, gleiche Dauerhaftigkeit bey einem Mauerwerke zu erhalten. Berlin 1776.
43	Perspectiva practica, oder vollständige Anleitung zur Perspektiv-Reißkunst, von J. Ch. Rembold. Augsburg 1710.
44	Das Zeichnen, und die damit verwandten Künste, aus dem Französischen übersetzt von Mehes, 1ster Theil, mit Kupfern. Breslau 1798.
45	Gerh. de Lairesse Grundlegung zur Zeichenkunst. Nürnberg 1727, m. Kupf.
46 — 47	G. de Lairesse großes Mahlerbuch. Nürnberg 1728, mit vielen Kupfern, 2 Bände.
48	Raccolta de' varj ornati, da L. Zuchi. Lipf. 1743, lauter Kupfer.
49	Collection de divers plans & façades (sans titre, sehr alt).
50	Der römische Carneval, von Göthe, mit illuminirten Kupfern.
51	Praktische Anweisung zur Pastelmahlerey, von Günther. Nürnberg 1762.
52	Ueber den Raub der Cassandra, auf einem alten Gefäße von gebrannter Erde, 2 Abhandl. von H. Meyer und Böttcher, m. K. Weimar 1794.

193

Nro.

53 Manuſkript mit vielen Handzeichnungen; Pizlers Reiſe-Beſchreibung durch Deutſchland, Holland, Niederlande, Frankreich und Italien, 1685.

54 Ueber theoretiſche und praktiſche Zeichenkunſt, mit Kupfern. Königsberg 1799.

55 Oſſervazioni iſtorico-architettoniche ſopra il panthéon, da L. Hirt. Roma 1791.

56 G. Chr. Adler ausführliche Beſchreibung der Stadt Rom, mit Kupfern. Altona 1781.

57 A Treatiſe of theatres, by G. Sacenders. London 1790, mit Kupfern.

58 Sammlung landſchaftlicher Darſtellung der ſchönſten Landſitze und Parks in England.

59 Beſchreibung des Gartens zu Machern, mit Kupfern. Berlin 1789.

60 Ueber die Mahlerey der Alten, ein Beytrag zur Geſchichte der Kunſt, von Rode und Riem. Berlin 1788, mit Kupfern.

61 Coſtüme der älteſten Völker von Dandré Bardon, aus dem Engliſchen, 4 Hefte, jedes mit 1 Kupfer.

62 Avis aux ouvriers en fer, ſur la fabrication de l'acier, publié par ordre du comité de ſalut publique, mit Kupfern.

63 Piſé, or the art of building ſtrong and durable walls, with nothing but earth, by H. Holland.

64 Briefe über die Kunſt, an eine Freundin, vom Herrn zu Racknitz. Dresden 1792.

65 Inland navigation, or ſelect plans of the ſeveral navigable canals troughout Great Brittain, mit Kupfern.

66 — 68 Hiſtoire de l'art de l'antiquité, par M. Winkelmann, traduit de l'allemand par Huber. Lipſ. 1781, 3 Bände.

69 Praktiſche Anleitung zur Conſtruktion der Faſchinenwerke an Flüſſen und Strömen, von J. A. Eytelwein. Berlin 1800, mit Kupfern.

70 Verſuch einer Numismatik für Künſtler, oder Vorſchriften wie auf alle Fälle Münzen im römiſchen Geſchmack zu entwerfen, von G. Uhlich. Lemberg 1792.

71 Il foreſtiere iſtruito delle coſe più rare di architettura &c. della città di Vicenza, da O. B. Scamozzi. Vicenza 1761, mit Kupfern.

72 De af beeldinge der voornaamſten gebouwen van Amſterdam, door P. Schenk, blos Kupfer.

194

Nro.	
73	Projet d'un monument consacré a l'histoire naturelle, dedié à M. le C. de Buffon.
74	Eigentliche Beschreibung des Doms zu Magdeburg, 1720, mit Holzschn.
75	Vollständiger Lehrbegriff der Optik nach R. Smiths, von A. G. Kästner. Altenburg 1755.
76 — 82	Sammlung nützlicher Aufsätze und Nachrichten die Baukunst betreffend, für angehende Baumeister und Freunde der Architektur, mit Kupfern.
83 — 84	Voyage d'Egypte & de Nubie, par F. L. Norden, Paris an III, zwey Bände, mit schönen Kupfern.
85	Description de l'Arabie, par C. Niebuhr. Amsterdam 1774, m. Kupf.
86	Voyage de M. Shaw dans la Barbarie & le Levant, aus dem Englischen.
87	Relation d'un voyage fait au Levant, par du Thevenot. Paris 1665.
88 — 89	Keyßlers Reise durch Deutschland, die Schweiz, Italien :c. Hannover 1776, 2 Bände, mit Kupfern.
90 — 92	Richard Pocokes Reise nach dem Morgenlande, aus dem Englischen. Erlangen 1754, mit Kupfern, 3 Bände.
93	Description du Théâtre de Vincence. Paris 1780, mit Kupfern.
94 — 95	Handbuch der Landbaukunst, von D. Gilly. Berlin 1798, mit illuminirten Kupfern, Velinpapier.

In Octavo.

1	An essay on the construction and building of chimneys, including an enquiry into the common causes of their smoking, by R. Clavering, mit 1 Kupfer.
2	Traité d'architecture par Monroy. Paris 1785, mit Kupfern.
3	The builders Price book. London 1796.
4	Versuch einiger Beyträge über die Baukunst, von C. v. Dalberg. Erfurt 1792.
5	Geschichte der Baukunst der Alten, von Ch. L. Stieglitz. Leipzig 1792.
6	Vitruvii Architektur, ins Kurze gefaßt von Perrault, übersetzt von Müller. Nürnberg 1757, mit Kupfern.
7	M. Vitruvii Pollionis de architectura libri X. Florentiae 1522, mit Holzschnitten.

195

Nro.	
8	Architecture générale de Vitruve, reduite en abrégé par Perrault. Amsterdam 1681, mit Kupfern.
9 — 11	Milizia Grundsätze der bürgerlichen Baukunst, aus dem Italiänischen. Leipzig, 3 Bände.
12	Observations sur les ombres colorées, à Paris 1782.
13	J. H. Lamberts freye Perspektive. Zürch 1774, mit Kupfern.
14	J. H. Lamberts kurzgefaßte Regel zu perspektivischen Zeichnungen, vermittelst eines Proportional-Zirkels. Augsburg 1772, mit Kupfern.
15	J. H. Lamberts freye Perspektive. Zürch 1759.
16	Lamberts Grundregeln der Perspektive, herausgegeben von Hindenburg. Leipzig 1799, mit 1 Kupfer.
17	Gründliche Anweisung zur Perspektive, von A. Bürja.
18	Der Transparentspiegel, oder Beschreibung eines neuen Instruments zum Zeichnen, von C. B. Meyer. Aurich 1789, mit 1 Kupfer.
19	Versuch die mathematischen Regeln der Perspektive für den Künstler ohne Theorie anwendbar zu machen, von Mönnich. Berlin 1794, m. Kupf.
20 — 24	Dasselbe Werk noch fünfmal, ungebunden.
25	Versuch einer Erläuterung der Reliefs-Perspektive, von Breysig. Magdeburg 1798.
26	Skizzen, Gedanken, Entwürfe ꝛc. die bildenden Künste betreffend, von Breysig. Magdeburg 1799, mit 1 Kupfer.
27	Briefe über die mahlerischen Perspektive, von Horstig. Leipzig 1797, mit Kupfern.
28 — 29	Handbuch der Aesthetik, von J. H. G. Heusinger. Gotha 1797, 2 Bände.
30	Briefe ästhetischen Inhalts, mit Hinsicht auf die Kantsche Theorie, von Schmidt Phiseldek. Altona 1797.
31	Ueber Anmuth und Würde, an C. v. Dalberg in Briefen, von Schiller. Leipzig 1793.
32	System der Aesthetik, 1ster Band, von Heidenreich. Leipzig 1790.
33 — 34	Charis, oder über das Schöne und die Schönheit in den nachbildenden Künsten, von Ramdohr. Leipzig 1793, 2 Bände.
35 — 36	Archibald Alison, über den Geschmack, verdeutsche und mit Anmerkungen von Heidenreich. Leipzig 1792, 2 Bände.
37 — 40	Allgemeine Theorie der schönen Künste, von J. G. Sulzer. Leipzig 1786, 4 Bände.

196

136

197

58 Unterſuchung über den Charakter der Gebäude, und über die Verbindung der Baukunſt mit den ſchönen Künſten. Leipzig 1788, mit Kupfern.

59 Les loix des bâtiments, ſuivant la coutume de Paris, conſeignées par M. Desgodets. Paris 1787.

60 Meiſters Abhandlungen über die Pyramiden. Frankfurt 1781, mit 1 Kupfer.

61 Ueber den Gebrauch der Grotesken und Arabesken. Leipzig 1790.

62 J. Howards Nachrichten von den vorzüglichſten Krankenhäuſern in Europa, aus dem Engliſchen. Leipzig 1791, mit Kupfern.

63 Abbildung und Beſchreibung eines engliſchen Milchhauſes, mit 1 Kupfer. Leipzig.

64 Anfangsgründe der mechaniſchen Wiſſenſchaften, von Fiſcher, mit Kupfern. Jena 1793.

65 Gedanken von den Urſachen, Wachsthum und Verfall der Verzierungen in ſchönen Künſten. Leipzig 1759.

66 Conſidérations ſur les arts du deſſein en France, par Quatremere de Quincy. Paris 1791.

67 Procès de la première ſéance du Jury des arts, nommé par la convention nationale an II.

68 Ueber die chineſiſchen Gärten, eine Abhandlung, 1773.

69 Deſcription hiſtorique & chronologique des monuments de ſculpture, réunis au muſée des monuments françois, par A. Lenoir, à Paris an V.

70 Abhandlung von den Odeender Alten. Leipzig 1767.

71 Beſchreibung alter Denkmäler in allen Theilen der Erde, von C. Meiners. Nürnberg 1786.

72 Ueber den Theater-Vorhang im Charlottenburger Schauſpielhauſe. Berlin 1791.

73 Ueber die Wegführung der Kunſtwerke aus den eroberten Ländern nach Rom, von Völkel. Leipzig 1798.

74 Ueber die Mittel gegen die Verletzung öffentlicher Anlagen und Zierrathen. Berlin 1792.

75 Herzens-Ergießungen eines Kunſtliebenden Kloſterbruders. Berlin 1797.

76 Recherches ſur la préparation que les Romains donnoient à la chaux, par de la Faye. Paris 1777.

77 Mémoire pour ſervir de ſuite au livre precédent. Paris 1778.

78 Ueber

198

Nro.	
78	Ueber Leichenhäuser, als Gegenstand der schönen Baukunst, von J. Atzel, mit Kupfern. Stuttgard 1796.
79	Kurze Einleitung in die römischen Antiquitäten, von Schatzen. Büdingen 1726.
80	Anthusa, oder Roms Alterthümer, von C. Ph. Moritz. Berlin 1791.
81	J. C. E. Winken antiquarische Anmerkungen über ein altes schätzbares zu Quedlinburg aufbewahrtes Gefäß. Leipzig 1761.
82	Essai sur la Peinture en Mosaïque. Paris 1768.
83	Anweisung zur Verfertigung und Gebrauch des allgemeinen Zeichen-Instruments ohne Gläser, mit Kupfern. Ansbach 1780.
84	Neue Manier Kupferstiche von verschiedenen Farben zu verfertigen, nach Art der Zeichnungen, von Bylärt, aus dem Französischen, mit Kupfern. Amsterdam 1773.
85	Vermuthungen über die Barberini, jetzt Portland Vase. Helmstädt 1791.
86	De la composition des paysages sur le terrain, par Gerardin. Genève 1777.
87	Raph. Mengs Gedanken über die Schönheit und den Geschmack in der Mahlerey. Zürch 1774.
88	C. L. Junker Grundsätze der Mahlerey. Zürch 1775.
89 — 90	Direzioni à giovani studenti nel disegno dell' architettura civile, da F. G. Bibiena. Bologna 1745, mit Kupfern, 2 Bände.
91	Krubsacius wahrscheinlicher Entwurf von des jüngern Plinius Landhaus und Garten. Leipzig 1768, und über die Orientalische Gartenkunst, aus dem Englischen. Gotha 1775.
92	C. R. Reinhold Akademie der bildenden schönen Künste. Osnabrück 1788, mit Kupfern.
93	Entwurf einer Geschichte der zeichnenden schönen Künste, von A. Fr. Büsching. Hamburg 1781.
94	Versuche über die Architektur, Mahlerey, und musikalische Oper, aus dem Italiänischen des Gr. Algarotti. Cassel 1769.
95	D'Arclais de Montamy Abhandlung von den Farben zum Porcellain und Emailmahlen. Leipzig 1767.
96	Theorie der Verbreitung des Schalles für Baukünstler, von Rhode. Berlin 1800.
97 — 98	Betrachtungen über die Mahlerey. Leipzig 1762, 2 Bände.

C

In Octavo.

99	Kurzgefaßtes Handwörterbuch über die schönen Künste. Leipzig 1795, 2ter Band.
100	Fr. Junius von der Mahlerey der Alten, aus dem Lateinischen. Breslau 1770.
101	Versuch über das Alter der Oelmahlerey, von v. Budberg. Göttingen 1792.
102	Dictionaire portatif des beaux arts, par Lacombe. Paris 1753.
103	Dictionaire portatif de peinture, sculpture & gravure avec un traité practique des differentes manières de peindre, par A. J. Pernetti, à Paris 1757, mit Kupfern.
104—105	Handbuch der römischen Alterthümer, entworfen von Alex. Adam, aus dem Englischen, von Meyer. Erlangen 1796, mit Kupfern, 2 Bände.
106—107	Vies des fameux architectes depuis la renaissance des arts, par Dazincourt. Paris 1787, 2 Bände.
108	Verzeichniß der Casselschen Gemählde-Sammlung. 1783.
109	J. S. Semlers Erläuterung der egyptischen Alterthümer. Leipzig 1796.
110	Chr. Cellarii compendium antiquitatum romanarum, auctore Walchio. Halle 1748.
111	D'Alembert Abhandlung von dem Ursprung, Fortgange und Verbindung der Künste und Wissenschaften, aus dem Französischen. Zürch 1763.
112	A catalogue of the pictures in the Shakespear-Gallery. London 1796.
113	Laokoon, oder über die Grenzen der Mahlerey und Poesie, von G. E. Lessing. Berlin 1766.
114	Recherches historiques sur la nature & l'étendue d'un ancien ouvrage des Romains, appelé communement: Briquetage de Marsal. Paris 1740, mit Kupfern.
115	Recueil historique de la vie & des ouvrages des plus celebres architectes, par Felibien. Loudon 1705.
116	Kritische Anmerkungen, den Zustand der Baukunst in Berlin und Potsdam betreffend. Berlin 1776.
117	Ueber den großen Tempel und die Statue des Jupiters zu Olympia, von L. Völkel. Leipzig 1794.
118	Von der Puzzolane und deren Gebrauch bey den Bauanlagen, aus dem Französischen. Dresden 1784, mit Kupfern.
119	Geschichte des Luxus der Athenienser von den ältesten Zeiten bis auf den Tod Philipps von Macedonien, von C. Meiners. Lemgo 1782.

Nro.	
120	Einleitung in das Studium der alten Kunstwerke für Künstler und Kunstliebhaber, von P. F. A. Nitsch. Leipzig 1792.
121	M. J. Daums Schilderer und Mahler, herausgegeben von E. Bertram. Leipzig 1755.
122	G. Ch. M. v. Eilano ausführliche Abhandlung der römischen Alterthümer, herausgegeben von G. Ch. Adler. Altona 1775, mit Kupfern, 1r B.
123—126	Dasselbe Buch complett, in 4 Bände.
127	Ueber den Nutzen und Gebrauch der alten geschnittenen Steine und ihrer Abdrücke, von Kloß. Altenburg 1768.
128	Traité de la peinture en migniature. A la Haye 1708.
129—130	Beschreibung des Zustandes der Römer, nach den verschiedenen Zeitaltern der Nation, von Nitsch. Erfurt 1790.
131	Scythische Denkmäler in Palestina, von E. Fr. Cramer. Hamburg 1777.
132	Commentatiuncula de arcubus triumphalibus. Lips.
133	Justi Lipsii de amphiteatro liber. Antwerpen 1584.
134	Justi Rycquii de Capitolio Romano Commentarius. Lugd. Batav. 1696.
135	Traité de la construction des chemins. Paris 1722, mit Kupfern.
136	Nitsch Beschreibung des Zustandes der Griechen. Frankfurt 1791, 1ster Theil.
137	Reise des Gr. Choiseul-Gouffier durch Griechenland, aus dem Französischen, mit Kupfern und Carten, 1ster Band.
138—140	Moritz Reise nach Italien in 1786 — 88. Berlin 1792, 3 Bände.
141	Description du Colisée, elevée aux champs Elysées sur les desseins de M. de Camus, à Paris 1771.
142	Beschreibung aller Seltenheiten der Kunst und übrigen Alterthümer in Charlottenburg. Berlin 1768.
143	Promenade ou Itineraire des jardins d'Ermenonville, à Paris 1788, mit schönen savirten Kupfern.
143	La vera antichità di Pozzuolo, descritta da G. C. Cappaccio. Roma 1652, mit Kupfern.
143	Julii Caesaris Portus Iccius. Illustratus auctoribus Somnero & du Fresne. Oxonii 1694.
144	Erklärung eines Plans von Sanssouci.
145	Description de l'hôtel de ville d'Amsterdam, mit Kupfern.

202

Nro.	
174	H. M. A. Cramers Nachrichten zur Geschichte der Herkulanischen Entdeckung. Halle 1773.
175	Bonnor's copper - Plate perspective Itinerary, lauter schöne Kupfer. London 1796 (im Futteral).
176	Beschreibung des grünen Gewölbes, oder der Schatzkammer zu Dresden, und der Schatzkammer zu Wien. Leipzig 1786.
177—178	Beschreibung von Berlin und Potsdam. Berlin 1786, 2 Bände.
179	Anhang zur Beschreibung von Berlin und Potsdam, welcher Nachrichten von den dortigen Künstlern enthält. Berlin 1786.
180	Le guide ou nouvelle description d'Amsterdam, 1772, mit Kupfern.
181	A pittoresque tour troughout a part of Europe, Asia and Africa. London 1793, (Velinpapier) mit schönen Kupfern.
182—183	Guide des amateurs & des étrangers voyageurs, à Paris 1788, 2 B.
184	Lamotte Vorschläge zur Abfuhr der Unreinigkeiten von den Straßen in einer großen Stadt.
185	Einige Vorschläge dem Holzmangel abzuhelfen, vorzüglich durch Einführung der Lehmbacksteinhäuser, von Siegling 1795.
186—187	Le guide de ceux qui veulent bâtir, par le Camus de Meziéres, architecte. Paris, 2 Bände.
188	An essay of vertical and horizontal Windmills, by R. Beatson. London 1798, mit Kupfern.
189	The manner of securing all sorts of buildings from fire. London.
190	Lettres à M. Bailly, sur l'histoire primitive de la Gréce, par Rabaut St. Etienne. Paris 1787.
191	L'origine dell academia olimpica di Vicenza, con una breve descrizione del suo teatro, opera di Scamozzi. Vincenza 1790, m. K.
192	Historische Erklärung der Gemählde, welche Herr G. Winkler in Leipzig gesammelt, 1768.
193—194	Lettres familiéres de M. Winkelmann (schöne Ausgabe). Amsterdam 1781, 2 Bände.
195	Neues mythologisches Wörterbuch, von P. F. A. Nitsch, 1793.
196	Essai sur les lieux & les dangers des sépultures dans les villes.
197—198	Grundriß einer schönen Stadt. Hamburg 1776, 2 Bände.
199	Sépulture des anciens, par Olivier. Marseille 1771.
200	Versuch über den Geschmack in der Baukunst. Leipzig 1788.

203

In Octavo.

204

Nro.	
239	Winkelmanns Briefe an seinen Freund. Berlin 1781.
240	De l'utilité de joindre à l'étude de l'architecture celle des sciences & des arts, par Blondel. Paris 1771.
241	Die Baukunst der Alten. Ein Handbuch für Freunde der Kunst, von Stieglitz. Leipzig 1796, mit Kupfern.
242	Abhandlung über die alten Denkmäler der Kunst, von Casanowa, aus dem Italiänischen. Leipzig 1771.
243	Introduction à l'étude des pierres gravées, par A. L. Millin. Paris an IV.
244	Ueber Verzierung gymnastischer Uebungsplätze durch Kunstwerke in antiken Geschmack, von Böttcher. Weimar 1795, mit Kupfern.
245	Handbuch zum Gebrauch bey Vorlesungen über die Geschichte der Litteratur und der Kunst, von Dahler. Jena 1788.
246—247	J. Gillies's Geschichte von Alt-Griechenland, aus dem Englischen. Leipzig 1787, 2 Bände.
248—249	Pausanias Reisebeschreibung von Griechenland, aus dem Griechischen übersetzt, und erläutert von Goldhagen. Leipzig 1766, 2 Bände.
250	Observations sur l'architecture, par l'abbé Laugier. A la Haye 1765.
251	J. Kants Kritik der Urtheilskraft. Berlin 1790.

Klein Format.

1	Les Jardins, ou l'art d'embellir les paysages, poëme par l'abbé de Lille, à Paris 1782.
2	Abgebildetes altes Rom, aus dem Italiänischen. Arnheim 1662, m. K.
3	— — neues Rom, — — — — — — —1662, m. K.
4	— — unterirrdisches — — — — — — —1662, m. K.
5 — 7	Le voyageur à Paris, tableau pittoresque & moral. Paris an V, 3 Bände.
8	Dissertation sur un monument antique, découvert à Lyon en 1704, mit 1 Kupfer. Lyon 1731.
9	Mythologischer Almanach für Damen, herausgegeben von Moritz. Berlin 1792, mit Kupfern.
10	Notice des desseins originaux, cartons, gouaches du musée central des arts, première partie. An V.

205

Klein Format.

11 Annuaire du Lycée des Arts. Pour l'an III. Paris.

12 — — — — — — — IV. —

13 Exposition des Tapisseries des gobelins, porcellaines de Severs à St. Cloud, & description des tableaux existans au château de St. Cloud. Paris an V.

14 Antiquitatum graecarum praecipue atticarum brevis descriptio, autore L. Bos. Bern 1716.

Kupferstiche.

Blatt.

1 Darstellung antiker Gegenstände, von Piranesi.   12

2 Abbildung antiker Vasen.   12

3 Recueil de Vases, d'ornements, & de figures, tirées de l'antique par Willemin.   66

4 Verschiedene Blätter aus Montfaucon antiq. expl.   39

5 Darstellung diverser antiker Gegenstände.   64

6 Aus den in Nürnberg herausgekommenen Herkulanischen Alterthümern.   21

7 Die berühmte Meduse des Solon, von einer Gemme ins Große gebracht, vom Ritter Hier. Odam.   1

8 Antike Gemmen und Münzen.   14

9 Darstellung der Ruinen von Pästum, von Jollis gezeichnet und Morghen gestochen.   5

10 Illuminirte Prospekte aus dem Innern der Ruinen der Villa des Hadrians zu Tivoli.   2

11 Eine geheftete Sammlung mit der Feder gezeichneter und etwas ausgetuschter Landschaften, nach der Natur gezeichnet.

12 Veduta della porta di Levante, von F. Morghen.   1

13 Darstellung von Ruinen und architektonischen Ornamenten, meistens von St. Non radirt.   35

14 Darstellung der Egyptischen Pyramiden und des Sphinxes von Gissa.   2

15 Arc d'Orange, von Mignard gestochen.   1

16 Miscellanea per i Giovani studiosi del disegno, publicata da Gioc. Albertoli. Milano 1796, vorzügliche   20

17 Dar

Kupferstiche.

D

207

208

Kupferstiche.

209

D 2

Kupferstiche.

84 | Desseins des meilleures peintures des Pays-Bas, d'Allema-
gne & d'Italie, gravé par Prestel, ganz vorzügliche Sammlung von bunten 12

85 | Ein Heft Plane und Prospekte aus italiänischen Städten. .

210

Anhang.

212

In Quarto.

Nro.	
1 — 2	Homers Iliade, übersetzt von J. H. Voß. Altenburg 1793, 2 Bände.
3 — 4	— Odyssee, — — — — — — — 2 Bände.
5	Schreiben des Ritters v. Hamilton an die Akademie zu London, über das Erdbeben in Calabrien und Sicilien, aus dem Französischen. Strasburg 1784.
6	Recueil de questions proposées à une société de savants, qui par ordre du Roi de Dannemark font le voyage de l'Arabie, traduit de l'allemand. Amsterdam 1774.
7	J. Jansen Struys Reysen door Italien, Griekenlandt, Oost-Indien. Amsterdam 1676, mit Kupfern.
8 — 9	Histoire de la milice françoise depuis l'établissement de la monarchie françoise, jusqu'à la fin du règne de Louis le Grand, par Daniel. Amsterdam 1724, mit Kupfern, 2 Bände.
10	Onuphrii Panvinii Romanorum principum & eorum quorum maxima in Italia imperia fuerunt, libri 4. Basel 1558.
11	Onuphrii Panvinii Reipublicae Romanae commentariorum, libri 3. Francof. 1597.
12	Stollens Anleitung zur Historie der Gelahrtheit. Jena 1724.
13	Commodiani, poetae Christiani, Instructiones. Vitemb. 1705.

In Octavo.

1	Griechisches Lesebuch für die ersten Anfänger, von Gedike. Berlin 1791.
2	Anfangsgründe der griechischen Sprache, entworfen von J. G. Trendelenburg. Leipzig 1790.
3	Italiänisches Lese- und Wörterbuch, von Leonini. Berlin 1797.
4	Gedichte, aus dem Griechischen übersetzt von Chr. Gr. zu Stollberg. Hamburg 1782.

214

Nro.	
5	Q. Horatii, Eclogae, cura Gesneri. Lipf. 1772.
6	Schellers ausführliche lateinische Sprachlehre. Leipzig 1790.
7	Nieuport rituum Romanorum explicatio. Berol. 1767.
8	Anleitung zur Kenntniß der allgemeinen Welt- und Völkergeschichte für Studirende, von Ch. D. Beck.
9	Veneroni, italiänischer Sprachmeister. Frankfurt 1789.
10	Réponse au livre de M. de Maux. intitulé conference avec M. Claude, Miniftre de Charenton. A la Haye 1683.
11	Einige in Kupfer gestochene Handschriften.
12	Entwurf eines historischen Gemähldes der Fortschritte des menschlichen Geistes. Nachlaß von Condorcet, übersetzt von Poffelt. Tübingen 1796.
13 — 14	Effais fur le Département de la Seine inférieure. Paris an III, zwey Bände.
15	Vues générales fur l'Italie, Malte, & les limites de la France à la rive droite du Rhin. Paris an V.
16	J. E. Fisch Reise durch das mittägliche Frankreich vor der Revolution. Zürch 1795.
17	Historisch- und politische Abschilderung der englischen Manufakturen, Handlung, Schiff-fahrt und Colonien, von J. W. Taube. Wien 1774.
18 — 20	G. Jars Metallurgische Reisen. Berlin 1777, 2ter, 3ter und 4ter Band.
21 — 22	Voyage hiftorique d'Italie. A la Haye 1729, 2 Bände.
23	Die Bestimmung des Menschen, von Fichte. Berlin 1800.
24 — 25	Reise durch einigen Provinzen Englands, von Wendeborn. Hamburg 1793, 2 Bände.
26 — 29	Der Zustand von Großbritanien, gegen das Ende des 18ten Jahrhunderts. Berlin 1785 — 88, von Wendeborn, 4 Bände.
30 — 33	Géographie hiftorique & littéraire de la France, pas Lamésangère.
34 — 38	C. Plinius Secundus Naturgeschichte, übersetzt von G. Groffe. Frankfurt 1781 — 1787, 5 Bände.
39 — 41	Géographie ancienne abrégée par M. d'Anville, avec Cartes. Paris 1768, 3 Bände.
42	Weltgeschichte nach ihren Haupttheilen im Auszuge und Zusammenhange, von A. L. Schlözer. Göttingen 1785.

43 Die

Nro.	
43	Die symbolische Weisheit der Egypter, aus den verborgensten Denkmälern des Alterthums, herausgegeben von C. Ph. Moritz. Berlin 1793.
44	C. Plinii Secundi historiae mundi, libri 37 ex editione J. Dalechampii. Francof. 1608.
45	Orbis antiqui monumentis suis illustrati primae lineae. J. J. Oberlilinus. Argent. 1790.
46	Handbuch für Reisende aus allen Ständen, nebst Carten. Leipzig 1d84.
47	Beschreibung des Einzuges Friedrich Wilhelm II. in Ansbach. Nürnberg 1792.
48	Kurzer Entwurf der alten Geographie. Leipzig 1789.
49 — 50	P. Septimins, oder, das letzte Geheimniß des Eleusinischen Priesters, von Bouterwek. Halle 1795, 2 Bände.
51	Ansichten vom Niederrhein ꝛc., von G. Forster. Berlin 1791.
52 — 54	Geschichte des Verfalls und Unterganges des Römischen Reichs, abgekürzt nach Gibbon, aus dem Englischen, 1790, 3 Bände.
55 — 62	Histoire des empereurs romains depuis Auguste jusqu'à Constantin, par M. Crevier. Dresde 1750, 8 Bände.
63	Ueber alte und neue Mysterien. Berlin 1782.
64	Description du parc de Berlin. Berlin 1792.
65	Mémoires sur les eaux minérales & les établissements Thermaux des Pyrénées. Paris an III.
66	Geschichte der Schiffbrüche der berühmtesten Seefahrer, aus dem Französischen, 1ster Band. Berlin 1791.
67 — 68	N. Bailey englisch-deutsch und deutsch englisch Wörterbuch. Leipzig 1796, 2 Bände.
69	J. Ch. Gatterers Versuch einer allgemeinen Weltgeschichte, bis zur Entdeckung Amerika's. Göttingen 1792.
70	Fragmente über Italien, aus dem Tagebuche eines jungen Deutschen, 1ster Band, 1798.
71	Chemische Grundsätze der Gewerbkunde, entworfen von J. F. Gmelin. Hanover 1795.
72	Handbuch der klassischen Litteratur, von Eschenburg. Berlin 1787.
73	Neue Reise durch Italien, von Fr. Schulz. Berlin 1797.
74	Litterarische Chronik. Bern 1786, 2ter Band.

215

Nro.	
75	Anfangsgründe der Naturlehre, entworfen von Erxleben, mit Zusätzen von Lichtenberg. Göttingen 1784, mit Kupfern.
76	S. Geßners Schriften, zter Band.
77	The school for scandal, a comedy by Sheridan. Berlin 1790.
78 — 84	J. A. B. Bergstraß. rs Real-Wörterbuch über die klassischen Schriftsteller der Griechen und Römer. Halle 1772, 7 Bände, bis Equus.
85	Remarks ou several parts of Italy, by J. Addison. Glasgow 1754, mit 1 Kupfer.
86 — 91	Osservazioni letterarie d'Italia. Verona 1737, 6 Bände, mit Kupfern.
92 — 93	Hamburgische Dramaturgie, von G. L. Lessing, 2 Bände.
94	Diodori Siculi Bibliothecae historicae libri XV. reliqui. Hannoviae 1611.
95	Leggiadrie dello stile Italiano, o sia raccolta di pezzi scelti de più eccelenti scrittori, publ. da Mertens, 1778.
96 — 99	J. G. Krügers Naturlehre, mit Kupfern und Register. Halle 1771, 4 B.
100	Dillenius griechisch-deutsches Wörterbuch für die Jugend. Leipzig 1784.
101	C. Salustii Crispi quae extant opera. Paris 1774.
102—104	C. Cornelii Taciti quae extant opera. Recensuit Lallemand. Paris 1760, 3 Bände.
105	J. P. Millers Grundsätze einer weisen und christlichen Erziehungskunst. Göttingen 1771.
106	Betrachtungen zur Veredlung des menschlichen Herzens, von J. F. W. Herbst. Berlin 1792.
107	Geschichte der Polarländer. Berlin 1778, 4 Theile.
108	Kurze Biographie der berühmtesten Römer. Berlin 1792, 1ster Band, mit Kupfern.
109	C. Corn. Tacitus über Wohnungen und Lebensart germanischer Völker, übersetzt von J. F. Schwedler. Halle 1795, mit 1 Carte.
110	Le nouveau testament, à Berlin 1741.
111	Gallische Alterthümer, oder Sammlung älterer Gedichte, aus dem Gallischen. Leipzig 1781.
112—120	J. Bruckers Fragen aus der philosophischen Geschichte vom Anfange der Welt bis auf Christi Geburt. Ulm 1731, 9 Bände.
121	M. A. Lucani Pharsalia, libri X. Lips. 1726.
122	Franklin der Philosoph und Staatsmann, Gedicht in 5 Gesängen, von J. J. Meyer. Alt-Stettin 1787.
123	Chrestomathia Ciceroniana, herausgegeben von Fischer. Leipzig 1775.
124	Explication abrégé des coutumes & cerémonies chez les Romains, aus dem Lateinischen des Nieuport. Paris 1741.

216

144

217

Klein Format.

Nro.	
5	M. T. Ciceronis Epiſtolae ſelectae. Halae 1775.
6	L. Annaei Flori Romanum, libri 4. Rotterdam 1680.
7	Recueil de cantiques, hymnes, & odes pour les Theophilantropes. Paris an VI.
8 — 10	Année religieuſe des Theophilantropes, 3 Bände.
11	Le culte des Theophilantropes.
12	Manuel des Theophilantropes.
13	Inſtruction élémentaire ſur la morale religieuſe.
14	Schleſiens Bardenopfer für 1786 geſammelt, von Rauſch.
15 — 17	T. Livii Patavini Hiſtoriarum, quae extant, 3 Bände.
18	C. Claudius Claudianus ex optimorum codicum fide. Amſt. 1628.
19	M. Accii Plauti comoediae viginti, 1609.
20	C. Cornelius Tacitus. Amſterdam 1665.
21	Novum Teſtamentum graecum. Lipſ. 1736.
22	P. Virgilii Maronis opera. Amſterdam 1577.
23	P. Ovidii Naſonis opera. Amſterdam 1751, 1ſter Band.
24	L. Annaei Senecae & aliorum, tragoediae. Amſterdam 1568.
25	Cornelii Nepotis quae extant. Traj. ad Rhen. 1665.
26	Juſtini Hiſtoriarum, libri 44. Halae 1780.
27	Juſtini Hiſtoriae Philippicae, cura Burmanni. Lugd. Batav. 1722.
28	Schillers Muſenalmanach für 1799. Tübingen.
29	Gartenkalender für 1782, herausgegeben von Hirſchfeld.
30	Kalender der Muſen und Grazien für 1796, mit Gedichten von F. W. A. Schmidt.
31 — 32	Almanac Pariſien, 2 Bände, mit Kupfern.
33	— — du voyageur à Paris, par Thiery. Paris 1785.
34	— — hiſtorique & généalogique pour l'année 1792, mit Kupfern.
35	— — — — — — — 1793, mit Kupfern.
36	Hiſtoriſches Taſchenbuch für 1798, enthaltend Macartneys Reiſe nach China, mit Kupfern.
37	Hiſtoriae Romnae Epitome- Lugd. Bat. 1648.
38	T. Livii Patavini Hiſtoriarum ab urbe condita, Tom. 1. Halae 1777.
39	Eine Menge incompletter Journale.

Bibliography

PRIMARY SOURCES

Most of Gilly's drawings and manuscripts were lost or destroyed during World War II. His personal library (see Appendix 2) and the portfolios with some two-thirds of his drawings and notes, at that time kept in the library and archives of the Technische Hochschule, now the Technische Universität Berlin, were completely destroyed. A number of Gilly's drawings survived the war because they were housed elsewhere. Today they can be found in the collections of the Staatliche Museen Preußischer Kulturbesitz, Berlin, in the Kunstbibliothek, the Kupferstichkabinett, and the Nationalgalerie; in addition a small group of drawings belongs to the Märkische Museum Berlin. Most of the archival material relating to Gilly was destroyed as well. The Geheimes Staatsarchiv Preußischer Kulturbesitz, Abteilung Merseburg, which keeps the archives of the Oberste Preußische Baubehörde (Supreme Prussian building administration), holds in its files a few documents related to Gilly's appointment and tenure as professor at the Bauakademie.

1796   "Über die vom Herrn Oberhof-Bauamts-Kondukteur Gilly im Jahr 1794 auf-
        genommenen Ansichten des Schlosses der deutschen Ritter zu Marienburg in
        Westpreußen." In J. W. A. Kosmann and Th. Heinsius, eds., *Denkwürdigkeiten und
        Tagesgeschichte der Mark Brandenburg* 1 (June 1796): 667–76.

1796   "Zusatz zu dem Aufsatz des Herrn Oberhof-Bauamts-Kondukteurs Gilly über
        Marienburg; im 6ten Stück der Denkw. S. 667." In J. W. A. Kosmann and Th.
        Heinsius, eds., *Denkwürdigkeiten und Tagesgeschichte der Mark Brandenburg* 2 (August
        1796): 892.

1799   "Beschreibung des Landhauses Bagatelle bey Paris." *Sammlung nützlicher Aufsätze
        und Nachrichten, die Baukunst betreffend: Für angehende Baumeister und Freunde der Ar-
        chitektur* 3, no. 3 (1799): 106–15. Reprinted in Alfred Rietdorf, *Gilly: Wiederge-
        burt der Architektur*, 152–62. Berlin: Hans von Hugo, 1940.

1799   "Einige Gedanken über die Notwendigkeit, die verschiedenen Theile der Bau-
        kunst, in wissenschaftlicher und praktischer Hinsicht, möglichst zu vereinen."
        *Sammlung nützlicher Aufsätze und Nachrichten, die Baukunst betreffend: Für angehende
        Baumeister und Freunde der Architektur* 3, no. 2 (1799): 3–12. Reprinted in Alfred

Rietdorf, *Gilly: Wiedergeburt der Architektur,* 170–77. Berlin: Hans von Hugo, 1940.

1799   "Beschreibung des Landhauses Rincy unweit Paris." *Sammlung nützlicher Aufsätze und Nachrichten, die Baukunst betreffend: Für angehende Baumeister und Freunde der Architektur* 3, no. 2 (1799): 116–24. Reprinted in Alfred Rietdorf, *Gilly: Wiedergeburt der Architektur,* 163–69. Berlin: Hans von Hugo, 1940.

1801   "Einige ausgehobene Bemerkungen aus dem Reise-Journal des verstorbenen Professors und Ober-Hoff-Bauinspektors Gilly." *Sammlung nützlicher Aufsätze und Nachrichten, die Baukunst betreffend: Für angehende Baumeister und Freunde der Architektur* 5, no. 1 (1803): 126.

SELECTED SECONDARY SOURCES

Adler, Friedrich. "Friedrich Gilly—Schinkels Lehrer." *Zentralblatt der Bauverwaltung* 1, no. 1 (1881): 8–10; 1, no. 2 (1881): 17–19; 1, no. 3 (1881): 22–24. Reprinted in idem, *Zur Kunstgeschichte: Vorträge, Abhandlungen und Festreden,* 141–57. Berlin: Mittler, 1906.

Beenken, Hermann. *Schöpferische Bauideen der deutschen Romantik.* Mainz: Matthias Gruenewald, 1952.

Fontane, Theodor. *Wanderungen durch die Mark Brandenburg.* Vol. 1, *Die Grafschaft Ruppin.* Berlin: W. Hertz, 1862. Rev. ed. Berlin: Aufbau-Verlag, 1987. (See the chapter on Schinkel, pp. 113–14, which was rewritten for the edition of 1864.)

———. *Wanderungen durch die Mark Brandenburg.* Vol. 2, *Das Oderland.* Berlin: W. Hertz, 1863. Rev. ed. Berlin: Aufbau-Verlag, 1987. (See the chapter on Steinhöfel, pp. 475–76.)

Galland, George. "Ein früh Verstorbener: Friedrich Gilly." *Baugewerks-Zeitung* 10 (October 1878): 114–15.

Giedion, Sigfried. *Spätbarocker und romantischer Klassizismus.* Munich: F. Bruckmann, 1922.

Herrmann, Wolfgang. *Deutsche Baukunst des 19. und 20. Jahrhunderts.* Part 1, *Von 1770 bis 1840.* Breslau: Ferdinand Hirt, 1932.

Internationale Bauausstellung Berlin 1987. *Friedrich Gilly, 1772–1800, und die Privatgesellschaft junger Architekten,* exh. cat. Berlin: Willmuth Arenhövel, 1984.

Johannes, Heinrich. "Das Denkmal Friedrichs des Großen von Gilly." *Die Kunst im Deutschen Reich,* ed. B (August/September 1942): 157–61.

"Die Jubiläumsausstellung der bildenden Künste in Berlin," part 10. *Zentralblatt der Bauverwaltung* 6, no. 39 (1886): 387–89.

Klinkott, Manfred. "Friedrich Gilly: 1772–1800." *Dortmunder Architekturausstellung 1977: Fünf Architekten des Klassizismus in Deutschland*, exh. cat., 11–13. Dortmunder Architekturhefte, no. 4. Darmstadt: n.p., 1977.

Kugler, Franz. *Karl Friedrich Schinkel: Eine Charakteristik seiner künstlerischen Wirksamkeit*. Berlin: George Gropius, 1842.

Lammert, Marlies. *David Gilly: Ein Baumeister des deutschen Klassizismus*. Berlin: Akademie-Verlag, 1964. Reprint. Berlin: Mann, 1981.

Landsberger, Franz. *Die Kunst der Goethezeit: Kunst und Kunstanschauung von 1750 bis 1830*. Leipzig: Insel, 1931.

Levezow, Konrad. *Denkschrift auf Friedrich Gilly, königlichen Architekten und Professor der Academie der Baukunst zu Berlin*. Berlin: Georg Reimer, 1801. Reprinted in *Internationale Bauausstellung Berlin 1987. Friedrich Gilly, 1772–1800, und die Privatgesellschaft junger Architekten*, exh. cat., 217–42. Berlin: Willmuth Arenhövel, 1984.

Moeller van den Bruck, Arthur. "Gilly." In idem, *Der preußische Stil*, 109–29. Munich: R. Piper, 1916. 2nd ed., 143–64. Munich: R. Piper, 1922.

Neumeyer, Alfred. "Die Erweckung der Gotik in der deutschen Kunst des späten 18. Jahrhunderts: Ein Beitrag zur Vorgeschichte der Romantik." *Repertorium für Kunstwissenschaft* 49 (1928): 75–123, 159–85.

Neumeyer, Fritz. "1786–1848, Zwischen zwei Revolutionen: Das Experiment Poesie." In *750 Jahre Architektur und Städtebau in Berlin*, exh. cat., edited by Josef Paul Kleihues, 65–94. Stuttgart: Gerd Hatje, 1987.

Niemeyer, Wilhelm. "Friedrich Gilly, Friedrich Schinkel und der Formbegriff des deutschen Klassizismus in der Baukunst." *Mitteilungen des Kunstvereins zu Hamburg* 7 (1912): 1ff.

Oncken, Alste. *Friedrich Gilly, 1772–1800*. Berlin: Deutscher Verein für Kunstwissenschaft, 1935. Reprint. Berlin: Mann, 1981.

Pauli, Gustav. *Die Kunst des Klassizismus und der Romantik*. Propyläen Kunstgeschichte, vol. 14. Berlin: Propyläen, 1925.

Peschken, Monika. "Friedrich Gillys Aufenthalt in Paris im Jahr 1797." *Die Bauwelt* 76, Heft 38 (1985): 1531–45.

Posener, Julius. "Friedrich Gilly, 1772–1800." In *Berlin zwischen 1789 und 1848: Facetten einer Epoche*, exh. cat., edited by Sonja Günther, 105–22. Berlin: Akademie der Künste, 1981.

Rabe, Friedrich. "Beschreibung des zu Paretz über der Eisgrube erbauten Lusthauses." *Sammlung nützlicher Aufsätze und Nachrichten, die Baukunst betreffend* 4, no. 2 (1800): 123–24.

Rave, Paul Ortwin. "Friedrich Gilly." *Deutsche Rundschau* 64 (1938): 98–104.

Reelfs, Hella. "Friedrich und David Gilly in neuer Sicht." *Sitzungsberichte der Kunstgeschicht-*

lichen Gesellschaft zu Berlin, n.s. 28/29 (1981): 18–23.

Riemer, Horst. *Friedrich Gilly's Verhältnis zum Theaterbau, unter besonderer Berücksichtigung seiner Skizzen nach französischen Theatern und seines Entwurfes für das Nationaltheater in Berlin.* Ph.D. diss., Friedrich-Wilhelms-Universität, Berlin, 1931; Bochum, n.p.

Rietdorf, Alfred. *Gilly: Wiedergeburt der Architektur.* Berlin: Hans von Hugo, 1940. Reprint. Berlin: Hans von Hugo, 1943.

Rodenwaldt, Gerhart. *Griechisches und Römisches in Berliner Bauten des Klassizismus.* Berlin: Walter de Gruyter, 1956.

Ross, Erhard. "Friedrich Gillys unbekannter Entwurf für ein Theater in Stettin (1789)." *Zeitschrift für Ostforschung* 38, no. 3 (1989): 391–401.

Salewski, Wilhelm, ed. *Schloß Marienburg in Preußen: Das Ansichtswerk von Friedrich Gilly und Friedrich Frick: In Lieferungen erschienen von 1799 bis 1803.* Düsseldorf: Galtgarben, 1965.

Schmitz, Hermann. "Die Entwürfe für das Denkmal Friedrichs des Großen und die Berliner Architektur um das Jahr 1800." *Zeitschrift für bildende Kunst,* n.s. 20 (1909): 206–14.

———. *Berliner Baumeister vom Ausgang des achtzehnten Jahrhunderts,* 38–41. Berlin: Ernst Wasmuth, 1914.

———. "Die Baumeister David und Friedrich Gilly in ihren Beziehungen zu Pommern." *Monatsblätter der Gesellschaft für Pommersche Geschichte und Altertümer* (June 1909): 81–87, 108–11.

———. *Die Gotik im deutschen Kunst- und Geistesleben.* Berlin: Verlag für Kunstwissenschaft, 1921.

———. "Friedrich Gilly." *Kunst und Künstler* 7 (1909): 201–6.

———. *Kunst und Kultur des 18. Jahrhunderts in Deutschland.* Munich: F. Bruckmann, 1922.

Simson, Jutta von. *Das Berliner Denkmal für Friedrich den Großen.* Berlin: Propyläen, 1976.

Waagen, Gustav Friedrich. "Karl Friedrich Schinkel als Mensch und als Künstler." *Berliner Kalender auf das Gemein Jahr 1844.* Reprint. Introduction by Werner Gabler. Düsseldorf: Werner, 1980.

Watkin, David, and Mellinghoff, Tilman. *German Architecture and the Classical Ideal.* Cambridge: MIT Press, 1987.

Wollenschlaeger, Günter. "Dem Baumeister der Berliner Frühromantik, Friedrich Gilly." *Mitteilungen für die Geschichte Berlins* 68, no. 6 (1972): 146–52.

Wolters, Rudolf. "Das Berliner Friedrichsdenkmal." *Die Kunst im Deutschen Reich,* ed. B (August/September 1942): 154–57.

Zucker, Paul. "Ein vergessener Berliner Künstler: Friedrich Gilly." *Neudeutsche Bauzeitung* 9 (September 1913): 696–98.

INDEX

Friedrich Gilly:
Essays on Architecture,
1796–1799

INTRODUCTION BY FRITZ NEUMEYER
TRANSLATION BY DAVID BRITT

Fritz Neumeyer received his doctorate (*Habilitation*) in engineering from the Technische Universität Berlin, where he now holds a chair in theory of architecture. He has also taught at the Universität Dortmund in Germany, Princeton University, the Southern California Institute of Architecture, the Graduate School of Design at Harvard University, and at the University of Louvain in Belgium. His publications on architecture and urbanism from the eighteenth through the twentieth century include *The Artless Word: Mies van der Rohe on the Building Art* (MIT Press) and *Oswald Mathias Ungers: Architetture 1951–1990* (Electa). He is coeditor, with Tilmann Buddensieg and Martin Warnke, of *Artefact*, a series of monographs published by the Akademie Verlag, Berlin.

Born in Bournemouth, England, in 1939, David Britt was educated there and at Cambridge University, where he received a degree in French and German. Soon afterward he translated his first book (Hans Richter's *Dada*, 1965) and then joined the staff of the London publishers Thames & Hudson, where, for more than twenty years, he was an editor of art books, including many translations. Since 1987 he has been translating full-time. In addition to books for Prestel-Verlag in Munich, Thames & Hudson and Yale University Press in London, and Rizzoli and Abbeville Press in New York, he has translated many catalog texts for museums and galleries in Britain, France, Germany, Switzerland, and the United States. His forthcoming translations in the Getty Center's TEXTS & DOCUMENTS series include titles by J.-N.-L. Durand, Julien-David Le Roy, and Aby Warburg. He lives with his wife, Sue, and their three children in Muswell Hill, North London.

Designed by Lorraine Wild.
Composed by Wilsted & Taylor, Oakland,
in Weiss (introduction),
Walbaum (translation and heads), and Poster Bodoni (heads).
Printed by Gardner Lithograph, Buena Park, California
on Mohawk Superfine 80 lb., white and off-white.
Bound by Roswell Book Bindery, Phoenix.

Texts & Documents
Series designed by Laurie Haycock Makela and Lorraine Wild

Library of Congress Cataloging·in·Publication Data

Gilly, Friedrich, 1772–1800.
Friedrich Gilly : essays on architecture, 1796–1799 / introduction
by Fritz Neumeyer ; translation by David Britt.
p. cm. —(Texts & documents)
Translated from German.
Includes bibliographical references and index.
ISBN 0-89236-280-4 (hard) : $39.95 — ISBN 0-89236-281-2 (soft) : $24.95
1. Neoclassicism (Architecture)—Germany. 2. Architecture, Modern—
17th–18th centuries—Germany. 3. Neoclassicism (Architecture)—France.
4. Architecture, Modern—17th–18th centuries—France. 5. Architecture—
Composition, proportion, etc.
I. Getty Center for the History of Art and the Humanities.
II. Title. III. Series.
NA 1066.G55 1994
720'.9—dc20   93-23386
                                              CIP